Burden of History

Burden of History

Assam and the Partition—Unresolved Issues

U<small>DAYON</small> M<small>ISRA</small>

OXFORD
UNIVERSITY PRESS

Oxford University Press is a department of the University of Oxford.
It furthers the University's objective of excellence in research, scholarship,
and education by publishing worldwide. Oxford is a registered trademark of
Oxford University Press in the UK and in certain other countries.

Published in India by
Oxford University Press
22 Workspace, 2nd Floor, 1/22 Asaf Ali Road, New Delhi 110002, India

First Edition published in 2017
Sixth impression 2022
Digitally Printed in 2024

ISBN-13: 978-0-19-947836-1
ISBN-10: 0-19-947836-8

Typeset in Berling LT Std 9.5/13
by The Graphics Solution, New Delhi 110 092
Printed in India by Manipal Technologies Limited, Manipal

For Titul

CONTENTS

PREFACE

My interest in the subject of pre- and post-Partition politics and Assam has been spurred by the fact that the issues that were central to the region's society and politics during the 1940s, such as land, immigration, identity, and language, continue to occupy major public space seventy years after the Partition and Independence. It is as if all other issues, for instance, those relating to human development, have been pushed to the margins. The effects of the Partition continue to hang as a spectre over the entire region, and the more one tries to talk of present issues and search for solutions to them, the more one gets enmeshed in the relatively recent past. While it is true that all small nationalities struggling to assert their identities go back to the past and even try to recreate it to suit their identity concerns, in Assam's case its recent history seems to have subsumed its 'glorious past', with geography playing a crucial role in determining its present position vis-à-vis the Indian state. When armed insurgency broke out in Assam sometime in the 1980s, there was apparent confusion in the Assamese mind as to how this was possible with a people who were part of the Indian freedom struggle and who prided themselves on their strong socio-cultural links with the rest of the country. One could understand why nationalities that had never participated in the struggle for Indian independence often rejected their association with the Indian federation and demanded separation and an independent status. But it was certainly a different case with Assam. That is exactly why it was felt by many that the challenge posed by Assam held more serious consequences for the Indian state than even those put forth by the Nagas, the Manipuris, or the Mizos. And, in order to understand this, even if partially, one needed to go back to the developments that took place in the years preceding the Partition and Independence—developments that have etched their effect on the society, politics, and economy of Assam and also the entire Northeast region in an indelible manner. Romila Thapar in her preface to her latest collection of essays entitled *The Past as Present: Forging Contemporary Identities through History* talks of how 'the present draws on the past not necessarily always to better understand the past but to use the past to legitimize the present'.[1] Referring to her ideas over the past fifty years, Romila Thapar says: 'My ideas today are not substantially different from what they were a few decades ago although the emphasis on nuances may differ. I must confess that in re-reading the essays in order to revise them, I was saddened that the issues remain contentious and our movement towards a solution seems distant.'[2] In the case of Assam too, the contentious issues thrown up during the pre- and post-Partition years continue to influence the society and politics of the state even today and they are far from being resolved. Instead, these issues are taking on ever new complications and shades. My purpose in this book is merely to try to understand the present contentious issues of my state, which seem to defy any solution and which are increasingly adding to the growing human tragedy of the region, in the light of developments that occurred in the pre- and post-Partition years. However, if, in the process, some of the happenings of present-day Assam are 'legitimized', it is a different matter.

Notes

1. Romila Thapar, *The Past as Present: Forging Contemporary Identities through History* (New Delhi: Aleph Book Company, 2014), pp. xiii, 2.
2. Thapar, *The Past as Present*, p. 2.

ACKNOWLEDGEMENTS

I would like to sincerely thank the Indian Institute of Advanced Study (IIAS), Shimla, India, for offering me a national fellowship to work on a topic that has been engaging my attention for some time. The excellent academic atmosphere of the IIAS, combined with the warmth and friendship of the director and fellows, as well as the unstinting cooperation of the entire staff of the institute helped me to complete the first draft of my work within the scheduled period of a year. Friends at the institute put a lot of critical inputs into my work and I gained immensely from these, though it is not possible for me to name them individually. My sincere thanks to all of them. I am grateful to several young friends such as Madhumita Das, who helped me collect material for the work, and Saswati Chaudhury, who helped me with data on certain portions of the work. My sincere thanks to the team at Oxford University Press for making the manuscript ready for publication. A special word of thanks to Sanghamitra Misra for having meticulously gone through the manuscript and coming out with some really insightful suggestions and to Rahul Govind for evincing keen interest in the work. Arindam, Jaya, and Ani were a source of love and support for me while writing. Tilottoma has been with me always, through every stage of this work.

21 July 2017

Udayon Misra
National Fellow
IIAS, Shimla

I

INTRODUCTION

The focus of this introductory chapter is on how pre- and post-Partition politics created ruptures in Assam's relationship with the rest of the country, which are yet to heal; of how Partition turned the region into a landlocked one almost overnight and triggered long-range changes affecting its economy, its politics, and its society; of how the Centre's perception of the region came to be coloured by considerations of security associated with the periphery or borderland; of how the region's economy and politics came to be increasingly influenced by its post-Partition geography and how this, in turn, fostered the growth of an isolationist mindset as has been manifested in the rise of separatist insurgency. While discussing all of this, an attempt has been made to answer the riddle as to how a region that was culturally so integrated with the rest of India, nourished its socio-cultural and religious ties with the subcontinent, and whose economy had been integral to the nation's colonial as well as postcolonial history could eventually spawn militant separatism, which has cost thousands of lives and which, despite being contained in large measure, continues to be a central force in a state's politics.

The greater part of the area today known as the Northeast was, till about forty years ago, known as Assam. The process of the break-up of the territorial area of Assam started just after Independence. Although the then premier of undivided Assam, Gopinath Bardoloi, had taken a leading role in framing and incorporating the Sixth Schedule in the Constitution of India with a view to ensuring the maximum possible autonomy to the hill districts, yet this did not prevent the break-up of the state.[1] Interestingly, the States Reorganization Commission of 1955 had also recommended the inclusion of Manipur and Tripura in Assam. But the newly emerging middle classes amongst the different hill tribes eventually demanded their share of political power, and movements were started for separate statehood. Thus, the history of Assam took a different turn and from the 1960s onwards several new states were carved out of it. The Naga Hills district of the state was made into Nagaland in 1963, to be followed by the creation also of Meghalaya in 1972 and Mizoram, first as a union territory in 1971 and then as a state in 1987. Today, the state of Assam is primarily made up of the Brahmaputra and Barak Valleys and the hills of Karbi Anglong. It shares its international border chiefly with Bangladesh and Bhutan. And, there being currently no regular land and river route through Bangladesh, the state is virtually landlocked, being connected with the rest of the country by a small strip of land known as the Siliguri Corridor.

This work attempts to show how the shadow of the Partition continues to fall over the society and politics of Assam and how issues that were central to the years immediately preceding and following Independence and Partition continue not only to retain their relevance but are gaining an extra edge today. Moreover, many of the issues such as immigration, identity, and demographic change have gained a new sense of urgency in the contemporary politics of Assam. In the archive of the postcolonial state, the reader is confronted with strong resonances of the region's colonial past: for instance, while one goes through the Assam Legislative Assembly debates of the late 1940s, one discovers that many of the sociopolitical issues that occupied centre stage in the debates still continue to be of great importance to the Assam of today. Just as the Legislative Assembly debated immigration and identity issues in the 1940s, if one goes through the proceedings of the Assam Legislative Assembly of the 1980s and 1990s one would similarly find debates centred on immigration from Bangladesh, demographic change, and the perceived threat to the Assamese identity. Just as in the 1940s the fear of being included in a larger Bengal seemed to dominate the Assamese mind, in the 1980s and 1990s too, the fear of becoming a part of Bangladesh dominated the social discourse that found reflection in the Assembly proceedings. Interestingly, even the question of identifying who is actually an Assamese that figured in the pre-Independence debates finds a reflection several decades later in the debates that took on a new edge in the closing period of the nineteenth century and continue to engage civil society even today.[2] Most people in the Brahmaputra Valley had thought that with the Partition and the Referendum in Sylhet, Assam would finally result in a homogenous homeland for the Assamese-speaking people.[3] But the historical effects of the Partition have had a long afterlife in the region. Not only did Partition radically transform the political geography of the region and turn it overnight into a landlocked one, its after-effects continue to be felt in the sociopolitical and economic life of the region in diverse ways. The refugee problem immediately after Partition and Independence, the downslide of the economy, the influx from East Pakistan of land-hungry, poverty-stricken Muslim peasants, the change in the demographic scenario and the accompanying rise of identity fears of the Assamese, to be followed by similar identity concerns of the other small ethnic nationalities of the region, the disintegration of Pakistan and the emergence of Bangladesh, the northeastern region becoming a theatre of Bangladesh's liberation war and a shelter for the huge influx of refugees, the rise of militant politics and the slide towards secessionism—all these and many other factors are linked, in some way or other, with Partition and its fallout. Seen from this angle, the Partition has perhaps had a more enduring impact on the north-eastern region than on the western part of the subcontinent.[4] Some scholars, while referring to the differences between the impact of the Partition in the west and that in the east, have said that Assam is still confronting a 'failed Partition'.[5]

To understand the consequences of the 'failed Partition', it would perhaps be necessary to go back a bit in history. A new dimension to the politics of the region was added when Assam was joined with the populous Bengali-speaking district of Sylhet of East Bengal to be made into a Chief Commissioner's Province in 1874. The inclusion of Sylhet, which had a population almost equal to that of the whole of the Brahmaputra Valley districts, brought about a sudden increase in the Bengali population of the province. The competition for jobs between the emerging Assamese middle class and its Bengali counterpart began, and was to be one of the major factors contributing to Assamese–Bengali conflicts in the succeeding decades. A substantial rise in the Muslim population through immigration also marked the beginning of a conflict that would assume frightening proportions from the 1930s onwards. The marginalization of the Assamese middle class was not only due to the British preference for Bengali officials and clerks to man the administration, but also because of the demographic changes that were taking place. According to Amalendu Guha, by 1901 'non-indigenous elements came to constitute at least a quarter of the population of Assam proper'.[6] Added to this was the serious imbalance triggered by the tea, coal, and oil industries between the fast-growing modern sector and the near-stagnant, traditional agricultural sector. The gap between the income accrued and the income disbursed within the state kept widening. Not only was the extracted surplus remitted to the United Kingdom in the form of fabulously high dividends, but a substantial part of the wage bill was also sent outside the province. The commercial cultivation of tea by the colonial state and the subsequent venturing of British capitalists into tea plantations from the 1830s onwards resulted in regulations such as the Waste Land Grant Rules of 1838 (Wasteland Rules) that made it possible for British planters to acquire large tracts of land on very easy terms. The Wasteland Rules were framed to help British tea planters acquire large tracts of land at very nominal revenue rates and they took advantage of the rules to grab as much land as was possible. By 1870 almost 7 lakh acres of land were held by British planters, although the actual area under tea cultivation was approximately just about 56,000 acres.[7]

Given the huge profits made by the tea gardens, the actual inflow into the state has been negligible. As from the extractive oil and coal industries, the local people benefitted little from the tea industry. Most of the profits went to business interests outside the province. For instance, the Bengal-based transportation companies pocketed the transportation charges, while almost everything needed for the industry, from brushes to paints to iron pans, hoes, and billhooks, were imported from England.[8] Till the middle of the 1850s, even the packing boxes were brought from England, although Calcutta (now known as Kolkata) and Chittagong became the main centres of such supplies later on. This policy continued well after Independence and only in recent years have some marginal changes occurred because of the pressure mounted by the indigenous people. Even today, Assam is deprived of crores of rupees as income tax because most of the major tea companies still have their head offices in Kolkata. With local labour not being readily available, the British planters brought thousands of indentured labour into the state, thereby adding a new dimension to the demographic picture. Once kept segregated from the local population, today this section of people constitutes a major element of the Assamese nationality and has come to play a vital role in the state's politics. Whatever development the British initiated at the level of infrastructure in the form of roads and railways was clearly meant to benefit the extractive colonial economy built around oil, coal, timber, and tea. It would be relevant to note here that even after Independence, Assam continued to be a sort of colonial hinterland for the rest of India.[9]

The first two decades of the twentieth century were marked by the growth of Assamese national consciousness and the gradual involvement of the people in the emerging struggle against British rule being led by the Congress. The decision of the Assam Chatra Sanmelan in 1920 to support Gandhi's programme of non-cooperation signalled Assam's entry into national politics. The Non-Cooperation Movement was a success in the province and this led to a swift mobilization of the masses. The rise in the level of political consciousness was reflected in the articulation of regional demands which included the rights of the 'sons of the soil' and safeguards against unchecked and unlimited immigration from the neighbouring provinces, particularly Bengal. Assamese public opinion started to be increasingly agitated over the occupation of cultivable land by the immigrants, and demands were made for protective measures. The overwhelming majority of the immigrants were Muslim peasants from East Bengal and an open clash of interests began to take place when the immigrants started occupying land held by the autochthons. There seems to be a generally accepted perception that the British colonial administrators, in the interest of producing more crops and obtaining increased land revenue, followed a consistent policy of opening up Assam to immigrant peasants from Bengal. The inflow of immigrant peasants also received support from the Assamese landowning class as may be seen in the Jorhat Sarvajanik Sabha's approach to the problem.[10] But it was the administrative backing to immigration that added a totally new dimension to the issue.

In a recent article, Binayak Dutta has shown how the priorities of the British administration started changing by the turn of the nineteenth century and the emphasis gradually shifted from making land available for the tea gardens to encouraging immigration so as to extend

the area under cultivation and grow more crops.[11] This shift was evident in the large influx of people from East Bengal into Assam, and
the flow of indentured tea labour into Assam was quickly replaced by
immigrant peasants from the neighbouring province. The coming of
the railways helped the flow particularly from Mymensingh district of
Bengal, and within just two decades a major demographic transformation took place in districts of Assam such as Goalpara and Kamrup. In
Goalpara district the density of population per square mile rose from
89 persons in 1891 to 115 in 1911[12] and 193 in 1921.[13] Of the 3 lakh
(1 lakh equals 100,000) immigrants who came to Assam as per the
1921 Census, as many as 1.5 lakhs settled in Goalpara.[14] In the light
of such swift demographic change and the attendant pressure on land,
British officials were forced to think of ways to stop this influx. This is
revealed in the census report of 1931 where the superintendent, C.S.
Mullan, clearly stated:

> Probably the most important event in the province during the last
> twenty five years—an event moreover, which seems likely to alter per-
> manently the whole future of Assam and to destroy more surely than
> did the Burmese invaders in 1820 the whole structure of Assamese
> culture and civilization—has been the invasion of a vast horde of land
> hungry Bengali immigrants, mostly Muslims, from the districts of East
> Bengal and in particular from Mymensingh.[15]

Though Mullan has been accused of stirring up indigenous Assamese
and ethnic fears about immigration,[16] his remarks actually are indica-
tive of the change in the perception of the colonial administration that
was taking place about the impact of immigration on the province. For
many a colonial administrator, it was no longer a question of encouraging immigration to increase crop production; it was also now a question
of social conflict arising out of the occupation of land by the immigrants. This eventually led to the adoption of new rules to regulate the
settlement of immigrants. Binayak Dutta, while referring to these rules,
states:

> The first set of rules to regulate and restrict the immigration of agricul-
> tural immigrants from Bengal to Assam was proposed in 1915, which
> inter alia introduced changes in the tenure of holdings. But such a
> proposal evoked protests among the Assamese public opinion on the
> ground that such rules would 'affect permanent heritable and transfer-
> able character of tenures'. In 1916 the then Director of Land Records

first came up with a proposal to regulate the migration and settlement of these migrants. The proposal was designed with the ostensible purpose of 'assisting the settlement of the incoming immigrants and coordinate the work of all districts into which immigration was going on'. But it was evident that by 1916 official perceptions about inter-provincial migration between Bengal and Assam had changed and the official patronage to migration was gradually withdrawn.[17]

Soon the Line System,[18] which aimed at protecting the land of the indigenous people from occupation by the immigrants, would be put into effect. It was this Line System which would come under sustained attack in the 1930s and 1940s from the leaders of the immigrants under the banner of the Provincial Muslim League. The immediate pre-Partition years would be witness to the subversion of the Line System carried out in a systematic manner by the successive governments headed by Syed Muhammad Saadulla.

Although the entire process of migration was initially linked with the process of colonial development, it was soon to reach a saturation point because of the growing scarcity of cultivable land and the increasing pressure by immigrants on the tribal belts and blocks and the reserve forest areas. Soon it was to become a simple struggle for cultivable land between the immigrants and the autochthons. By the 1930s the situation arising out of immigration was already taking on serious proportions, with immigrant leaders such as Maulana Bhasani demanding the abolition of the Line System. Land became a major political issue of the state, and in just six years between 1930 and 1936 as many as fifty-nine grazing, forest, and village reserves were thrown open under the colonization scheme for settling the immigrants. The land-hungry immigrants did not appreciate the Assamese fears of being turned into a minority in their own land. They were clearly in search of a *Lebensraum*.[19] Thus, throughout the 1930s and 1940s the struggle between the immigrants and the autochthons continued, with successive governments headed/controlled by the Muslim League or its sympathizers encouraging state-sponsored immigration into Assam. The demographic change brought about by such immigration triggered indigenous Assamese fears of being eventually outnumbered in their own homeland. This, in turn, added a new complexity to the entire politics of the region, with issues of land, identity, and language gaining precedence over all other matters.[20]

The separation of Sylhet in 1947 seemed to assuage Assamese fears of being reduced to a minority, but the continued influx from East Pakistan and subsequently from Bangladesh resulted in a major transformation of the Assamese identity itself. Today, lakhs of Muslim migrants (known as neo-Assamese) have become a part of the Assamese nationality whereas several of the plains tribal communities have been alienated from the Assamese mainstream. One of the reasons for such alienation may be linked to the Assamese middle class's rather one-sided engagement with linguistic nationalism. Today, more than seventy-five years since the immigration issue received serious attention, illegal influx from Bangladesh continues to be a major political issue in the state. The 1991 Census had shown that while the Muslim population of India increased by 402 lakhs or 65.47 per cent over that of 1971, in Assam the increase has been 77.42 per cent. Muslims formed a majority in Dhubri (70.46 per cent), Goalpara (50.42 per cent), Barpeta (56.07 per cent), and Hailakandi (55.42 per cent). The 2001 Census figures confirmed the rising trend of Muslim population in the state, which is being linked by many observers to the increased influx from Bangladesh. The Muslim decadal growth rate in Assam during 1991–2001 was 29.35 per cent, while the Hindu decadal growth rate during the same period was only 14.9 per cent. The proportion of Hindus fell from 67 per cent in 1991 to 65 per cent in 2001, while that of Muslims rose from 28.4 per cent in 1991 to 30.9 per cent in 2001. The Muslim population in Assam has grown from 24.7 per cent in 1951 to 30.9 per cent in 2001 and 34.26 in the 2011 Census. The 2011 Census figures have raised a huge controversy in Assam, with the indigenous Assamese and tribal groups expressing the fear that in another two decades or so they would be turned into minorities in their own state. In the four districts bordering Bangladesh (Dhubri, Goalpara, Hailakandi, and Karimganj), Muslims constitute more than 50 per cent of the population.[21] The released figures of the 2011 Census[22] have shown that while the Muslim population growth in the country came down from 29.52 per cent in 2001 to 24.6 per cent in 2011, Assam recorded the highest growth of the Muslim population from 30.9 per cent in 2001 to 34.2 per cent in 2011, a 3.3 per cent rise. This growth rate has been substantially higher than that of states such as Jammu and Kashmir and West Bengal.[23] By contrast the Hindu population growth in the state has fallen from 32.88 per cent in 1991 to 29.52 per cent in 2001 and 24.6 per cent in 2011. The share of Hindu population stands today at 61.47 per cent, registering a decrease of 4.4 per cent during the period between 2001 and 2011.[24] In the districts bordering Bangladesh, the rise in Muslim population has been much higher, with Muslims constituting a majority in nine of the twenty-seven districts of Assam.[25] As per the 2011 Census, the total population of Assam stood at 3,11,69,272, while in the 2001 Census it was 2,66,38,407. The growth rate has been 16.93 per cent. According to a report published in a local daily:

> Out of the 27 districts of Assam, eight districts registered a rise in the decadal population growth rate. Muslims dominated the districts of Dhubri, Goalpara, Barpeta, Marigaon, Nagaon and Hailakandi, record-ing growth rates ranging from 20 per cent to 24 per cent during the last decade. On the other hand, the eastern Assam districts mostly of upper Assam registered around nine per cent growth. These districts do not share any international border.[26]

Thus, the census figures of 2011 are being seen by many as an official acknowledgement of the apprehensions of the indigenous people that they may be eventually turned into minorities in their own homeland. Census figures have always remained a highly contentious issue in Assam, for every time these are released, uncertainty about the future identity of the autochthons take on a new edge.

The identity debate in Assam goes back to the closing decades of the nineteenth century. The status of the Assamese-language speakers has for long been a part of the central discourse in the region. The struggle for the restoration of the status of the Assamese language has a long history starting with the colonial times. The high point for Assamese linguistic nationalism was reached in 1960 when Assamese (along with Bengali in the Barak Valley) was made the official language of the then undivided state of Assam. This, paradoxically, instead of strengthening the base of Assamese nationalism, only helped to weaken it by alienating not only the hill tribes but also a large section of the plains tribe living in the Brahmaputra Valley. The quest for an exclu-sive Assamese homeland where the Assamese language would reign supreme has, however, met with several roadblocks. Though the num-ber of Assamese speakers registered what may be called a phenomenal rise in the 1951 Census, subsequent censuses have shown a steady decline in their numbers.[27] This has occurred despite the fact that a substantial number of the Bengali Muslim immigrants started returning Assamese as their mother tongue. For the first time in the 2001 Census, Assamese speakers in the state fell below the 50 per cent level while the number of Bengali speakers rose to almost 28 per cent. In the year 1971, Assamese speakers comprised 60.89 per cent of the population while Bengali speakers were only 19.85 per cent. The 2011 Census has triggered apprehensions that the number of Assamese speakers has further gone down while Bengali speakers have almost touched the 30 per cent mark. This drop in the number of Assamese speakers and the rise in the Bengali-speaking population has become a major concern for Assamese nationalist organizations, which attribute the crisis to increased immigration from Bangladesh. That the erosion of the tribal base of Assamese nationalism is a major factor contributing to the fall in the number of Assamese speakers is a fact which organizations such as Asom Sahitya Sabha, the All Assam Students' Union, and so on, refuse to acknowledge. Whatever the immediate and long-term reasons behind this change, the fact remains that the crisis being faced by the Assamese language has once again taken centre stage in the state's sociopolitical scenario. The Assamese national consciousness is today gripped by the feeling that the threat to the majority status of their language is a threat to the very identity of the Assamese people.

Assam is currently caught in the vicious circle of underdevelopment and insurgent politics. Rising unemployment,[28] tardy economic growth, and lack of infrastructural facilities combined with swift demographic change and growing pressure on cultivable land have all contributed to the rise of militant politics in the region. Over and above these, there seems to be another important factor that has contributed to the growing alienation of the Assamese people from what is considered to be mainstream politics. This feeling has been substantially nourished by the Centre's overall attitude towards this region, which many feel has been characterized by a colonial mind-set and guided by security interests. To understand this, it is necessary to go back to the pre-Independence days when the overwhelming public opinion in Assam, cutting across linguistic, tribal, and ethnic lines, was galvanized by the provincial Congress to successfully resist the Cabinet Mission proposals, which had grouped Assam with Muslim-majority Bengal. It would also be relevant to discuss in brief the position taken by the members from Assam in the Constituent Assembly on issues relating to financial and political autonomy of the states. When the Cabinet Mission Plan of grouping Bengal and Assam together was announced, fear gripped the minds of the people of Assam who felt that this would ultimately lead to the amalgamation of their province with Pakistan. A general feeling of being betrayed by the Congress high command swept the province. The Assam Congress under the leadership of Gopinath Bardoloi[29] put up a spirited fight against the proposals, and this pitted them against leaders such as Nehru, Patel, and Azad. Eventually, with Mahatma Gandhi's support the Assam Congress managed to make the proposals infructuous, even though the Congress Working Committee had accepted the Cabinet Mission Plan in August 1946. Assam's stand was one of the major reasons why the Cabinet Mission Plan fell through. But the feeling persisted in the province that the central leadership of the Congress and the country at large had betrayed the interests of the region. This feeling of being indifferently treated by the central leadership was reinforced substantially during the Constituent Assembly debates. It was during these debates that the members from Assam unequivocally demanded greater financial and political autonomy for the states. The Assam premier, Gopinath Bardoloi, demanded the 'fullest possible autonomy' for the states and in this he was supported by hill leaders such as J.J.M. Nichols Roy.[30] Almost all the members from Assam demanded that the Central List should not be made unduly long and that the powers of the states should not be reduced. There was a strong unified demand that the rights of the Assamese people be protected through constitutional safeguards and that the economic exploitation of the region by the Centre be stopped.[31] But once the fight to keep the residual powers with the states was lost and the rights over mineral resources went to the Centre, the leaders from Assam insisted that the percentage of share should be high enough to meet the needs of economically backward states such as Assam. During the discussion on Article 253 (Article 272 of the final draft), relating to the sharing of Union duties of excise among the states and the Centre, several members from Assam demanded that 75 per cent of the excise duty of tea and oil should accrue to the states producing them. The Drafting Committee refused to accept these amendments, and even the plea that Assam be treated as a special case, in view of the colonial pattern of extractive exploitation that the state had been subjected to under the British, found little support in the House. One could argue that in the refusal of Assam's demand for greater financial and political autonomy lay the grounds for the eventual rise of secessionist politics.

Assam lost its fight in the Constituent Assembly to secure greater autonomy for the provinces. But the issues relating primarily to Centre–state relations that were raised in the debates were to assume important dimensions in the years to come. The sharp differences on matters covering issues such as financial aid, refugee rehabilitation, and immigration, which marked Assam's relationship with the Centre during the period immediately following Independence, would, in the years to follow, manifest themselves in new forms of protest culminating in the rise of militant separatism symbolized by organizations such as the United Liberation Front of Assam (ULFA) in the 1980s. The rise of militant separatism in Assam clearly poses a greater threat to the Indian nation state because unlike areas such as Nagaland, Mizoram, or even Manipur, Assam has had centuries-old socio-historical and cultural links with the rest of India. In the first two decades or so after Independence, popular protest was related to demands for the speedy industrialization of the state. This was reflected in the movements for the setting up of the first and second oil refineries and in other economic demands related to employment for locals, the setting up of industries and improvement of road and rail communication, and so on. Soon, however, the course of popular protests changed with the influx of immigrants and land alienation becoming central issues as was reflected in the Assam Movement (1979–85). The long-held Assamese fear of losing their ethnic identity found expression in a highly populist movement which, given the massive participation, may be said to have been largely peaceful but which, nevertheless, was marked by several major outbursts of communal violence. The movement brought about certain ruptures in Assamese society and also paved the way for the ethnic assertion of several of the plains tribes,[32] including that of the Bodos that led to the establishment of an autonomous region (Bodoland Territorial Autonomous District) within Assam.

Today, however, separatist militancy notwithstanding, there seems to be a general awareness, both at the governmental and civil society levels, about the need to move away from fragmentary politics to a more cohesive effort towards development involving all the states of the region. Assam's relationship with states such as Nagaland, Arunachal Pradesh, and Meghalaya has been marred by boundary disputes, and a collective endeavour towards coordinated development of the region has been missing till now. Of late, however, swift economic progress of the region is being increasingly viewed as the most effective antidote against insurgency and for this the 'Look East' Policy is being actively put forward. There has been a marked shift in the perception of the Centre, which has, in recent years, come to see the northeastern part of the country as having a large degree of commonality with the South East Asian countries. It has come to be accepted that the 'landlocked' Northeast has more to gain by way of trade and commerce with its South Asian neighbours than with the Indian mainland. Subregional cooperation and cross-regional projects between the northeastern region and the South East Asian countries are being viewed as important take-off points in the road to overall economic prosperity of the entire region. In the light of all this the Bay of Bengal Initiative for Multi-Sectoral Technical and Economic Cooperation (BIMSTEC) meets, the South Asian Growth Quadrangle (SAGQ), and South Asia Subregional Economic Cooperation (SASEC) have assumed great relevance. Opening up of communication routes with Myanmar, Thailand, and China have assumed great importance and the India-ASEAN Car Rally, flagged off from Guwahati amidst much hype and fanfare, is a part of the endeavour to forge trade and cultural links with the South East Asian countries. Trade and industry circles in India have been asserting that such exercises would bring great commercial benefits to the northeastern region. But, while it is an undeniable fact that opening up of trade and commerce with the South Asian neighbours is long overdue, to insist that the 'region-state' should get priority over the nation state would be to eschew the realities of the ground situation. The idea of transnational neighbourhood and fluid borders must be seen against the background of changing international politics after the 9/11 attacks and the strengthening of the nation state in Europe and America. The Look East Policy must be viewed keeping in mind the interests of the people of the northeastern region and the problems of immigration, demographic change, and growing pressure on land which they have been facing. If opening up trade opportunities means turning the northeast region into a trade corridor and nothing else, then the benefits would obviously accrue to the Indian capitalist class. Further, whatever nominal economic and industrial infrastructure the northeastern region possesses today would come under severe strain from outside competition. The future of the Northeast's handicrafts, handlooms, and cottage industries would become uncertain in the face of competition from cheap and attractive goods from its South East Asian neighbours. For instance, the fate of the Assamese peasant could also be in jeopardy because of possibly cheap rice imports from Myanmar. Added to all this would be the drug and arms menace that would accompany the easing of the borders. Therefore, the questions thrown up by the Look East Policy must be analysed deeply and adequate safeguards must be provided to the economy of the northeastern region. For ensuring these safeguards and accelerating the pace of economic growth through cooperation with the South East Asian neighbours, the different states of the Northeast must learn to work from a common platform. The issues which Assam and her neighbours are facing today seem to be too complex to be wished away by economic liberalization and transnational region-building. Any attempt to understand these issues would necessitate looking into those momentous years before and after Partition which triggered long-standing changes in the polity, economy, and social life of the region while at the same time redefining the region's relationship with the Indian mainland in a variety of ways.

An attempt has been made in the succeeding chapters to show how the shadow of the Partition continues to fall over the society and politics of Assam, and how issues that were central to the years immediately preceding and following Independence and Partition continue not only to retain their relevance but are gaining an extra edge today. While delving into the politics of those momentous years, one discovers that even today Assam and the northeastern region have not been able to move away from the politics of the pre- and post-Partition days. On the contrary, many of the issues such as immigration, identity, and demographic change have gained a new sense of urgency in the present-day politics of Assam. It is this, one feels, which has added a sense of relevance to the work. What would perhaps invariably attract anyone working on the effects of the Partition on the region would be the time warp in which Assam seems to have been caught over all these decades since Independence.

It is said that geography often determines the politics of a region. Although the view about biogeography influencing the society and politics of a region is not accepted by many scholars, yet without being deterministic, one may say that the post-Partition geography of Assam and the northeastern region has, in many ways, influenced its economy, politics, society, and even the overall mindset. These factors have all been determined, in some way or other, by Partition which almost overnight cut off Assam's communication links with the rest of the Indian mainland and turned it into a region that shared 95 per cent of its borders with foreign countries. Referring to the effect of geography on a region's history, Jared Diamond, in his book *Guns, Germs and Steel*, says:

> Naturally, the notion that environmental geography and biogeography influenced societal development is an old idea. Nowadays, though, the view is not held in esteem by historians, it is considered wrong and simplistic or it is caricatured as environmental determinism and dismissed.... Yet geography obviously has some effect on history; the open question concerns how much effect, whether geography can account for history's broad pattern.[33]

Certainly, the post-Partition geography of Assam has had an effect on its post-Partition history precisely because it snapped the region's centuries-old physical links with the rest of the Indian subcontinent, thereby having a spin-off effect on its social, cultural, and religious links as well.[34] That Partition had a long-term effect on the economy and politics of this region is evident from the fact that we are still struggling to resolve some of the issues that surfaced during the pre- and post-Partition period and seventy years after Independence, the shadow of Partition is still with us precisely because it turned Assam into a part of the periphery and borderland of India. That is exactly why to arrive at a balanced understanding of many of our present socio-economic and political problems, it is necessary for us to understand Partition and its politics of geography. Suddenly becoming a part of a borderland[35] brought with it its own problems. The Centre increasingly started viewing the region from the vantage point of security and interpreted different expressions of people's discontent as a sign of their separatist intentions and lack of allegiance to the idea of India. It was felt that the laws which were meant for the rest of the country were not sufficient to tackle the people's protests in the northeastern region. The Centre would, of course, maintain that laws such as the Disturbed Areas Act and the Armed Forces (Special Powers) Act were needed to fight armed militancy in the region. But the unsavoury fact remains that in the majority of cases, these laws were used to suppress different forms of democratic protests.

Not to speak of autonomist movements and popular agitations, even matters relating to the development of the economic and industrial infrastructure of the region came to be dominated by security considerations. One of the earliest manifestations of such an approach was evident when the Centre refused to set up a refinery in Assam because the defence ministry did not approve of it for security reasons. This approach continues till the present day and was recently best illustrated when an Assamese school student sought clarification from the Government of India about a reference to security considerations in a lesson on Assam's tourism potential.[36] Though the National Council of Educational Research and Training (NCERT) has been asked by the Ministry of Tourism, Government of India, to drop the 'careless sentence' in the Class X textbook, which stated that tourism has not been encouraged in the Northeast because of 'strategic reasons', the entire matter runs much deeper. This apparently careless sentence did not come from nowhere. It was part of a wider perception about the northeastern region which has been nourished by the Centre ever since Partition. It is clear that a borderland or periphery needs special laws and dispensations which are otherwise not applicable to the rest of the country! But there was a time when Assam was not just a part of a borderland region or a periphery.[37]

Thus, just as geography determined in large measure the attitude towards the newly created borderland or periphery of the nation state, so did people's perceptions about the Centre and the rest of the country start undergoing a change. It was increasingly felt that the distant Centre was too prejudiced to listen to the voices of the northeastern region and the relatively few elected representatives from the region in the country's parliament could make little impact on the framing of national policy. Now, how does a particular region overcome this politics of geography? There has been much talk for several years now about opening up the northeastern region as part of the Look East Policy.[38] But why has the Look East Policy not brought any dividends to Assam and other northeastern states? How can one really talk of opening up a region without developing its infrastructure? Surely the northeastern region would not wish to be just an export corridor for goods manufactured in other parts of the country. A necessary precondition for developing connectivity with the South East Asian countries and China is to develop connectivity within the states of the Northeast as also with the rest of the country. It needs to be remembered that trade and commerce is between people, and when we talk of people we also need to discuss the politics of perceptions and mindsets involved that might facilitate or restrict economic cooperation.

While it is true that prejudices have long coloured the Centre's approach to this region, it is also a fact that for several decades the people of this region have been subjected to the exclusivist politics of the worst kind. It just would not do to try to sweep under the carpet the violence that has marked the different forms of identity politics in the northeastern region. Perhaps we have reached that juncture in history when identity issues cannot be solved just by creating more and more political spaces in the form of ethnic homelands. The very heterogeneity of the northeastern region poses a challenge to this. Ethnic nationalism, whatever its historical roots, derives its strength from exclusivist politics, and community passions quite often tend to drown the individual voice. Social analysts might rightly argue that such exclusivist politics, often attended by violence, has its historical as well as economic and political roots that have been nourished by a highly unequal political system. But it is equally true that in today's increasingly globalized world there is a need to move away from the narrow groove of fragmentary politics into a more inclusive social space. Only then shall the northeastern region, and particularly Assam, be able to shed the burden of history that Partition has bequeathed it.

Though it is now been seventy years since the country was divided into two, any discussion on Assam must still begin by referring to Partition. For, the immediate impact of Partition on Assam and the Northeast was that it was suddenly cut off from the rest of the country. A region that was from time immemorial a part of the continuous land mass stretching across the Gangetic plains into the plains of Bengal and spreading across to the Brahmaputra and Barak Valleys was suddenly turned into a landlocked region connected to India only by a tenuous stretch of 27 kilometres of land called the Siliguri Corridor. Centuries-old trade links with neighbouring East Bengal were disrupted and in the course of time, as relations between India and Pakistan deteriorated, the river traffic along the mighty Brahmaputra, which was responsible in British days for most of the trade and commerce, stood disrupted, thereby further adding to the northeastern region's isolation. This geo-political distancing and isolation virtually wrought havoc on Assam's

economy. The disruption of traditional trade links and the sudden geographical isolation of the region had a negative impact on the economy
of the entire region. Assam, which had a gross domestic product (GDP)
equal to the all-India average at the time of Independence, started slid-
ing down the economic scale and is today considered as one of the
poorer states of the Indian Union, contributing only about 1.5 per cent
to the national income. This despite the fact that the state produces
more than half of the country's tea and has considerable reserves of
oil, gas, minerals, and great hydropower potential. The immediate
post-Independence years were marked by sluggish industrial and agricultural growth, rising unemployment, and little effort being spent in
developing the infrastructure of the region. The 1950s and 1960s were
marked by popular agitations demanding speedy industrialization and
this was soon followed by the rise of armed insurgency in the region.
A part of the Government of India's policy for checking the rise of
militancy included programmes aimed at the economic development
of the region, and the Look East Policy is part of such an initiative.

The Partition dealt a major blow to the northeastern region's connectivity with the rest of the country by cutting off rail and road
links. But despite the loss of access to Chittagong port,[39] it was the
eventual complete closure of the region's access to the sea through the
Brahmaputra that hurt the economy the most. Waterways had always
been the main lifeline of trade and commerce in Assam. During colonial
rule and after the setting up of the tea plantations by the British and
the exploitation of oil resources as well as timber, the importance of the
Brahmaputra as a major waterway of commerce increased manifold.[40]
Yet, despite the Partition, river transport continued to play a vital role
in the state's economy.[41] River transport continued to be the main
means of transporting goods not only during the period from 1947
to 1949, when the region had no rail connectivity with India, but also
much later. Discussing this, S.B. Medhi says:

> Before the completion of the Assam Rail link in 1949 the river services
> had their most busy years. The J.S. Companies, the most prominent
> among the private companies, continued to carry about 80% of tea, 90%
> of jute and large volume of petroleum products from Assam to Calcutta
> till 1963–64 and also moved in large volume of imports. However, even
> after the construction of the Rail Link when the railways connected
> internal markets with other states, the importance of the waterways did

not decline.... After the Partition of 1947 the river transport had a spe-cial role in movement of traffic to and from Cachar district.[42]

It is significant to note that even ten years after Partition, import of goods to Assam by river services was much higher than by rail. While referring to the 1960s, Medhi quotes from the report of the Committee on Transport Policy and Coordination to show that of the 'total annual traffic of 2.5 million tonnes between Assam and Calcutta, water trans-port accounted for about one million tonnes in recent years'.[43] A report prepared by the Inland Water Transport Committee in 1959 stated that while the railways were handling 35 per cent of the total traffic of Assam, about 50 per cent 'of the traffic requirements of Assam will still have to be met by Inland Water Transport'.[44] All this shows how vital waterways have been to the economic development of Assam and what irreversible damage was done to it when the river route was closed and river traffic came to a standstill with the outbreak of hostilities between India and Pakistan in 1965. Commenting on this, S.B. Medhi says:

> So far as the external trade was concerned, 1964 was the last year of the glory of the steamer services in Assam as the Indo-Pak hostilities of 1965 led to the closure of the river route and river services came to a standstill. After the closure of the Indo-Pak river route, about 22 steam-ers and 40 fleets remained in Assam waters. River craft belonging to the R.S.N. Company and cargo in transit valued at about Rs. 3.19 crores [1 crore equals 10 million] were detained in East Pakistan.[45]

The economic cost of this disruption has been really huge and only recently efforts have been geared up to reopen regular river traffic via the Brahmaputra between India and Bangladesh. [46]

Rail connectivity between Assam and the rest of the country was cut off by the Partition and one of the most important effects of this was the loss of access to Chittagong port as also the closure of access to Calcutta port. The Partition left the region without a single railway workshop.[47] The construction of the Assam Rail Link started in 1948 and was completed in 1949. The railway link was opened to goods traffic in December 1949 and to passenger traffic from January 1950.[48] But the capacity of the railway connecting Assam with the rest of the country was severely limited, severe congestion on the single metre gauge line and shortage of wagons being major contributing factors.[49] As a result, the economy of the region suffered immensely because for 'quite a few years after the Link was established, railways could not play a significant role (especially in imports) in comparison to river transport.... Imports by rail declined by about 88 per cent and exports also went down by about 17 per cent in 1953–54 as compared to 1939–40.'[50] The effect of the Partition on rail connectivity and transport in Assam may be gauged by the fact that 'in 1954–55 the capacity of the rail Link route to Assam was about 25 per cent of Assam's pre-war rail traffic of 14.4 lakh tones of imports in 1939–40'.[51]

Another major area of connectivity which was disrupted by the Partition was in the sphere of roads. Although Assam did not have well-developed road connectivity within the state or with the rest of the country before the Partition, yet along with the waterways, roads, mostly *kutcha* (unmetalled) ones, served as major means of movement of people and goods. In 1937–8 there were some 900 kilometres of metalled and some 4,000 kilometres of unmetalled or kutcha roads in the state, although most of these were substandard. During the Second World War, the construction of roads for defence purposes received a boost and road connectivity improved marginally. Since early times, the economy of the region was well integrated with that of Bengal and India, and in providing access to markets both road and water connectivity played a vital role, with the railways coming in at a later stage.[52] It is generally accepted that prior to Partition, Assam and the northeastern region were connected by road infrastructure, however deficient this might have been. But with Partition the roads which were the lifeline of trade and commerce with neighbouring Bengal[53] were totally severed as was the rail network. All that was left in the name of connectivity with the rest of the country was now the bottleneck of the Siliguri Corridor. The negative fallout of this on the economy of Assam and the entire region has been tremendous and even after seventy years of Independence it is still to recover from it.

It is significant that for the first ten to twelve years after Partition, till the early 1960s, road connectivity between Assam and the northeastern region and the rest of the country was in a pitiable state and the state of the roadways was a major hindrance to the development of the economy of the region. After much popular agitation, the construction of the first bridge over the Brahmaputra was started in January 1959 amid deteriorating India–China relations following India's granting of asylum to the Dalai Lama,[54] and was completed in November 1962, just a month after the outbreak of the Sino-Indian border war.[55] It was clearly because of defence needs that the Brahmaputra Bridge was completed within three years. It was also because of security reasons that following the Indian debacle at the Sino-Indian border attempts were initiated to improve road connectivity with Assam and the northeastern region. The National Highway 31, connecting Guwahati with the rest of the country through the Siliguri Corridor, was speedily improved and within another two years, by April 1964, four major concrete bridges were built on this highway, thereby eliminating the ferry crossings. This shows that security considerations played a central role in the Government of India's attempts to improve connectivity with the region. It was again defence needs that compelled the Centre to extend the broad-gauge line from New Jalpaiguri to Jogighopa via New Bongaigaon, and it has been said that 'to a great extent the major railway projects in Assam since independence are the result of forces external to the railways'.[56] Security concerns speeded up the improvement of the railways in such a manner that during the years 1965–6 alone about 220 kilometres of track was opened to traffic. But this sense of urgency has nowhere been evident in projects relating to the development of the industrial or agricultural infrastructure of the state or for that matter in the power sector. In these sectors, the Indian state's approach was, to say the least, lackadaisical because these did not involve immediate security considerations.

Assam today typifies a syndrome of what economists call 'resource curse'—the high availability of natural resources does not necessarily augment economic growth in the region. There is a general acceptance of the fact that reduction in transaction and communication costs is essential for increasing the region's interaction with the world economy. Increased efficiencies together with improvements in quality, productivity, and technology are crucial for attaining greater market competitiveness. The planned development approach pursued by India since 1951 to do away with regional imbalances and foster holistic growth and development aimed at the uplift of the marginalized sections of society did not bring about any marked changes in the northeastern region, and even the few enterprises that were set up under the public sector failed to meet their goals. To understand the gradual deceleration in the economic growth of Assam, it would be essential to delve into the asymmetric fiscal federal structure that went hand in hand with the delineation of political boundaries of the states on the basis of languages after the partition of 1947 to reorganize the Indian states. Typically, separate religious, caste, ethnic, or tribal identities within these boundaries were not the basis for further divisions of the provinces in new India. One major exception to this has been the northeastern region of India, where there exist distinct differences in ethnicity from the rest of India and the population sizes of the states are also markedly different. Of the states in northeast India, only Assam has a population comparable to other typical Indian states. However, by the 1970s as many as three states were carved out from Assam and some were upgraded from the status of union territories. This reclassification gave them, at one level, a political status equivalent to that of larger states such as Madhya Pradesh and Uttar Pradesh.[57] States in India have, till recently, been classified into special category states and non-special category states based on certain parameters. States of the northeast region were accorded this status based on topography of hilly terrain, sparsely populated habitation, and high transport costs leading to high delivery cost of public services. The importance of apparently non-economic factors in determining the structure of federalism is underscored by the fact that the economic viability of the special category states has been questioned.

The growing concentration of fiscal manoeuvrability with the central government over the years has also been responsible for differences across states with respect to public infrastructure and investment. Notwithstanding the growth impetus stimulated by the plan development process in the initial decades, it, however, remains a fact that adoption of planning led by the public sector as the post-Independence strategy of development and emergence of the Planning Commission (PC)—a body not envisaged in the Constitution—gave the central government an unquestionably dominant role in fixing economic policies and priorities and also as a dispenser of central funds to the constituent states of the republic. The expenditure policies of the states, therefore, were bound to be influenced by the Centre as the former were required to draw up their five-year and annual plans as approved by the PC. The annual plan approval proved to be a major mechanism for the Centre to control state expenditure. Over and above the plans approved by the PC, the states were made to increasingly implement Centrally Sponsored Schemes (CSS), supposedly initiated in national interest.

The Centre's intervention in areas such as rural development, health, and family welfare that under the Constitution belonged primarily to the states consistently grew over the years, particularly in the post-1991 period. The concentration of economic decision-making at the level of the Centre and reliance on the public sector were primarily the result of distrust in the market system because of its imperfections, and essentially aimed at promoting domestic industries. Various acts and laws on the movement of goods across states, especially agricultural produce, and origin-based taxes were introduced, which distorted the domestic market and the states that were low in production base suffered the most.

While it has been maintained in some quarters that the northeastern states are overwhelmingly dependent on central transfer of funds and most of these states are not economically viable, such an argument is not necessarily applicable to Assam. It may be true, as Rao and Singh argue,[58] that one of the important reasons for large transfers to these states may be found in the political bargain that brought these areas firmly into the Indian Union and keeps them there; this is particularly true for not only the formal, separate induction into the Indian Union of states such as Sikkim and Kashmir, but also applies to cases such as Nagaland which was born out of an insurgent struggle, which refused to acknowledge and accept the Indian Constitution, and was finally brought under some control through the granting of statehood with special provisions; and this implicit political bargain may require continuing transfers beyond the average. Yet such a cosmetic fiscal federalism of northeastern India, which is assumed to have affected its growth, is perhaps not true for Assam which has had thriving business and trade relations with neighbouring countries in the pre-Partition days. During the colonial period, the tea, oil, and coal industries were developed in the province and the infrastructure of railways and roads was laid. It needs to be recalled that while in the pre-Partition period much of the present-day northeast India came under excluded or partially excluded areas, where economic activities of the areas were left unto themselves, and the British administration did not intervene in the local economic spaces as long as they brought in the requisite revenue, this was not the case with Assam which was a place for commercial possibilities as it was getting increasingly integrated with the Indian market. Even in matters of intercommunity, interregional, and inter-country trade Assam was quite ahead of the other regions with its innumerable local *haats* and fairs. But this process came to a stop with the partition of the country. What was once normal trade within the same colonial administration, now came under the aegis of international trade, and interstate movement of goods were subjected to a new set of regulatory framework. The breaking down of the existing trade arrangements and the evolution of the same under a new state regulatory framework with a communication bottleneck had a severe impact on economic resurgence in the post-Partition period. India's developmental model in the post-Independence era has channelled public spending to meet the critical gaps in infrastructure and, therefore, it is obvious that regions which have natural accessibility have been able to take advantage of government policies to build their infrastructural base. On the other hand, Assam and the rest of northeast India, which became a landlocked region post the Partition, fell behind as the connectivity with the rest of the country across hilly and mountainous contours became more and more cost intensive. Also, the local economic transactions waned under the regulatory framework of the market transactions. Thus, institutional weaknesses, remoteness from markets, and difficult access have taken their toll and left Assam without substantial agglomerations of commercial and industrial activities. While it is an accepted fact that accessibility to markets and sources of raw materials are critical for the growth of a region, it is equally true that economic activities are invariably attracted towards locations that have good market access because this lowers transport costs. This has been borne out by that fact that those coastal Indian states which have good port facilities have been able to attract substantially higher investments than those regions which are geographically handicapped.[59] It is true that geographical disadvantages can be compensated by positive business investments and good administrative policies, yet in the case of a state such as Assam this, too, seems to be have been badly affected by a long-drawn insurgency and continuing identity movements resulting in an unstable political situation and a slew of ad hoc measures by the government, which have had a negative impact on economic growth. As a result, Assam has fallen far behind the other Indian states comparable to it in size and population in areas of communication, power, and transport—the three core sectors determining the infrastructural base. Incidentally, the state's infrastructural base is still amongst the lowest in the country.

A leading economist of the region, Professor Atul Sarma, argues that the two main factors which have been hindering the economic growth of the region are the 'over-emphasis on security/strategic considerations rather than a development perspective in development efforts' and 'minimum intervention in the traditional systems and institutions of the hill economy, which is what has led to their non-compatibility with the growing penetration of market forces in the process of economic development efforts'.[60] He points out the fact that when the North Eastern Council (NEC) was formed, ostensibly to speed up the economic growth of the entire northeastern region, it was initially placed under the Ministry of Home Affairs because of security reasons.

> But even this [NEC] was designed to serve more a security interest than to promote integrated development of the NER [northeastern region]. This is clear from the fact that the NEC was placed for long under the administrative control of the Ministry of Home, GOI, and under the chairmanship of one of the governors of the northeastern states but not under any development ministries or the Planning Commission. Only recently has the NEC been reorganized as a regional planning body, though it has continued to function as a rudderless body so far.

The fact that a refinery was denied to Assam in the 1950s further validates Sarma's arguments about the Centre's approach towards Assam. This skewed approach, combined with lack of governmental initiative to bring the traditional systems of the economy in line with modern needs, has hampered the economic growth of the region. Nonetheless, from the mid-1990s efforts were made to accelerate the economic growth of the region and integrate the economy with that of South East Asia. It was during this time that the much-hyped Look East Policy, aimed at freeing the region from the fetters of geopolitical isolation, was announced and worked out in detail in the Vision 2020 prepared by the NEC.[61] But as Sarma has said, for the vision to become operative new inputs in foreign, defence, and international trade policy are needed and, before anything else, the economy of the different northeastern states must be integrated through better infrastructure and market facilities. This, unfortunately, has not happened despite the fact that the Ministry of Development for the Northeastern Region (DONER), set up in 2001, has spent thousands of crores for the development of the region. There seems to be a general agreement amongst economists and analysts of the region that mere pumping in of money without attempting to integrate the economies of the northeastern states and building up the necessary infrastructure to facilitate trade and commerce, not only with the rest of the country but within the northeastern states as well, would not yield positive results. This is exactly why the Look East Policy is yet to take off. Meanwhile, Assam and the northeastern region continue to be trapped in the geographical isolation into which they were pushed into by the Partition.

When the Look East Policy was announced in 1992, plenty of expectations were raised throughout the northeastern states and especially in Assam because it happens to be the most advanced state of the region in terms of trade and commerce and is the virtual gateway to the Northeast. But, apart from spectacular shows such as the India-ASEAN Car Rally, nothing tangible has emerged in the last one decade or so. While it is true that the Look East Policy has gained a lot of acceptance amongst administrators and policy planners and this has led to a radical change in perceptions about an integrated South Asian market, certain constricting factors have been preventing a take-off. It is now being increasingly realized that if states such as Assam are to benefit from the Look East Policy then meaningful and effective measures must be taken to develop the industrial and institutional infrastructure of the region. Otherwise, given its present position in the development graph of the country, Assam would remain only a transit state for goods that would move between India and the South East Asian nations as well as other neighbours such as Bangladesh, Bhutan, and China. It is also being realized that unless radical steps are taken to do something about the deplorable power and communication scenario in the state, it would be very difficult for Assam to derive any benefits from the opening up and integration of the Indian market with that of South Asian states.

The need, therefore, has arisen to make a thorough study of the socio-economic scenario of Assam and identify those areas that have contributed towards making the state's economy moribund and stagnant. It must be realized that unless the economic and industrial scenario of Assam is made viable, the main aspects of the Look East Policy would never be translated into reality. That is exactly why there must be a shift in emphasis towards identifying the weak links in the chain in states such as Assam and then initiating such steps as may be necessary to help integrate the economy of this region with that of the rest of the country as well as with the South Asian states. One cannot expect

Assam to be a viable partner in the Look East project with a GDP that is much below the national average, an agricultural growth rate that is almost stagnant, and industrial growth way below the national figures. It is clear that there cannot be any substantial growth in the service sector of Assam unless changes for the better take place in the agricultural and industrial sectors. Recurrent floods, scanty progress in the irrigation sector, lack of a scientific approach in the use of chemical fertilizers and pesticides coupled with poor connectivity have severely affected the agriculture sector which happens to be the mainstay of the economy of Assam. Erosion by the Brahmaputra, the Barak, and their tributaries has been a major challenge to the economy of Assam. The area eroded since 1954 has been 3.68 lakh hectares, some 7 per cent of the total area of the state.[62] Every year hundreds of thousands are affected by the floods and erosion, and thousands seek shelter in the raised portions of national highways and other roads which turn into their semi-permanent homes for years.[63] There has been no major initiative on the part of either the central or the state government to tackle this continuous threat to the economic growth of the region. Added to natural calamities is the increasingly unstable law and order situation created by continuing insurgency. Efforts to improve connectivity by upgrading existing rail and road networks were initially resisted at several places by the insurgents, for example, in parts of Karbi Anglong and North Cachar Hills.

Thus, a weak and moribund Assam cannot contribute towards the success of the Look East Policy. In order to be a viable partner in the trade and commerce of an expanding market, not only would it be necessary to improve the communication network with the other northeastern states but also within Assam itself. This, along with improvement in the power sector, would help in integrating the economy of Assam with that of the rest of the Northeast by providing an effective boost to trade and commerce. Assam's geographical position, its huge hydropower potential, its experience as one of the world's largest producers of tea, its natural resources in the form of petroleum and coal are only a few of the positive points which give it a premier position as far as trade and commerce of the Northeast is concerned. But owing to the factors already mentioned, this resource-rich state is today way down in the development graph and is several decades behind not only other large Indian states such as Gujarat and Maharashtra but also smaller ones such as Himachal Pradesh, not to speak of the South East Asian countries to which it is expected to open up. It is certain that in its present state of industrial and institutional infrastructure and its sluggish economy, Assam will not be in a position to reap the benefits of the Look East Policy. Rather, there are apprehensions that its opening up to trade could have an adverse effect on the people's lifestyle and culture and would bring in changes to which the people as a whole would not be able to adjust.

Therefore, the clue to a successful Look East Policy lies in a vibrant Northeast economy which would depend not only on better connectivity but also a better understanding between the sister states leading to a meaningful sharing of resources based on the development of a common economic policy. Added to this would be the need to improve the present state of relations with countries such as Bangladesh and Bhutan, two of the major trading partners of Assam and the Northeast. The few steps that have already been initiated to formalize much of the 'illegal' trade that goes on between these countries and the northeastern states have already shown results. However, much more needs to be done on this front and areas must be identified where more effective and coordinated measures can be initiated to increase the flow of trade. But it remains an unpleasant fact that policies relating to trade and commerce are often influenced by the ground realities of the political situation and this is the case with India's relations with Bangladesh. Both sides suffer from certain inbuilt prejudices and perceptions, with the issue of illegal influx further complicating the situation. Despite all these roadblocks, recent years have seen a change in the situation as far as trade relations are concerned and a comprehensive policy worked out by Assam and Bangladesh could be of great benefit to them, both of whom share a long history of trade ties. Given these factors, the perspective of Assam and the northeastern region regarding the Look East Policy is bound to be different from that of the Centre. The possibilities as well as the doubts and apprehensions, stemming from a weak and undeveloped economy being swamped by much more developed ones, need to be taken into account when the Look East Policy comes up for discussion. The apprehensions and doubts of small ethnic communities about the challenges that would surface in the wake of globalization must be attended to. Only when the human dimensions of the entire issue of opening up the market are properly addressed would trade and commerce with neighbouring countries gain new strength, and Assam and the other northeastern states would be able to be effective partners in a South East Asian market.

Finally, it may be said that there have been long-range after-effects of the Partition in the case of Assam. On the political front, one witnessed polarization along communal lines, which gave a totally new dimension to the issue of influx from the then East Bengal/East Pakistan; it also helped the growth of concerns of autonomy among the small nationalities of the region because of the fear of it going to Pakistan. On the economic front, trade and commerce stood disrupted and infrastructure and development suffered a major setback, which in turn triggered waves of dissension among the less developed communities/nationalities, thereby laying the seeds of future militant movements. On the governance angle, security concerns dominated all other aspects and rule of law and distributive justice were marginalized. Added to all this was the growth of an isolationist mindset, which consciously started to move away from the Indian mainland and the civilizational concerns it represented. Any attempt, therefore, to understand the reasons behind the rise of secessionist militancy in provinces such as Assam, which have had centuries of socio-historical and cultural relationship with the Indian mainland and its civilizational ethos, must look back into those pre- and post-Partition days when the entire northeastern region was pushed into a state of flux and uncertainty, and how after the Partition both geography and politics underwent a radical change. Thus, among many other things, one of the long-range effects of the Partition may be seen in the growth of not only a separatist mindset among the younger generation but, more important, an isolationist attitude. While some work has been done on the psychological impact of the Partition in western India, we do not see any serious study relating to the northeastern region. Once cut off from the Indian mainland and surrounded by regions not easily accessible, a new psychology of isolationism developed. This was certainly not so in the pre-Partition days when the movement of people across the plains of the Indian subcontinent into the Assam plains and further onwards was quite common. Partition seriously disrupted, if not totally put an end to, such interaction. Those who were angry with the Indian leadership's insensitivity towards this region started looking eastward and, in doing so, tried to disown the cultural and political links with the rest of the subcontinent. The process of rewriting and reinterpreting the history of the region began and the 'Indian' link was sought to be assiduously discounted. This tendency was to be seen in the agenda of the militant outfits who swore by their East Asian neighbours, whose culture and civilization they tried to emulate.[64] The security concerns of the Indian mainland, the failure to empathize with the people of the region, the reluctance to invest capital and develop the much-needed infrastructure of the Northeast, the attempts to rule the region through draconian laws, and, most important, continuing to view the region and its people as the 'other', all contributed towards alienating the northeastern region from the mainland.

However, in recent years, perspectives have begun to change and the great resilience and power of accommodation of the Indian Constitution have gone a long way in neutralizing the separatist tendencies and their thesis of civilizational difference. The carving out of new political and cultural spaces for the small nationalities of the region has brought with it its own problems in the form of constitutional rights of those non-tribal minorities who continue to be residents of ethnic homelands.[65] But such measures have also shown the willingness of the Indian nation state to accommodate the aspirations of the small nationalities within the expanding parameters of the nation state. But, even as peace negotiations are on with the different militant organizations, many of the issues thrown up in the pre- and post-Partition days are yet to be resolved. Primary among these are the question of ensuring the identity of the small nationalities, the problem of illegal infiltration from Bangladesh (erstwhile east Pakistan), swift demographic change, the alienation from land of the ethnic population, the rights of the states over their natural resources, and, to put it in broad terms, the restructuring of the quasi-federal relationship between the Union and the states into a truly federal one.

Notes

1. The Sixth Schedule of the Constitution of India [Articles 244(a) and 275(1)] provided for district councils in the tribal areas of undivided Assam, which were made into autonomous districts. Though the district councils, which had elected representation, were given wide-ranging powers over land, water, and even mineral resources, the relationship between

the councils and the state government, under which they functioned, was never clearly defined. Quite often the district councils were totally dependent on the mercy of the state governments for financial grants for their projects. Moreover, when most of these autonomous districts were turned into full-fledged states within the Indian Union, the role and function of the district councils was further marginalized.

2. The Assam Assembly session of March 2015 saw vituperative exchanges between members over the question of Assamese identity. The regional press was filled with reports and letters regarding this emotive issue. Assam's premier literary organization, the Asom Sahitya Sabha, was entrusted by the state government to find out an acceptable definition for the 'Assamese people'. But it failed to do so.

3. Mountbatten's pronouncement of 3 June 1947 provided for a referendum to be held in the Sylhet district of Assam in order to ascertain whether the people of that district wished to join Pakistan or continue stay in Assam (India).

4. While there are scores of excellent studies on the partition of the Punjab and Bengal, very few scholars have thought it fit to discuss the effects of Partition on Assam and the entire northeastern region. There are, of course, references to Assam's role during the Grouping and the Constituent Assembly debates in works by Joya Chatterjee and Bidyut Chakrabarty, for instance, but the discussion does not go beyond this, primarily because these works are about Bengal.

5. Refer to Sanjib Baruah, 'Assam: Confronting a Failed Partition', *Seminar*, vol. DXCI (November 2008): 34. Baruah states that 'for all its twists and turns, politics in post-independence Assam has been mostly about a single issue: dealing with the failure of the 1947 Partition'.

6. Amalendu Guha, *Planter Raj to Swaraj: Freedom Struggle and Electoral Politics in Assam 1827–1947* (New Delhi: Indian Council of Historical Research [ICHR], 1977), p. 39.

7. Since the late 1990s, there has been a phenomenal increase in the number of small tea gardens in the state. Thousands of small tea gardens have sprung up over the years, although almost all the large estates are controlled by the corporate sector. The total land held by tea gardens today is estimated at some 8 lakh acres. Small tea gardens started mushrooming after the Janata government (1978–80) of the state lifted the restrictions on the cultivation of tea in Assam.

8. Amalendu Guha, *Medieval and Early Colonial Assam: Society, Polity and Economy* (Guwahati: Anwesha Publications, 2015), p. 196.

9. Refer to Tilottoma Misra, 'Assam: A Colonial Hinterland', special article, *Economic and Political Weekly*, vol. XV, no. 39 (9 August 1980): Bombay.

10. The Jorhat Sarvajanik Sabha, set up in 1874, was an organization of Assamese landowning peasants or revenue-paying ryots. It had a mass peasant base but the leadership was invariably in the hands of the emerging middle-class elite, many of whom felt that it was in their economic interest to support immigration.

11. Binayak Dutta, 'The "Stout Fanatical Mahomedan" and Mullan's Burden: The History of Bengali Immigration in Colonial Assam (1871–1931)', *Man and Society: A Journal of North-East Studies*, vol. XI (Winter 2014): ICSSR North Eastern Regional Centre, Shillong.

12. In the report on the 1911 Census, the census commissioner referred to the 'peaceful invasion of Assam by advancing hordes of Mymensinghia army'.

13. As per the 2011 Census the population density in Assam is 397 per square kilometre, amongst the highest in India.

14. Dutta, 'The "Stout Fanatical Mahomedan"', p. 78.

15. C.S. Mullan's note, *Census of India*, vol. XII, part-1A Report (Shillong: Municipal Printing Press, Government of Assam, 1954), p. 73.

16. Amalendu Guha calls Mullan's observations 'mischievous and blatantly fallacious' and accuses Mullan of 'irresponsible and unfounded utterings' aimed at increasing friction between the autochthones and the immigrants. He holds Mullan responsible for fanning 'chauvinist' fears through his 'false prophesy'. But recent census figures have proved that Mullan was not entirely wrong in his prediction.

17. Dutta, 'The "Stout Fanatical Mahomedan"', pp. 78–9.

18. The idea of a line dividing the immigrants from the indigenous peasants was first mooted in 1916 and finally adopted as an administrative measure in 1920. According to the Line System, a line was drawn in those districts which were under pressure from immigrants so that they could be settled in segregated areas specified for their exclusive settlement. The system was first put into action in 1920 in Nowgong district and in the Barpeta subdivision of Kamrup district. Later, the system was applied to most of the lower Assam districts. Under the system, the villages were divided into three groups: (*a*) 'open villages' in which immigrants might settle freely; (*b*) 'closed villages' in which immigrants could not settle at all; and (*c*) 'mixed villages' in which a line was drawn so that immigrants could settle on one side only. But continuous encroachment by immigrants into lands earmarked for indigenous peasants ultimately made the Line System quite ineffective.

19. Guha, *Planter Raj to Swaraj*, pp. 212–13.

20. The Congress, which had emerged as the main political organization of the Brahmaputra Valley during the 1930s, gave articulation to these apprehensions and became the chief platform of anti-immigration politics.

Its election manifesto of 1946 clearly states its intention of securing an Assamese homeland.

21. Dhubri (74.29 per cent), Barpeta (59.37 per cent), Hailakandi (57.6 per cent), Goalpara (53.7 per cent), Karimganj (53.2 per cent) [2001 Census].

22. The United Progressive Alliance (UPA) government headed by Manmohan Singh held up the release of the religious break-up fearing social turmoil in Assam. The figures were finally released by the National Democratic Alliance (NDA) government in August 2015.

23. In Jammu and Kashmir it was 1.3 per cent, from 67 per cent to 68 per cent, while that in West Bengal was 1.8 per cent, from 25.2 per cent to 27 per cent.

24. As per the 2011 Census the Hindu population stood at 1,91,59,751 (60.49 per cent), while that of Muslims stood at 1,06,66,124 (34.2 per cent).

25. Four more districts were formed in January 2016. According to a report published in a local Assamese daily, Bengali Muslims and Hindus constitute a deciding force in some 47 assembly constituencies of the state's 126 constituencies. The paper quoted the peasant leader Akhil Gogoi as saying that according to the 2011 Census, in thirty-one constituencies of the state immigrant Muslims make up to 50 per cent or more of the population while in another eight constituencies they constitute around 40 per cent of the population. (The 'Asomiya Jatiye Siddhanta Lobo Lagibo Jatiatabad ne Hindutva' [The Assamese Nationality Must Decide Whether It Should Be Nationalism or Hindutva], *Amar Asom*, Guwahati, 17 September 2015, pp. 1, 8.) Also refer to D.N. Bezboruah, 'A Crippling Load of Aliens', *The Assam Tribune*, Guwahati, 20 September 2015, p. 6. The Muslim majority districts are Dhubri (79.67 per cent), Barpeta (70.74 per cent), Goalpara (57.52 per cent), Nagaon (55.36 per cent), Morigaon (52.56 per cent), Karimganj (56.36 per cent), Darrang (64.34 per cent), Bongaigaon (50.22 per cent), and Hailakandi (60.31 per cent) [2011 Census].

26. Kalyan Barooah, 'State Records 7 pc Rise in Muslim Population', *The Assam Tribune*, Guwahati, 2 September 2014, p. 1.

27. In the 2001 Census, when the Bengali-speaking populous district of Sylhet was a part of Assam, the number of Assamese speakers stood at 21.6 per cent. In the 1931 Census it was 31.4 per cent. Following the separation of Sylhet from Assam in 1947, the percentage of Assamese speakers registered a sharp rise and the 1951 Census put the figure at 56.7 per cent. Many observers questioned this sudden rise.

28. The state had some 14 lakh educated unemployed people registered in Employment Exchanges in 2010; the total number of unemployed registered was more than 19 lakhs.

29. Gopinath Bardoloi (1890–1950) was the foremost Congress leader of Assam during the struggle for independence. He led a consistent fight

against the pro-immigration policies of the Saadulla government and also successfully steered the province's struggle against the grouping scheme of the Cabinet Mission. Gandhi extended his support to Bardoloi on the grouping issue. When he took over as the premier of Assam in February 1946, following the Congress's victory in the elections, he initiated measures to evict illegal encroachers from government reserves. Following Independence, Bardoloi had serious differences with Nehru over the settlement of refugees in Assam, and successfully held his ground against the central leadership of the Congress. Bardoloi was posthumously awarded the Bharat Ratna by the Government of India.

30. James Joy Mohan Nichols Roy was a Khasi legislator and a minister. Though he served as a minister in two of Saadulla's ministries, his opposition to the politics of the Muslim League drew him closer to the Congress. Nichols Roy was vocal on the issue of immigration from East Bengal and opposed the Muslim League's efforts to make Assam a part of Pakistan. As a member of the Constituent Assembly, he played a leading role and may be said to be one of the few hill leaders of his time who acquired a national standing in the country's politics. In post-Independence India, Nichols Roy was a minister in the Bardoloi government but he gradually became disillusioned with the Congress politics of the state dominated by the Assamese middle class and veered towards the Hill State Movement which stood for a separate Khasi–Jaintia–Garo state.

31. Interestingly, these very points were to come up again in the Assam Accord, which was signed between the All Assam Students' Union and the central government following the Assam Movement of 1979–85.

32. Six other plains tribes in Assam have been given 'autonomous councils' in an attempt to accommodate their growing demands for recognition of their separate identities. These are the Rabha Autonomous Council at Goalpara, Deori Autonomous Council at Lakhimpur, Mishing Autonomous Council at Dhemaji, Thengal Kachari Autonomous Council at Titabor, and Sonowal Kachari Autonomous Council at Dibrugarh. These tribal autonomous councils are not within the Sixth Schedule of the Constitution and are somewhat like developmental bodies. The three autonomous councils created under the provisions of the Sixth Schedule of the Constitution are the Karbi Anglong Autonomous Council (KAAC), the Dima Hasao District Autonomous Council (DHDAC), and the Bodoland Territorial Council (BTC).

33. Jared Diamond, *Guns, Germs and Steel: A Short History of Everybody for the Last 13,000 Years* (London: Vintage Books, 2005), pp. 25–6.

34. The huge Indo-Gangetic plain extended into the Brahmaputra Valley through the plains of Bihar and north Bengal, with the mighty

Brahmaputra River being the lifeline between Assam and the rest of the Indian subcontinent.

35. Although certain scholars have maintained that Assam and the northeastern region was considered as a frontier territory during colonial rule and its links with the Indian mainland were quite tenuous, the growth of the tea and oil industries, for instance, went a long way in integrating the economy of the region with that of the rest of the country. Hence, there is great difference between the frontier or borderland of colonial times and the isolated and landlocked periphery that emerged following the Partition of 1947.

36. 'A Class X student from Assam has made the 50-year-old National Council of Educational Research and Training erase a "careless sentence" from one of its textbooks. The NCERT, the national agency publishing textbooks, has removed a controversial reference about tourism in the Northeastern states only after Kavya Barnadhya Hazarika, the schoolboy from Guwahati, pointed it out. The NCERT removed the sentence that attributed the slugging [*sic*] tourism sector in the hilly states to "strategic reasons".' The sentence in the chapter on 'Lifelines of National Economy' in the NCERT-published geography textbook for Class X read: "There is vast potential of tourism development in the northeastern states and the interior parts of Himalayas, but due to strategic reasons these have not been encouraged so far."' (Basant Kumar Mahanty, 'Assam Boy Forces Textbook Revision', *The Telegraph*, Calcutta, 6 February 2014.)

37. Interestingly, it was during the colonial period that the first oil refinery in Asia was set up at Digboi in upper Assam in 1901, the railways were laid, and Dibrugarh was connected to Chittagong for the purposes of export of tea. Moreover, it was in the latter half of the nineteenth century that the tea estates were established, bringing in thousands of indentured labour from other parts of India. Even during the Ahom period (1228–1826) there was a vibrant trade between Assam and neighbouring Bengal, although some of the Ahom rulers were known to have followed an isolationist policy.

38. The present NDA government has changed the nomenclature from Look East Policy to Act East Policy, although the parameters have remained the same.

39. As early as 1904, Dibrugarh in upper Assam was connected by rail to Chittagong port primarily for the export of tea, jute, and petroleum products. Tea was easily the most import item of export through Chittagong port.

40. Up to 1882, steamer companies carrying cargo took eighteen days to reach Dibrugarh from Goalando in Bengal. In 1883, a daily steamer service on the Brahmaputra was introduced and this could reach Dibrugarh from

Goalando in just a week. Refer to S.B. Medhi, *River Transport and Economic Development in Assam* (Guwahati: Publication Board, 1978), p. 22.

41. Medhi, *River Transport and Economic Development in Assam*, pp. 26–35.

42. Medhi, *River Transport and Economic Development in Assam*, pp. 28–9.

43. According to the Regional Transport Survey of Assam, in 1963 more than 47 per cent of goods moved between Assam and Calcutta by waterways as against 46 per cent by railways in 1963–4.

44. Medhi, *River Transport and Economic Development in Assam*, p. 32.

45. Medhi, *River Transport and Economic Development in Assam*, p. 35.

46. While in pre-Partition days ships carrying tea, coal, and timber reached Calcutta from Dibrugarh in just over a week, a ship from Kolkata to Guwahati nowadays takes more than twenty-five days due to lack of night navigation and customs formalities at various points.

47. As per agreement with Pakistan, repairs of carriages and wagons of the then Assam Railway were periodically carried out at the Saidpur workshops of the Eastern Bengal Railway in East Pakistan. Refer to Medhi, *River Transport and Economic Development in Assam*, p. 87.

48. Assam and the northeastern region's only link with the rest of the country was now through a 27-kilometre wide stretch of land called the Siliguri Corridor or the 'chicken's neck'.

49. For instance, a substantial quantity of tea had to be sent by road to Calcutta because the railways could not provide enough wagons, thereby adding to the costs. Road transport costs were much higher than river transport, which was costlier than rail transport.

50. Medhi, *River Transport and Economic Development in Assam*, p. 89.

51. Medhi, *River Transport and Economic Development in Assam*, p. 90.

52. The first major road network was built by King Naranarayana in the sixteenth century and this 400-kilometre road in the north bank of the Brahmaputra connected Cooch-Behar with upper Assam. During Ahom rule (1228–1826), too, many embankments, which were used as roads, were built connecting upper and lower Assam in the south bank of the Brahmaputra.

53. For instance, the then Khasi Hills district of Assam (present-day Meghalaya) was highly dependent on trade with the areas bordering East Bengal. Partition snuffed out all trade outlets.

54. The Dalai Lama arrived in the Tawang sector of the then The North-East Frontier Agency (NEFA) and present-day Arunachal Pradesh on 31 March 1959.

55. The Brahmaputra Bridge, also known as the Saraighat Bridge, was opened to goods traffic in October 1962 and to passenger traffic in January 1963. On the entire length of the Brahmaputra River from Dhubri to Sadiya

which covers almost 900 kilometres, there are only three bridges till date, while two more are under construction.

56. Medhi, *River Transport and Economic Development in Assam*, p. 93.

57. For detailed analysis, refer to Dr Chanchal Kumar, 'Federalism in India: A Critical Appraisal', *Journal of Business Management and Social Sciences Research* (JBM&SSR), vol. III, no. 9 (September 2014): 31–43.

58. M. Rao Govinda and Nirvikar Singh, *Political Economy of Federalism in India* (New Delhi: Oxford University Press, 2005).

59. For elaboration and details, see World Bank, *India: Investment Climate and Manufacturing Industry* (Washington DC: World Bank, 2004), available at http://siteresources.worldbank.org/INTKNOWLEDGEFORCHANGE/Resources/491519-1199818447826/IC-IndiaUpdateDraft.pdf.

60. Atul Sarma, 'A Unified North East Economy: Road to Gainful Economic Integration with South East Asia', J.B. Ganguli Memorial Lecture, delivered at Tripura Central University on 11 April 2011. Also refer to Atul Sarma, 'Why the Northeastern States Continue to Decelerate', *Man and Society: A Journal of North East States*, vol. I, no. 1 (Spring 2005): 12–14.

61. Vision 2020 was envisaged by the Centre in 2005 and the draft document, prepared by DONER, was made public in May 2008. The aim of the document was to speed up the socio-economic development of the eight states of northeastern region and bring them in line with the rest of the country. For this, stress was laid on the development of infrastructure, grass-roots level growth, good governance, and making the northeastern region central to India's economic ties with South East Asia.

62. *Economic Survey of Assam 2011–2012*, Directorate of Economics and Statistics, Assam, Planning and Development Department, Government of Assam, Dispur. The total area of the state of Assam is 78,438 square kilometres.

63. More than 1,50,000 families have been displaced in the past decade alone. Refer to Amarjyoti Baruah, 'Assam's Nowhere People', *Down to Earth* (1 October 2015), available at www.downtoearth.org.in/nowhere, last accessed on 29 February 2016.

64. This feeling was also motivated by the fact that most of the insurgent groups had their bases in eastern Nagaland or northern Myanmar and their leaders made frequent trips to Thailand. In the 1990s the ULFA had also succeeded in establishing links in southern China.

65. Refer to Udayon Misra, 'Ethnic Homelands and Citizens' Rights', Nehru Memorial Srikant Dutt Lecture, 26 November 2012, Nehru Memorial Museum Library (NMML), New Delhi.

2

THE CRITICAL FORTIES I

This chapter takes up for discussion the turbulent 1940s when the issues of immigration, land, and identity gained an urgency that had never been witnessed before. Under the different ministries led by Syed Muhammad Saadulla, immigration of Muslim peasants from East Bengal received a new impetus from the 1930s onwards, and the issue of land became a contentious one. Following the All India Muslim League's (AIML's) Lahore Resolution of 1940, which, for the first time, laid down the idea of a separate Muslim homeland, the issue of immigration acquired grave political overtones all of a sudden and became inextricably linked with the question of land and the identity of the indigenous Assamese and tribal populations. In order to give the reader an idea of the change that was occurring, extensive details from the Assam Legislative Assembly debates of the 1940s over the occupation of government reserves and grazing lands have been included. These debates reveal the diametrically opposite positions held by the Indian National Congress and the Muslim League on immigration, land, and identity. Through these debates, the reader gets a comprehensive view of the contentious issues of land and identity and how the massive inflow of immigrants, actively aided and abetted by the party in power, led not only to swift demographic change but also to new political equations; of how the question of identity came to occupy a central place as far as the indigenes were concerned; and of how occupation of cultivable land and the attempt to do away with administrative measures such as the Line System, aimed at protecting indigenous life patterns, created a highly explosive situation in the state.

Issues of Land, Immigration, and Identity

The 1940s were indeed critical years for Assam when its very existence as a separate state seemed to be under threat, when politics took on different and contradictory hues, and when religious and community divides got perilously sharpened. This was the period when issues centred on land, immigration, identity, and language surfaced as never before and eventually determined, in many ways, the future course of Assam and the entire northeastern region and its people. It was also the period when the Congress came to dominate the politics of the region[1] and met with increasing opposition from the Muslim League, which began to gradually veer around to the idea of a separate Muslim homeland. The 1940s also saw frequent change of ministries, with Syed Muhammad Saadulla[2] heading as many as five different ministries from 1937 to 1946. The frequent formation and collapse of ministries bore evidence of the delicate demographic balance of the region that was being increasingly threatened by continued influx from East Bengal—which was encouraged by the Saadulla ministries and backed by the political parties of Bengal.[3] While the activities of the Muslim League primarily centred on immigration, and land added a clear communal dimension to the entire issue, the Assam Congress, by putting up a concerted fight to prevent grouping under the Cabinet Mission proposals, succeeded to a large extent in keeping the separatist tendencies at bay. But the entire politics centred around grouping, where the Central Congress leadership initially displayed a marked insensitivity towards Assam's position, was to colour the province's and the northeastern region's relationship with the Centre in the post-Independence years. Thus, the politics that led up to Partition may be said to have given shape to many an equation that marked the region's, and especially Assam's, post-Independence relationship with the Centre as well as with the rest of the nation. That is exactly why it is necessary to have a comprehensive idea of the social and political cross-currents of the period that preceded Partition and Independence and the period that immediately followed it. To say the least, the burden of the history of those momentous years still rests heavily on Assam's contemporary political scenario, marked as it is by a variety of identity struggles and ethnic strife.

The land question in Assam, which was inextricably linked with the issue of immigration from East Bengal, assumed serious dimensions in

the years immediately preceding Partition. It was the central political issue in the Assam of the 1940s and was debated at length in the
Assam Legislative Assembly. The members were sharply divided on
the issue of immigration and the occupation of the government forest reserves and grazing plots. The Congress led by Gopinath Bardoloi
was pitted against the immigrant lobby led by Syed Saadulla, Maulana
Hamid Khan Bhasani,[4] and the Muslim League. Though he was with
the Muslim League, Saadulla was repeatedly attacked by Bhasani and
his supporters for not doing enough for the immigrants. One would get
an idea of the contrary pulls that the Congress and the League were
exerting on the land question if one takes up the debates that took
place on the floor of the Legislative Assembly in the 1940s. The immigration issue got swiftly politically polarized once the Muslim League
adopted its Lahore Resolution of 1940, calling for a separate homeland
for India's Muslims. The controversial Land Settlement Resolution[5]
was adopted by the Muslim League-supported Saadulla ministry[6] just
a year after the Lahore Resolution. It was clearly intended to reduce
the effectiveness of the Line System[7] and open up as many government
forest land and grazing reserves to the immigrants as possible.[8] As it was,
during the 1930s, under the 'colonization scheme', thousands of acres
of government land had been opened up to immigrants. Commenting
on this, the social historian Amalendu Guha observes:

> During the six years preceding 1936, as many as 59 grazing, forest
> and village reserves had been thrown open in Nowgong under the
> Colonisation Scheme for settling the immigrants. Out of the district's
> total occupied area of 5,41,160 acres—sown and fallow—in 1936,
> 2,04,078 acres or 37.7 per cent were under immigrants' occupation,
> as against 62.3 per cent still in the hands of indigenous people.... The
> land hungry Muslim immigrants, segregated and pitted against all odds,
> never appreciated the Assamese point of view. If all men were equal in
> the eyes of Allah, why should thousands of acres of land remain waste,
> particularly when men in search of a livelihood and *lebensraum* were
> available to turn them into smiling fields? ... They wanted the Line sys-
> tem to go. If only it would concede them the right to a new home, they
> would even follow the Congress flag.[9]

The Assamese viewpoint was very different from that of the immigrants. With several of the plains tribes still accustomed to shifting cultivation, government reserves, grazing reserves, and village community

land were a part of their life pattern. These lands were integral to their ethos of living and they did not consider them only from the point of view of crops and revenue. These two very different approaches to land and life were bound to clash, with the Assamese increasingly viewing the immigrant occupation of land as a threat to their identity and culture. This apprehension took on ominous overtones even as the Muslim League geared up its efforts to communalize the situation by claiming Assam as a part of its proposed Muslim Pakistan. Meanwhile, the Saadulla ministries from 1939 to 1945[10] took full advantage of the situation to keep on encouraging immigrant settlement in the lower Brahmaputra Valley districts. It is significant that pressure for opening up the government reserves was also mounted on the Assam government by neighbouring Bengal.[11] Partly in response to this pressure, the Saadulla government initiated schemes that tried to justify the further settlement of immigrants in reserves and grazings in the name of increased food production to meet the war needs. Immigration, which till the 1930s was an essentially economic issue, had now become a hugely political issue and along with the issue of land, now got entwined with the issue of the future of Assamese nationality itself. This change is adequately reflected in the legislative assembly debates from the 1940s onwards.

The closing years of the 1930s were marked by major political changes in Assam. It was largely due to the efforts of Subhas Chandra Bose that a Congress coalition government was formed to replace the Saadulla ministry and put a check on its pro-immigration policies. The first coalition ministry headed by Bardoloi,[12] which lasted for barely fourteen months, tried to initiate certain measures aimed at protecting the indigenous peasantry from encroachment by the immigrants. The new ministry stated its intention of evicting immigrant settlers from village and professional grazing reserves (PGRs) as well as from lands reserved for the tribals and backward classes. The government also made its intention clear that it would give preference only to those settlers who had come before 1937.[13] The Government Resolution on this stated that land settlement would not be made with anyone in the village and PGRs, that regulated settlement of landless people, including immigrants would be made on wastelands subject to a holding of 30 *bighas* per family,[14] and that all immigrants would be evicted from protected tribal blocks in the submontane regions.[15] The decision of the government naturally drew the ire of the immigrant lobby, and Maulana Bhasani declared jihad against the Assam government in the first session of the Assam Provincial Muslim League held in November 1939. Bhasani, in the course of his speech, declared that 'it is not possible to solve this problem without resorting to jihad for the sake of Allah' and that the 'days have come now to get your demands fulfilled by becoming sahids [shahids] in the path of Allah'.[16] From this speech it is clear that the question of land occupation by immigrants was no more an economic issue but one that had been imbued with distinctly religious implications and turned into an almost exclusively Muslim issue. For leaders like Bhasani, the struggle for land of the immigrants had yet another dimension. This was the fight for the Bengali language and culture. Criticizing Saadulla for not doing enough for the immigrants, and justifying his disassociation with Saadulla's Assam United Party, Bhasani accused the former of joining hands with those who were out to kill the Bengali[17] language and culture. Thus, the communalization of the politics of the province on lines of religion and language had taken on new dimensions.

Once the Bardoloi-led ministry resigned in November 1939, a new ministry headed by Saadulla[18] took over and the issue of land settlement for the immigrants took on a new edge. That the Saadulla government was determined to undo all that was attempted by the previous Bardoloi-led government became clear in Saadulla's budget speech of March 1940, where he, while talking of safeguarding the interests of the indigenous people, emphasized the need for settlement of land by immigrants. In this budget speech he announced that his government would introduce a new land development scheme. Accordingly, in May–June 1940 he convened a meeting of all the parties to discuss the Line System, and it was here that the decision was reached on putting a ban on all settlements on wastelands by immigrants entering Assam after 1 January 1938. It was also decided that the indigenous landless along with eligible immigrants would be given settlement. The Government Resolution of June 1940 endorsed the ban on settlements by pre-January 1938 immigrants. The Development Scheme was published in the *Assam Gazette* of 4 December 1940. It envisaged settlement of indigenous landless peasants and pre-1938 immigrants on government land without doing harm to the forest reserves and grazing lands. But there was a catch in the Government Resolution of 1940.

It also provided for the accommodation of people affected by flood and erosion who had been illegally staying in government reserves or 'lined' villages. This proviso was taken full advantage of by the officials working under the Saadulla government to settle immigrants who came after January 1938 on government reserves and grazing lands. Any attempts by the Saadulla government, however feeble, to maintain the Line System in favour of the indigenes was fiercely resisted by the Muslim League, which seemed to have adopted a one-point agenda of getting the Line System abolished.[19] The Muslim League's agenda was pushed forward by the Saadulla government through the initiation of the Land Development Scheme, which apparently was meant to provide land to indigenous landless peasants but in actuality aimed at helping to further immigrant settlements.[20]

Meanwhile, popular resentment against Saadulla's Land Development Scheme was mounting and the politics of the province was taking new turns. Saadulla was finally forced to resign in December 1941 and there was a brief period of Governor's Rule.[21] The governor scrapped the Land Development Scheme in March 1942, and Amalendu Guha writes: 'It was stated that the policy of wastelands settlement, if continued further, would seriously prejudice "the interests not only of the indigenous population, but also of those who have already come from Bengal and settled in the last twenty or thirty years." The pressing need of extending forests and preserving grazing grounds was particularly emphasized.'[22] During the brief period of Governor's Rule, the entire issue of land settlement found a new focus and the administration's policy was geared towards preventing fresh immigrant settlements while trying to evict encroachments upon the PGRs. The new policy of the government stressed on the non-availability of wasteland for the fresh wave of immigrants and said that further settlements would seriously prejudice the interests not only of the indigenous people but also those of settled immigrants.[23] However, government efforts to evict encroachers during this period did not have much effect because the organized lobby of the immigrants went all out to foil them.

The Quit India resolution of the Congress led to the arrest of almost all its top leaders in August 1942, and both the All India Congress Committee (AICC) and the Assam Pradesh Congress Committee (APCC) were declared as unlawful bodies. This helped Saadulla to come back to power and the fourth Saadulla ministry was formed on

25 August 1942. Saadulla took full advantage of the Assam Congress leaders being in prison and the legal restrictions imposed on the party to push forward his policy on immigration. The Muslim League demands for the total abolition of the Line System became ever more strident and, with the revenue portfolio now being headed by pro-immigrant minister Munawar Ali, the stage was set for the further opening up of government-reserved land for immigrant settlement. To aid this process, the government initiated a Grow More Food campaign, ostensibly to help the British war efforts but actually to make full use of the situation. What the Land Development Scheme could not fully achieve was now being attempted through the Grow More Food campaign. Referring to this, Dev and Lahiri comment:

> In the new Saadulla Ministry the Revenue Portfolio was entrusted to Munawar Ali who was well-known for his active sympathy for the immigrants. Under his 'pilotship' and driving force, the immigrants got a new deal. The Grow More Food campaign provided a grand opportunity to keep the Line System in abeyance and make settlement of lands with the immigrants at an unprecedented pace. This could be done either by inducing immigrant cultivators to substitute rice for jute crops, by more widespread utilization of current fallow land or by settlement of new land with the immigrants primarily for cultivation of food crops and particularly all varieties of paddy. The last method was found to be more suitable to the Minister and as such at the government level it was proposed to relieve the Colonisation Officers in Kamrup and Darrang of all subsidiary and extraneous work to enable them to devote their full time to settlement of new lands with 'Mymensinghias' wherever possible. It was also proposed to throw open to cultivation village grazing reserves which were considered to be too large for the needs of local cattle. The Revenue Minister felt that the most effective form of securing a large increase in the cultivated area would be wholesale abolition of all restrictions imposed by the Line System. [24]

Discussing this, Amalendu Guha writes: 'Exactly a year after its formation, the fourth Saadulla Ministry, therefore, adopted a new resolution on land settlement under the slogan, "Grow more Food". What it really meant, according to the Viceroy, was "grow more Muslims".'[25]

Thus, in the name of the Grow More Food programme, all evictions of encroachers were stopped and the revenue minister, Munawar Ali, passed an order in December 1942 that stated that 'as the present government is committed to the policy of vigorous drive in their campaign of "Grow More Food", it would be nullifying the effect of that policy to be very rigorous in the matter of eviction of encroachers unless circumstances justified and made that urgently necessary'.[26] This clearly showed that the government was in favour of encouraging further immigration of Muslims from East Bengal into Assam and turning the Line System more and more ineffective. Not only this, but all old encroachers were also to be protected. A memorandum on the land issue drawn up by the government stated: 'Government are at present considering ways and means of throwing open more land for colonization by immigrants and contemplate de-reservation of some of their professional grazing reserves for this purpose.'[27] The Muslim League welcomed the government's move and skilfully combined the demand for the removal of the Line System with its demand for Pakistan.[28] But even Saadulla had his compulsions and could not go the whole hog to accommodate the demands of the Muslim League, which had become more strident after Bhasani took over its leadership in Assam. But the mounting pressure put up by the Muslim League, the procrastination of the Saadulla government, and the growing Assamese public opinion against the land policy of the Saadulla government resulted in a complex political scenario in the province. With the Congress finally returning to the legislature, Bardoloi and his fellow Congress legislators started mounting pressure on the government to shift the land settlement policy in favour of the indigenous people. The Saadulla government had already turned shaky because of the belligerence of the Muslim League and now it tried to find a way out by working out a land settlement policy with the opposition. This led to the All-Party Conference on Land Settlement in December 1944. Saadulla, who was already falling out with Muslim League leaders such as Bhasani and Rouf over occupation of government land by immigrants,[29] agreed to the Congress's suggestion of putting brakes on the immigration policy and settling lands with the indigenous population. Commenting on this, Amalendu Guha says:

> He [Saadulla] chose not to stand by the rigid Muslim League policy on this issue and agreed, in essence, to whatever was suggested by the Congress party. Reservation of thirty per cent of the available wastelands as provision for future expansion of the indigenous people, a planned settlement of the residual wastelands with the landless sons of the soil and the pre-1938 immigrants and a system of protection to

tribal people in belts specially reserved for them—these were the measures recommended by the conference. Besides, it was also agreed that
the integrity of the grazing reserves should be strictly maintained and all
the trespassers evicted.[30]

This agreement reached at the All-Party Conference was followed up by
the Government Resolution on the settlement of wastelands in January
1945, which was full of loopholes and which, when read between the
lines, provided fresh avenues for immigrants to settle. While the resolution entailed the settlement of wastelands with indigenous landless
people, it also included settlement provisions for all the pre-1938 immigrants. But it gave sweeping powers to the local land officials to allow all
encroachers who had squatted illegally on government grazing reserves
in the preceding three years[31] to continue to hold on to their land. This
meant that occupation by the post-1938 immigrants was being legal-
ized. Since the resolution defined a landless person as one owning less
than 5 bighas of land, it exempted from settlement all those poor indigenous Assamese peasants who held uneconomic plots of 5 bighas. Lastly,
on the question of the creation of tribal belts, clear guidelines were not
mentioned and this left the field open for manipulation by land officials,
who often sided with the immigrants. Referring to the rejection of the
Government Resolution both by the Muslim League and the Congress,
though for diametrically opposite reasons, Amalendu Guha observes:

> As expected, the resolution was not acceptable to the immigrant
> Muslims. A meeting of the Assam Provincial Muslim League Council,
> held at Guwahati under Bhasani's chairmanship on 28 January, 1945
> and attended by 525 representatives, demanded total abolition of the
> Line System.... The Assamese public opinion was adverse to the resolu-
> tion, because of a number of built-in loopholes. Most of the indigenous
> cultivators owned uneconomic holdings consisting of no more than five
> bighas of land. Hence they could not claim themselves to be landless
> under the prescribed conditions; the five-bigha clause operated as a
> handicap for them. Secondly, since tribal belts had yet to be delimited,
> much room was still left for manipulation and bungling. Contrary to the
> conference decisions, the resolution allowed wide discretionary powers
> to the local officers 'to keep in possession encroachers who had been
> in occupation of and cultivating land in the grazing reserves over three
> years'. This meant that even the post-1937 immigrants could get land if
> they were already in illegal occupation of plots in the grazing reserves.
> The Congress, therefore, refused to back the resolution.[32]

Thus, it was but natural that the Congress party rejected outright the Government Resolution as a ploy to further settle immigrants in government reserves. On the other hand, the Muslim League also rejected the government's stand by declaring that the Saadulla government was not doing enough for the immigrants by refusing to totally do away with the Line System. Faced with such a situation, Saadulla did not waste any time when the Congress offered him two choices: either to resign or agree to head a ministry that would be dictated by the Congress, although the latter would not be in the government.[33] Saadulla accepted the Congress proposal, resigned, and reconstituted his ministry.[34] He retained all the five Muslim League ministers of his earlier cabinet but they were shorn of the important portfolios of land revenue and finance. Four non-Muslim ministers selected by the Congress and a tribal minister chosen by the tribal groups became a part of the new Saadulla government. Political equations seemed to be changing fast in Assam, and the Muslim League was facing its first major roadblock in the form of united resistance to its policy of unrestrained immigration and occupation of land.

Interestingly, most of these contentious issues relating to immigration and land figured prominently in the budget session of March 1945 of the Assam Legislative Assembly.[35] This session is a significant one because it witnessed what could be said to be the final struggle between the Muslim League and the Congress, with the former making a last-ditch attempt in the Assembly to influence government policy in favour of the immigrants, while the latter putting up a fight to defend indigenous interests in land and identity. The session witnessed acrimonious debates on the land issue that were initiated by the Muslim League member Abdur Rouf, who brought serious charges against the Saadulla ministry for its policy of forced eviction of immigrants from the grazing reserves. Intervening in the debate, Rabi Chandra Kachari raised the land issue in relation to the tribals. He said that the tribals were being forced to move to less fertile areas and the tribal belts and blocks were being thrown open to the Mymensinghias.[36] Kachari, who was a plains tribal leader, declared that 'although a Tribal Belt has been opened in the Mangaldoi area of Darrang district, yet within a short span of time the said belt was opened up for settlement by Mymensinghia labourers' and that 'government officials were too eager to allot land to the foreign labourers'.[37] In his speech, Maulana Matiur Rahman Mia of the Muslim

League stated that out of the 17 lakh Muslims in the Assam Valley, as many as 13 lakhs were from Bengal (*banglaagata*), while only 4 lakhs were Assamese Muslims. But he did not wish to distinguish between the Muslims from Bengal and those who were indigenous to Assam and declared: 'The Muslims from Assam, Bengal, Punjab, Arabia, Egypt—all of us are brothers. I do not wish to differentiate between Assamese and Bengali Muslims. But we have been dubbed as Bengali Muslims and have been deprived of our rights as citizens in Assam.'[38] The member also called for 10 per cent reservation of jobs for immigrant Muslims in Assam. He also demanded an end of the Line System and said that immigrants be allowed to settle wherever they wished. He accused the Saadulla government of letting lose a reign of terror on the immigrants.

Countering such arguments, Beli Ram Das of the Congress raised the question of encroachment upon government reserves and said: 'The settlement policy of the government has been leading the country to civil war, breach of peace and lawlessness.' He declared that the limits of tolerance of the indigenous people had been reached, and demanded that there be a stop to all further settlements of land by the immigrants and 'little surplus land' should be kept reserved for the indigenous people. Sarveswar Baruah, another Congress member, rued the future of the Assamese people and declared that 'hordes of invaders from Bengal have occupied our land' and the future of the Assamese race, including the tribal people, was in jeopardy. He accused the Saadulla government of making the Line System ineffective by protecting unscrupulous officials. Referring to the Saadulla government's Development Scheme, Baruah said that it was meant only for the welfare of the immigrants and that in Nowgong district alone out of the 12,000 bighas settled only 2,600 bighas went to the sons of the soil, while 9,400 bighas were allotted to immigrants. Sarveswar Baruah stated: 'The entire government policy is being viewed with suspicion and will be viewed with suspicion and distrust so long as the government will not be prepared to bring about order in the matter of settlements by enforcing their orders by means of evictions.' Referring to the plight of the tribals in the face of large-scale immigration and occupation of their land, Baruah declared:

> The protection guaranteed to the Tribal people since the beginning of the present Constitution in their behalf, has been maintained more in their breach than observance.... The government policy of regularization

of encroachments has been carried to the extreme end. The safety of the Tribal and the indigenous people is now nil.[39]

Baruah condemned the Saadulla government for its 'unseemly haste' in settling land with immigrants in the government and grazing reserves in Nowgong district.[40] He saw the Grow More Food campaign as part of a greater design of 'converting Assam into Pakistan'.

Bardoloi supported Baruah and others on the land settlement question and said:

> I want to add only this much just now that all actions that have been taken by the government have gone to favour the immigrants and to throw out the graziers and local people out of the soil. Some Grazing Reserves are being settled on the plea that the decision in this regard had been taken previous to the present land policy was announced (sic!) This is distinctly against the spirit of the All-Party Conference[41] on Land Settlement.... Government wants to carry out a communal policy of complete aggressiveness.... As the adjournment motion tabled by honourable Mr. Buragohain[42] shows, local people are being driven out from possession of land although according to the decision of the aforesaid Conference they are entitled to stay at least for six months in the Reserves where they settled. On the other hand, new aggressions on almost all the Reserves have been taking place.... The Government Resolution, instead of taking note of it, went beyond the scope of the agreement in order to accommodate intruders and trespassers. [43]

Bardoloi put up a strong defence on behalf of the rights of the indigenous people when he pointed out that the Government Resolution on the land issue was clearly biased in favour of the immigrants and against the interests of the Assamese people, including the tribals. Speaking on a cut motion on the demand for grants in the Assembly, Bardoloi referred to the Line System Committee of 1937 and said that even before the recommendations of the committee could be taken up, the government resigned.[44] Subsequently, the Saadulla government held a meeting on land settlement and adopted the Land Development Scheme. But in that meeting the important question of grazing reserves was not discussed, although it was generally agreed that the 'reserves shall remain inviolable'. In 1943 when most of the Congress legislators were in jail, the Saadulla government took up the land settlement issue once again and proposed the de-reservation of grazing reserves. Bardoloi alleged that 'some of the decisions were dictated by the Premier' (Saadulla) and 'only portions of the Resolutions were read out to the members', while the full text was sent to them later. He said that 'the point of view of the indigenous people' was left out and some points were recorded in a manner that these could be interpreted against the interests of the indigenous people. Bardoloi stated:

> Much to our surprise we found that the Government Resolution[45] failed to convey our wishes and our desire to safeguard the interests of the indigenous people which were totally neglected.... The Government Resolution went out of its way to accommodate the immigrants.... As a party we are not opposed to settlement of land to the landless provided land is made available.... We are not guided by any communal consider-ations, but must deplore the League's efforts to find settlement only for Muslim immigrants from Bengal.[46]

Bardoloi further said that while he did not object to a proper and planned settlement that would benefit the landless, he was upset over 'the manner in which the claims of the people of the province have been ignored'. He said that his 'criticism is as much on behalf of the Sylhet Muslims and Hindus as of the people of the Assam Valley'. Joining issue with Saadulla over the fact that the Muslim League members of the ministry were party to the decisions of the 1941 Conference, although the two Congress members had disagreed with the findings, Bardoloi said that the League had secured what it wanted to and now wished to have even more:

> This new policy and its execution directly goes against the interests of the people of the soil—I mean thereby all communities of the prov-ince. For I would tell the Honourable Premier definitely that by this new policy and its execution, not only the interests of the Assamese Hindus have been affected seriously but also the interests of the Tribals, Assamese Muslims and the Scheduled Castes have been affected by its operation.[47]

Bardoloi argued out that the very definition of landless was flawed and meant to help the immigrants. Setting the benchmark at 5 bighas to determine a landless person had resulted in great discrimination against the indigenous peasants, whereas a landless immigrant could get as much as 30 bighas. He pointed out that this was 'one of the worst things done to my people'. He said that the government's refusal to accept the Congress demand that a family be defined as having five members would gravely harm the interests of the indigenous people and give the advantage to the immigrants. Had the Congress's suggestion been accepted, then an average family of five members would have had a holding of 30 bighas.[48]

Referring to the position of tribal peasants, Bardoloi said that the Government Resolution had no provision for tribal blocks in areas other than places that had been termed as 'tribal blocks'. This, he felt, made the position of the tribals impossible since tribal people, according to Clause 15 of the resolution, would have to move to the hills if they required land for settlement. Elaborating on this, Bardoloi referred to Clause 15 of the resolution:

> The area required for them will be calculated at double the area occupied by the present people in the government sub-montane tracts.... Superfluous lands in the present loosely defined tribal areas will be excluded and thrown open for settlements under the planned scheme. In other words, they are not to find lands in the areas which are now in occupation by them and they shall have to go to tribal areas. I consider this very iniquitous and extremely harsh. As the tribal people are living side by side with the other people, they should get lands adjacent to the lands given to the other people. And then the sentence that superfluous land in the present loosely defined tribal areas will be excluded from the Tribal Belt and be thrown open to settlement, will take away from the Tribals all that the Government Resolution for the protection of the Tribals seems to profess. Tribals do not want this. They want that these lands should continue as tribal land where they alone can settle.[49]

Here Bardoloi is clearly exposing the Saadulla government's policy of opening up the tribal areas for immigrant settlement while at the same time giving the impression that it was defending the tribal blocks. Bardoloi could see that whatever Saadulla's stated empathy for the tribals, his was clearly an agenda to settle the immigrants on government reserves. Hence, Bardoloi commented that although the stated objective of the Conference of 1941 was to provide land to all the landless including immigrants who had come to Assam before 1938, in effect it was made legal for all encroachers who had settled on government reserves in the space of the 'last three years'.[50] Summing up his frustration at the government move, Bardoloi said: 'Thus, in every way, Sir, the immigrants, irrespective of the time of their arrival in Assam, are going to be helped by the Government Resolution.'[51] Bardoloi

summed up his arguments by referring to the interests of the local
landless people—the Muslims, tribals, Kacharis, graziers—and said that
they were being pushed out of their land by the immigrant encroachers, that the government was encouraging the encroachers and refusing
to give settlement to the indigenous people. He ended with a warning
that 'posterity would blame us if we cannot protect their interests'.[52]

Intervening in the debate, the Muslim League leader Rouf declared
that 'no Assamese cultivator requires more than two bighas of land per
capita and no Assamese can therefore get more than one acre of land'.
He rolled out figures of landholding and population in the different
districts to justify his contention. Rouf said that in 1941 roughly out
of the approximate 13 lakh Muslims in the Assam Valley,[53] 9 lakhs
were immigrants, 4 lakhs were Assamese Muslims, while there were 4
lakh Bengali Hindus plus 'railway coolies and U.P. cultivators'. He put
the total number of immigrants at some 15 lakhs and said that they
got around 5,15,000 acres (15.5 lakh bighas) of land. Giving figures of
immigrant settlement from 1931–2 to 1941–2, Rouf complained that
during the ten-year period only about 5 lakh acres had been settled
with the immigrants. He said that in 1931–2 immigrants had secured
settlement on 3,35,000 acres, while in 1941–2 they had got 5,17,000
acres. He accused the Saadulla government of not doing enough for the
immigrants who had now to manage with some 16 lakh bighas of land
for some 15 lakh immigrants.[54] On the other hand, he accused that
the government had done nothing to stop the practice of 'squatting'
that was freely exercised by the Assamese. 'There is no prohibition to
squatting for the Assamese.... The government has befooled us [the
immigrants] by giving a free hand to the Assamese people to bring
under cultivation every inch of *khas* land [government land] so that
they may receive *pattas* [land deeds] for all the khas land available
in the country.' Regarding the grant of land to the tribal people, Rouf
referred to the Government Resolution and said: 'In some places, they
[the tribals] have already got more than twice the land they require,
and again they are going to be given twice the land they now possess
plus 30% of the entire *khas* land as it stood in the year 1940. This means
they will take nearly half of the *khas* lands now available.' Opposing
Bardoloi's contention that it was unjust to define an Assamese landless as one possessing less than 5 bighas of land, Rouf demanded that
'no discrimination should be made between the immigrants and the

Assamese'.[55] He described the move to reserve 30 per cent of the land for future generations as ridiculous.

Independent members Rohini Kumar Chaudhuri[56] and Surendranath Buragohain supported the Congress stand and stated that the interests of the indigenes were not being protected. Buragohain said that 'it is very unkind of this government to particularly lay their hands on the Assam Valley, leaving those of the Surma Valley and the hills'. He strongly opposed the throwing open of the government reserves in Nowgong, Darrang, and Kamrup districts for immigrant settlement. Chaudhuri declared that the Government Resolution of 15 January 1945 nullified everything and 'took away the security of the indigenous people of this Province'.[57] Chaudhuri said that it was earlier agreed that all PGRs would not be touched and that wastelands were to be given to only those immigrants who came before 1938, that it was also agreed that those immigrants who established themselves before 1936 by 'illegal means' would not be disturbed. He added, 'but whereas the Assamese landless are afraid of settling in the professional grazing reserves (PGR), the immigrants do so.... They come with sword in one hand and gold in another'. Regarding the limit set to determine the landless, Chaudhuri observed: 'If a person who does own five bighas of land is to be deprived of settlement, then in the future the bulk of the local people will not be entitled to land settlement at all, whereas anyone from outside the province will get settlement.' Finally, Chaudhuri asserted that all post-1938 encroachers be evicted from the grazing reserves, the definition given by the government for 'landless' should not apply to the Assamese people, and the tribal people should get their due since this was their land and they were the real cultivators.

Commenting on the land settlement policy of his government, Saadulla said:

> We have heard the immigrants' views. There has been a special plea on behalf of the Tribal people as well.... The last Conference was representative of all groups of people who are vitally interested in the land settlement policy in Assam. It will take a long time to go into the details of the land settlement policy, but the result arrived at recently can be summarized by this bold assertion on my part that this was a victory for all parties concerned.... To my Muslim friends, the immigrants, I would say that whereas previously the majority of the Hindu community was out against recognizing immigrants as entitled to settlement on

any land, through this conference they get the admission that those who
came earlier than 1938 would be treated as indigenous people entitled
to settlement of government waste lands in the province. That was a
very great concession made to those friends who have come from the
neighbouring province. To the great Hindu community, I would say that
whereas Government has already started delimitation of the professional grazing reserves on the advice of their agricultural experts that
5 bighas are sufficient for a buffalo and only one-third of this is enough
for a cow, government did not pursue that policy with a view to come to
an amicable arrangement with all the parties. They backed out of their
conclusions and withdrew their de-reservation plans. But for the sake
of humanity or rather on humanitarian considerations which was even
accepted by the leaders of the Hindu and other communities, those
encroachers who had settled on professional grazing reserves before
1938 and had converted barren waste land into smiling fields, should be
allowed to remain and anyone who had taken shelter there on account
of erosion of rivers or on account of military requisition of their land[58]...
should be allowed a period of grace so that government may find suit-
able land elsewhere for these people before they are evicted from the
professional grazing reserves. This was *a concession* that the government
gladly gave to the *popular opinion*.[59] (Emphases mine)

In the above speech, Saadulla clearly polarizes the land and immigration issue into a Hindu–Muslim one. He refers to the immigrants as 'my
Muslim friends', although he uses the term 'encroachers' for those who
settled on PGRs before 1938. All indigenous peasants, both Assamese
and tribal, are referred to as belonging to 'the Hindu and other communities'. Finally he also accepts the fact that 'popular opinion' in Assam
was against the encroachers. Referring to the demand from the immigrant lobby that those who encroached upon the PGRs before 1943
be allowed to remain, Saadulla said that this would have gone against
'popular opinion' and done great harm to the milk industry. But he
added that that his government had made efforts to reach a settlement
with 'parties with separate interests',[60] and that the colonization officer
of Nowgong had informed him that there was 'no difficulty in settling
12,000 bighas of land with immigrants who have been in the province
from 10 to 15 years before'. He also declared: 'Everyone will agree with
the policy "first come first served" and even in the case of land settlement this ought to be the guiding policy. No one who has *come recently*
would be preferred to those who have been waiting to get government

land settlement, say, from 7 to 10 years earlier' (emphasis mine). From this it is clear that the Saadulla government was keen to settle the immigrants phase-wise. Those who had come ten to fifteen years prior to 1945 had already been settled on government land and now it was the turn of those who had come just seven to ten years earlier. He, however, carefully avoids the dates for those who have 'come recently'.

Referring to the tribal peasants, Saadulla gave the impression that his government had given them plenty of concessions. This is what he has to say:

> On behalf of the Tribal people special concessions were sought in that Conference and the government as well as all the parties agreed to give those concessions. Whereas in the case of the other people, no more annual settlement was given, but annual *pattas*[61] will be issued to the tribal people for their protection and they are assured that the sub-montane area will be reserved for them. This was *a concession* which the tribal people got at the hands not merely of the government but also representations of *other interests*[62] that were present at the conference. These Tribal people want there should be a special officer to look after their interests and who will survey the landless amongst them and reserve sufficient[63] lands for them. They were given that officer and an officer of their own choice.... All these things gave the tribal people the concessions that they wanted as regards land settlement policy.[64] (Emphases mine)

Now, what are actually these concessions that Saadulla is repeatedly referring to? From this speech it becomes clear that in the face of continuous immigration, the tribal people were gradually losing their hold over their land and asking for safeguards. But these safeguards are seen by Saadulla and his government as concessions or favours that the immigrants and their promoters have deigned to grant to those very people who were the actual sons of the soil.

Saadulla and his government knew that the immigrants' quest for land would keep on increasing and that, in the long run, the decisions arrived at the Land Conference would be nullified, especially with the resistance being put up by the Muslim League under the leadership of Maulana Bhasani.[65] Hence, in this same speech, he warns the immigrant lobby not to subvert the agreement reached at the conference of December 1944. He said: 'If we go back upon the Resolution of 1944, the opposition of the great Hindu community against throwing open more lands for *encroachers* to remain on the grazing reserves will continue to grow in volume' (emphasis mine). Here Saadulla is asking the immigrants not to be overzealous in pushing forward their programme of taking over government land. It is interesting to note that he is here referring to the immigrant settlers as 'encroachers'. As an astute politician, Saadulla was aware of the possible backlash that could occur if the immigrants, spurred on by leaders like Bhasani, brazenly went ahead with occupying the reserves. Clearly, he was in favour of a slow takeover that would help him avoid friction with the indigenes. At the same time he was aware that the political scenario in the province was changing fast, and that the Muslim League was falling short of its plan to create a viable Muslim majority that would have edged out the Congress with the support of both the plains and hill tribes. The seasoned politician that he was, Saadulla was thinking of survival strategies that would reduce his total dependence on the League and at the same time provide him enough space to continue to work for the benefit of the Muslim community. For this, he was even prepared to seek the support of the Congress party. In a sense, his warnings to the extreme faction of the Muslim League gives one an inkling of the change that was about to come in ministry-making by the end of March 1945. Trained to survive in tricky situations, Saadulla now sidelined the Muslim League, led by Bhasani, and quickly accepted the conditional support offered to him by the Congress. The Saadulla–Bardoloi agreement, which led to the last Saadulla ministry in the province,[66] clearly shows that Saadulla was trying to marginalize his opponents in the Provincial Muslim League. Justifying his latest position on the land settlement policy, Saadulla wrote to Liaquat Ali Khan towards the end of March 1945 that the Government Resolution on land adopted in January 1945 was 'the maximum measure of concession obtained from the Hindus and the Plains Tribal people' and that 'barring 9 members' (of the Provincial Muslim League) others supported his move. In this letter, Saadulla tries to present himself as a saviour of the immigrants and says, 'I can assure all the Muslim Leaguers that the interests of the Muslim immigrants into Assam are safe in my hands and settlement with them is going apace. In the four lower districts of the Assam Valley these Bengali immigrant Muslims have quadrupled the Moslem population during the last 20 years.'[67] The struggle between Saadulla and Bhasani would intensify in the period immediately before Independence as is revealed in Saadulla's letter to Mohammad Ali Jinnah written in April 1947. In this letter, Saadulla directly accuses the Provincial Muslim League leadership, headed by Bhasani, of launching the civil disobedience movement without due approval of the parliamentary group of Muslim League in Assam and of trying to clothe himself in 'dictatorial powers'.[68]

In his summing up, Saadulla took a different position from that of the other Muslim League members when he said that 'the existing right of the indigenous people of getting land settlement anywhere and everywhere which goes by the name of "squatting" and which is based in our law, i.e., the Assam Land Revenue Regulations, was to continue'. But this assertion only seemed to cover the clever manoeuvres that his government indulged in to make settlement for immigrants easier.

Saadulla referred to the agreement reached at the Conference of 1944, which accepted 1938 as the cut-off year for immigrant settlement. He said that though he was aware of the need for safeguards for the indigenous people, his government had decided to open some reserves in 1943. (This was the time when most of the Congress legislators were in jail.) And, accordingly, three PGRs in Nowgong district were de-reserved for those who came after 1937. He justified his government's action by asserting that those who were settled in these reserves were people affected by floods and erosion or whose land had been taken over for military occupation. Saadulla further stated that his colonization officer had reported that these PGRs had already been settled with immigrants in June–July 1944 and since crops had already been raised, the settlers were not to be disturbed.

Regarding the tribals, Saadulla stated that the new land settlement rules favoured the tribals, and measures such as the appointment of a land settlement officer had been taken to protect their land. He said that the PGRs were being encroached both by the immigrants and the tribals and the 5 bigha limit for the Assamese was all right. However, it was while discussing the last paragraph of the Government Resolution of 15 January 1945 (subclause[c] to para 18) that Saadulla showed his guile in favour of the immigrants:

> Subject to (a) and (b) above[69] the PGRs will be kept intact and the D.Cs[70] will be directed to see that they are kept free of encroachment by eviction of trespassers—past, present or future. Government realize that cases of hardship are likely to arise among encroachers not included

in the categories dealt with in sub clauses (a) and (b) who have nevertheless been in occupation of and cultivating the land in the PGRs for
over three years and are prepared to direct the Deputy Commissioners
to use their discretion in affording them special consideration.... This
concession was made on humanitarian grounds. A *set of people* either
goaded by greed or land hunger or compelled by necessity had gone into
these PGRs, cleared very thick jungle or thick grass—these people had
undertaken trouble, putting forth much labour in making these lands fit
for cultivation and for three years cultivated these lands. If these people
are now evicted forthwith, great hardship may be caused; in order to
consider such cases that discretion has been given to the D.C. to evict
or not *but no direction has been given to keep them in the land*. If the D.C.
can find land outside these reserves, they may be given the same concession as in sub-clause (b) for 6 months and given land elsewhere.[71]
(Emphases mine)

From this is clear that Saadulla was protecting the interests of this
'set of people' by circumventing the provisions of the 1944 all-party
decisions on the land issue, while at the same time avoiding the strident
position of the Muslim League. On the surface the Saadulla government had not given any directions for the encroachers to be kept in
the PGRs. But by giving discretionary powers to the deputy commissioners, who were directly under the ministers, the path was cleared
for those immigrants who had already settled in the PGRs in the three
years before the Government Resolution was adopted. Moreover, it
would be impossible to enforce even the three-year frame for those
who had encroached upon the PGRs. This insensitivity towards the
tribal peasants of the Brahmaputra Valley would push them to the wall
and ultimately lead to violent clashes in the 1990s in the Bodoland
Territorial Autonomous District area as well as in the Rabha and Lalung
dominated regions.

The land and immigration issues continued to dominate the proceedings of the Assam Legislative Assembly in the budget sessions of
1946 and 1947. One may refer to the Assam Legislative Assembly
debates of the March 1946 session where immigration was directly
linked by several leading Congress members with the Muslim
League's wider political strategy. It is significant that the major part
of the discussion on the budget in the March 1946 session of the
Assam Assembly was taken up not by development matters but by
the question of immigration and the encroachment/occupation of

PGRs and wastelands. Clearly the Assembly was sharply divided into two segments—one against immigration and calling for measures to stop it, and the other openly espousing the cause of immigration. In this session of the Assam Legislative Assembly, Beli Ram Das directly accused the Muslim League of vile attempts to turn Assam into a Muslim-majority province and declared that 'Jinnah's demand for the inclusion of Assam in the Eastern Zone of his proposed Pakistan has been to a great extent responsible for the complication of the land problem in Assam, even though the problem is purely an economic one'. He was speaking in support of Medhi's contention that 'since after the Muslim League put the claim to include Assam in Pakistan Zone, a large number of immigrants practically began to invade Assam as if under a plan although there was no sufficient arable land even to provide the landless indigenous Hindus, Muslims, tribals and others who had no economic holdings'.[72] Medhi argued:

> The sudden influx of immigrants (specially during the war) imported by the Dewanias in various places, failing to get Waste Land began to encroach on the village grazing reserves and professional grazing reserves in direct violation of the law leading to serious clashes. These lands have been reserved of definite purpose and settlement is forbidden to all persons—immigrants and non-immigrants.[73]

He appealed to the government of Bengal not to encourage landless people from that province to come to Assam in search of land.[74] Medhi stressed on the maintenance of the reserves as these were integral to the village economy, and accused some ministers of the previous government of having pursued the 'shortsighted policy' of opening up the reserves to immigrant settlers. He further said that by-passing the claims of the indigenous people, the previous government, under its Grow More Food programme, had settled around 1.6 lakh bighas of reserve land. Interestingly, Medhi in his speech commended Saadulla for having realized the harm that the total opening up of the reserves would do to the indigenous people and he said:

> The entire people of the Assam valley were startled by such de-reservation and settlement of land to immigrants to the exclusion of the indigenous people. Sir Muhammad Saadulla fully realized the injustice done to the people of the soil and convened a conference of all parties which came to an agreement with the Honourable Gopinath Bardoloi and Srijut Rohini Kumar Chaudhuri. In pursuance of that agreement,

it was decided by the last Government that that recent encroachers should be forthwith evicted from all professional grazing reserves and a resolution dated 13 July, 1945 to that effect was published in the gazette. Unfortunately on some plea or other during the last election campaign, the resolution was not given effect to till the care-taker Ministry resigned.[75]

From Medhi's speech it appears to be clear that the Congress as well as Assamese public opinion seemed convinced that the flow of immigrants into Assam from the late 1930s to the 1940s was essentially part of a state-sponsored plan and had not been motivated 'exclusively' by economic consideration as was being claimed by the Muslim League and their supporters. What could have been an economic issue had now been given political dimensions not only through state-sponsored immigration, but also by linking this immigration with the clear political objective of making the province a part of Pakistan. This naturally gives an entire new political dimension to the issue of immigration into Assam.

The entire issue was summed up succinctly by the Congress member Beli Ram Das in the following points:[76]

1. Under the Grow More Food programme, valuable land, including PGRs and game sanctuaries, was thrown open to immigrants. The existence of the Assamese people was at stake. What the great Mughals could not achieve, Das contended, was achieved by the Muslim League.

2. The very fact that PGRs and game sanctuaries have been thrown open to immigrants shows that there is no sufficient cultivable wasteland in Assam.

3. 'The area of settled land in Assam was 206 lakh bighas in 1941 and the area per capita was about 2 bighas only. The Government of Assam has defined 20 bighas as an economic holding for a family of five and as such the number of landless would be somewhere around 50 per cent. Settlement of immigrants in 5 lakh bighas in about five years has made the situation even more complicated.'

4. In Assam there is no such thing as surplus land in the reserves, rather most of the reserves are deficit in area.

5. The immigration is primarily a political design. Das referred to the speech of Maulana Rouf at a League meeting at Barpeta on 7–8 March 1944 where Rouf is reported to have stated:

The same blood which runs through their veins even today took the rudder ... for a new conquest of Assam.... The souls of martyrs and devotees of past, are witnessing this new expedition of the Bengalee Muslims ... with increased vitality in the life of the community and with the help of numerous new reinforcements, the figure in the subdivision of Barpeta alone could be raised to 65,000.

6. 'The Government of India must not allow the conversion of a Hindu-majority province into a Muslim-majority one by undermining the legislative claims of the people of the province, even though it may be advantageous to their imperialistic design to create so many "Ulsters" in India.[77] The encroachment into the grazing reserves and also squatting on other land by the immigrants was being resisted by the Assamese people, especially the tribals, from the very beginning.... District officers were afraid of evicting encroachers because of government patronage under the league. The aim was to make Assam a Muslim majority province.'

7. The 1941 Census showed the tea labour as tribals. But earlier census reports had showed them as Assamese. Their population was around 14 lakhs but the Muslim league was trying to show them as non-Assamese. [78]

8. There were 106 lakh acres of good fallow land in Bengal. However, as many as 50 lakh people died during the Bengal famine and this vacuum could be filled up by Bengali immigrant peasants from Assam.

9. Nearly half of Assamese people were landless. According to Beli Ram Das, during the preceding twenty years, as many as 25 lakh bighas of land had been settled, thereby leading to serious apprehensions among the tribals. He highlighted tribal apprehensions about the land distribution policy of the previous Muslim League government.

10. The argument that immigrants have made Assam prosperous is not borne out by facts. According to Das, immigrants did not contribute to more than 10.1 per cent of the total outturn of food crops in Assam, whereas they consumed 29 per cent of the available crops.[79] Das supported Medhi's contention that 1.6 lakh bighas of land were given to immigrants and cited the case of Nowgong where 0.5 lakh bighas were settled in Bhurbandha, Borghuli, and Laokhowa—of those settled, as many as 95 per cent were Muslim

immigrants from Bengal. Das insisted that 'the leaders of the immigrants should take them back and re-settle them in the 106 lakh acres of fallow land in Bengal'.

11. Lands shown as fallow land were practically non-existent in Assam. Das argued that in the category of 'wasteland' waterbodies such as *beels*, marshes, and *dobas* as well as hillocks and roadside land often used for purposes other than cultivation were also included. He further pointed out that even parts of riverbeds that dried up in winter and were used for cultivation of one crop were shown as wasteland. If one deducted all these lands, then there would practically be no cultivable wasteland in Assam, Das reiterated.[80]

The Muslim League members strongly refuted these arguments by emphasizing that it was within the rights of the Muslim immigrants to settle in Assam, which was just another part of the same country. The counterargument that was built up by Muslim League leaders such as Rouf and Mayeen-uddin-Chaudhury was that the Assamese peasant was indolent by nature and that no Line System could ever protect him. Rouf claimed that the Assamese people got more land than they deserved and that the government had embarked on a cruel policy of evictions. He rounded off his speech by saying that the 'remedy to all the evils lie in the achievement of Pakistan and we have the right to have it. These criminals against humanity, worse than war criminals, can only then be brought to book and they shall be. Pakistan Zindabad'.[81] Another Muslim League member Khan Bahadur Maulvi Abdul Majid Ziaosh Shams intervened to say that if Assam was to be a part of the Congress's plan for a federation of India, then it was the duty of the province to help the rest of the country by opening up more and more areas to cultivation.[82] Yet another Muslim League member, Maulvi Mohammad Mafiz Chaudhury, refuted the Congress claims on immigration and said that 'nature itself has invited these Bengali cultivators to cross the *artificial provincial boundaries* and spread in some parts of Assam' (emphasis mine).[83] Mayeen-uddin-Chaudhury of the Muslim League added a new dimension to the debate by saying that the immigrant question since its inception was essentially an economic one, had, after the inauguration of provincial autonomy, taken on a 'communal colouring because political power has come to be stressed on the numerical strength of the different communities'.[84] But whatever these arguments, the essential point in the Muslim League agenda on land was that as much land should be seized by the immigrants as possible. Summing up this attitude, Muslim League member Abdul Matin Chaudhury stated that the Working Committee of the Assam Provincial Muslim League had resolved that the landless and evicted immigrants 'be advised to spread out and cultivate all surplus cultivable government waste lands'.[85] His argument was that the country was facing a famine-like situation and the immigrant encroachers were doing a great job by producing more food crops. Matin Chaudhury's was a clear call for the occupation of government land by the immigrants in violation of all laws. It is rather striking to note that when the Muslim League leadership under men like Maulana Bhasani was pushing its agenda of occupation of tribal belts and blocks by immigrant peasants in the 1940s, it was setting in motion a process that would, within half a century, lead to an unbridgeable gulf between the immigrant Muslim peasants and the plains tribal people of the lower Assam districts and by the close of the century erupt in severe violent clashes over land claiming hundreds of lives.[86]

The debate on land and immigration would take on a completely new dimension after a year or two after the Partition because the immigrant peasant from East Bengal would turn into a foreign national once the passport–visa system was introduced. While Partition put an end to the fear of Assam and the northeastern region being included in Pakistan, it now raised the fear of illegal infiltration from the newly created East Pakistan and, from the 1970s, from Bangladesh—a subject that would be at the core of the Assam Movement (1979–85). It is significant that in the years just after Partition, the government of Assam's attempts to convince the Centre about the dangers posed by such infiltration did not receive the necessary administrative response. Partition gave an entirely new dimension to the issue of land and immigration—an issue that continues to occupy central space in the political discourse of the region and something that seems to defy any logical solution.

Notes

1. Congress politics in the region was primarily concentrated in the Brahmaputra and Surma Valleys and most of the hill areas were out of its purview. Nevertheless, several hill leaders such as J.J.M. Nichols Roy were

closely acquainted with the politics of the Congress and gave it support during the struggle against grouping as announced in the Cabinet Mission proposals.

2. Sayed Muhammad Saadulla headed, in all, five different ministries in Assam from April 1937 to February 1946. An Assamese Muslim, Saadulla is seen as being largely responsible for the large-scale entry and settlement of Bengali Muslim immigrants from the then East Bengal. In just one year, 1939–40, the Saadulla government settled Bengali Muslim immigrants on 1 lakh bigha land in the Brahmaputra Valley. Saadulla joined the Muslim League in 1937 and supported the grouping scheme under the Cabinet Mission plan. But all through his political career, Saadulla tried to chart out an independent course by keeping in check the more radical elements within the Muslim League in Assam. He opposed at one stage the demand of the Bhasani-led Muslim League to do away with the Line System and throw open all available government land for occupation by the immigrants.

3. In this connection one may refer to the resolution of the Bengal Legislative Assembly in the pre-Partition period asking for the reserves meant for tribals to be opened up to immigrant peasants. Also refer to Saadulla's note to Humayun Kabir and his letter to Liaquat Ali stating that he was helping the cause of the Muslims.

4. Abdul Hamid Khan Bhasani, better known as Maulana Bhasani, was born in a peasant family of East Bengal. He was involved in the Khilafat and Non-Cooperation Movements and finally emerged as a prominent leader of the Muslim peasants of East Bengal where he organized them against zamindari oppression. Soon he became influential among the Bengali Muslim immigrants of Assam and was elected to the Assam Legislative Assembly in the year 1937. Bhasani led the immigrant peasants in a movement against the Line System in Assam and demanded that the belts and blocks reserved for the tribals be opened up for occupation. As the president of the Provincial Muslim League, Bhasani, with the active support from the Muslim Leaders of Bengal, planned a series of marches in lower Assam in February 1947 against the Line System. But the move fizzled out when the possibility of Assam becoming a part of East Pakistan receded. Bhasani was arrested during one of these demonstrations and finally left for East Pakistan just before independence. In East Pakistan he occupied a special space as one of the most distinguished peasant leaders.

5. As per the Land Settlement Resolution, the PGRs in Kamrup, Darrang, and Nowgong districts were de-reserved and opened up for settlement by immigrants, and the ban on land occupation by post-1938 immigrants was lifted for all practical purposes. This decision of the Saadulla ministry virtually opened up the floodgates of immigration for Muslim peasants

from East Bengal. Despite the fact that the special officer, S.P. Desai, appointed to identify the available wastelands and grazing reserves, clearly stated that no surplus land was available for settlement, the Saadulla ministry tried to justify its decision by saying that all this was being done as part of the Grow More Food Programme aimed at helping the British war efforts. Refer to Amalendu Guha, *Planter Raj to Swaraj: Freedom Struggle and Electoral Politics in Assam: 1826–1947* (New Delhi: ICHR, 1977), pp. 281–2.

6. The third Muslim League ministry in Assam headed by Saadulla (17 November 1939–25 December 1941).The first Saadulla ministry (1 April 1937–5 February 1939) had introduced the Land Development Scheme in January 1938. This was followed by the Act of 1940.

7. The Line System was a system by which Muslim immigrants from East Bengal, and particularly from Mymensigh, were required to settle in certain areas earmarked for them by the administration. The aim was to segregate the Bengali Muslim immigrants from the indigenous population, and it was a protective measure against indiscriminate settlement by immigrants in indigenous and, particularly, tribal land.

8. In just one year, 1939–40, over 1.6 lakh bighas (1 bigha is a land measurement equal to approximately one-third of an acre, that is, 0.33 acres or 0.133 hectares. 1 hectare is equal to 7.4 bighas or 2.47 acres.) of reserve land in the Brahmaputra Valley was given for settlement to Muslim immigrant peasants from East Bengal. See Bimal J. Dev and Dilip Kumar Lahiri, *Assam Muslims: Politics and Cohesion* (Delhi: Mittal Publications, 1985), p. 23.

9. Guha, *Planter Raj to Swaraj*, pp. 209–10.

10. From 17 November 1939 to 12 March 1945, Saadulla headed two ministries, his third and fourth ministries. During this period he actively encouraged Muslim immigration from East Bengal, although during his fourth ministry (25 March 1942–23 March 1945) political compulsions forced him to initiate certain measures aimed at protecting cultivable land held by the indigenous populations from immigrant occupation.

11. The Bengal Legislative Council carried a motion on 16 July 1943 calling upon the Government of India to take immediate steps to remove existing restrictions on the land-hungry immigrant cultivators from Bengal.

12. This was a Congress coalition ministry and lasted from 19 September 1938 to 16 November 1939 when it resigned following the Congress Working Committee's decision asking all Congress ministries to resign. Both Gandhi and Bose were against Bardoloi giving up office, particularly in view of the delicate political situation in Assam arising out of the machinations of the Muslim League. Had Bose had his way, perhaps the entire course of Assam

history during this period could have been different. Bose wrote to Nehru trying to dispel the latter's doubts about coalition ministries in the following manner:

> Will you tour the province of Assam for a fortnight and tell me if the present Coalition Ministry had been a progressive or reactionary institution? What is the use of your sitting in Allahabad and uttering words of wisdom which have no relation to reality? When I went to Assam after the fall of the Saadulla Ministry, I did not find a single Congressman who did not insist that there should be a Congress Coalition Ministry. The fact is that the province had been groaning under a reactionary Ministry.... If you only knew the improvement that has taken place in Assam, in spite of all the various obstacles and handicaps, since the Coalition Ministry came into office, you would change your opinion completely.

Quoted in Nirode Barooah, *Gopinath Bardoloi, 'The Assam Problem' and Nehru's Centre* (Guwahati: Bhabani Print and Publications, 2010), pp. 56–7; Barooah quotes from Jawaharlal Nehru, *A Bunch of Old Letters* (Bombay: Asia Publishing House, 1958), pp. 38–40.

13. Extracts from the proceedings of the Government of Assam in the Revenue Department No. 5216-R, dated 4 November 1939, as quoted by Dev and Lahiri in *Assam Muslims*, pp. 32–3.

15. Refer to Guha, *Planter Raj to Swaraj*, pp. 261–2.

16. Quoted by Dev and Lahiri, *Assam Muslims*, p. 33, from Assam Government Secret Records (special branch).

17. Dev and Lahiri, *Assam Muslims*, pp. 34–5.

18. This third Saadulla ministry lasted from 17 November 1939 to 24 December 1941.

19. The second session of the Assam Provincial Muslim League, held in January 1941, called upon the Assam government to do away with the Line System altogether.

20. Guha, *Planter Raj to Swaraj*, pp. 262–3.

21. Governor's Rule was from 26 December 1941 to 24 August 1942.

22. Guha, *Planter Raj to Swaraj*, p. 270.

23. Dev and Lahiri, *Assam Muslims*, p. 72.

24. Dev and Lahiri, *Assam Muslims*, p. 38.

25. According to Wavell, 'The chief political problem is the desire of the Muslim Ministers to increase this immigration into the uncultivated Government lands under the slogan "Grow More Food". But what they really wanted was to "Grow more Muslims".' (Archibald Percival, *Wavell: The Viceroy's Journal*, edited by Penderel Moon [London: Oxford University Press, 1978]; Guha, *Planter Raj to Swaraj*, p. 280.)

26. Dev and Lahiri, *Assam Muslims*, p. 39.

27. Dev and Lahiri, *Assam Muslims*, pp. 40–1.
28. In April 1944, a resolution was passed by the Assam Provincial Muslim League for the creation of a sovereign state of Eastern Pakistan made up of Assam and Bengal. Bhasani was elected the president in this session. In a subsequent session of the Muslim League held at Guwahati in January 1945, it was demanded that the Line System be totally withdrawn.
29. Saadulla vented his anger at the Muslim League's unabated campaign for the abolishment of the Line System and the unrestricted occupation of government land and reserves at a meeting of immigrants in April 1944 by comparing the situation in Assam with the unrestricted immigration of Jews into the Arab homeland of Palestine. Refer to Guha, *Planter Raj to Swaraj*, pp. 282–3.
30. Guha, *Planter Raj to Swaraj*, p. 284.
31. Last three years here seems to refer to the post-1939 period and especially the years between 1940 and 1944.
32. Guha, *Planter Raj to Swaraj*, pp. 285–6.
33. Prior to the formation of the new ministry, a tripartite agreement was reached between Bardoloi, Saadulla, and the independent member Rohini Kumar Chaudhuri. Among the terms of the agreement was the revision of the land settlement policy so as to accommodate the claims of the indigenous people.
34. Saadulla resigned on 23 March 1945 and reconstituted his ministry. This was the fifth Saadulla ministry (caretaker) which lasted from 23 March 1945 to 11 February 1946.
35. During this period the government was headed by Saadulla. This was the fourth Saadulla ministry (25 August 1942–23 March 1945). All references to the Assam Legislative Assembly Proceedings are from the records of the India Office Library Section of the British Library, London.
36. Usually most Muslim immigrants were referred to as 'Mymensinghias' because the large majority of them were from the district of Mymensingh in East Bengal/East Pakistan.
37. Proceedings of the Assam Legislative Assembly, March 1945, p. 191 (translated from Assamese by the present author).
38. Assam Legislative Assembly Proceedings, March 1945, p. 195 (translated from original Bengali by the present author).
39. Assam Legislative Assembly Proceedings, March 1945, p. 205. All references to Bardoloi's speeches are from the Assam Legislative Assembly Proceedings of March 1945.
40. The reserves mentioned were Laokhowa Game Reserve, Bhurbandha, Barghuli, Naliguri, and Soraguri grazing reserves.

41. The All-Party Conference of December 1944 that worked out certain guidelines for settlement of land among indigenes and immigrants.

42. Surendranath Buragohain was a leading independent legislator and served as a minister in the sixth and last Saadulla ministry, which was a caretaker one till the general elections of February 1946. Buragohain was a staunch defender of the land rights of the indigenous people.

43. Assam Legislative Assembly Proceedings, March 1945, p. 246.

44. The Line System Committee (also referred to as the Line Enquiry Committee) was set up in 1937 under the chairmanship of F.W. Hockenhull, the leader of the European party in the Assam Legislative Assembly, to enquire into the working of the Line System. Its report, also known as the Hockenhull Report, was submitted in February 1938 and recommended strict measures for the protection of tribal lands.

45. The Government Resolution of January 1945.

46. Assam Legislative Assembly Proceedings, March 1945.

47. Here, Bardoloi is referring to the All-Party Conference called by Chief Minister Saadulla, which, while approving the settlement of landless indigenous people and pre-1938 immigrants on government wastelands, also provided for a development scheme with plenty of loopholes in favour of the post-1938 immigrants.

48. A family of five would be eligible to 30 bighas of land.

49. Assam Legislative Assembly Proceedings, March, 1945, pp. 523–4.

51. Assam Legislative Assembly Proceedings, March 1945, p. 524.

52. This sounded prophetic in the sense that from the 1970s onwards social tension between the indigenous tribals and the immigrant settlers started escalating in several districts of lower Assam, soon erupting into a series of violent incidents, and reaching its peak in the 1990s.

53. Assam Valley refers to the Brahmaputra Valley area.

54. Rouf calculated this at some 6 bighas per family of five immigrants.

55. Assam Legislative Assembly Proceedings, March 1945, p. 502.

56. Rohini Kumar Chaudhury was an important independent Member of Legislative Assembly (MLA) who was part of several Saadulla ministries. He later fell out with Saadulla over the land-settlement policies.

57. Assam Legislative Assembly Proceedings, March 1945, p. 527.

58. Wartime regulations (World War II) empowered the government to acquire land for military purposes.

59. Assam Legislative Assembly Proceedings, March 1945, p. 522.

60. Clearly referring to the indigenous population and the immigrants.

61. Land deeds.

62. The 'other interests' here obviously refer to the immigrant lobby.

63. There seems to be no formula to determine what would be 'sufficient' for the tribal families.
64. Assam Legislative Assembly Proceedings, March 1945, pp. 248–9.
65. The Line System had already been made ineffective by the 1930s in districts such as Goalpara with immigrants acquiring large tracts of land in the 'lined villages'. Refer to Guha, *Planter Raj to Swaraj*, p. 262.
66. This Saadulla ministry that was a coalition between his United Assam Party and the Nationalist Party, headed by Rohini Kumar Chaudhuri, was supported by the Congress from outside. Its tenure was from March 1945 till February 1946.
67. Syed Saadulla's letter to Liaquat Ali Khan, dated 25 March 1945, Saadulla Papers, Sub-File 7, NMML, New Delhi.
68. Syed Saadulla's letter to Mohammad Ali Jinnah, dated 10 April 1946, Saadulla Papers, NMML, New Delhi.
69. Subclause (a) was for de-reservation for settled villages in the PGRs and subclause (b) was for de-reservation on account of erosion or loss on account of military requisition.
70. Deputy Commissioners.
71. Saadulla's speech at the Assam Legislative Assembly in March 1945, Assam Legislative Assembly Proceedings, March 1945.
72. Bishnuram Medhi (1888–1981) was a senior Congress leader who was a member of the Bardoloi cabinets both before and after Independence. He was the finance minister in the 1946 Bardoloi ministry. Following Bardoloi's death in August 1950, Medhi took over as the chief minister of Assam and continued in that post till 1957 when he was made the governor of Madras state. He was known for his strong position against immigration from then East Bengal/East Pakistan.
73. All references are from the Assam Legislative Assembly Proceedings of March 1946.
74. It may be mentioned that just three years back, in July 1943, the Bengal Legislative Council had passed a resolution which urged upon the Government of India to remove all existing restrictions on land imposed by the Assam government so that land-hungry immigrant peasants from Bengal could freely settle in Assam. It specially called for dereservation of the PGRs in the districts of Nowgong, Kamrup, and Darrang. Refer to Guha, *Planter Raj to Swaraj*, pp. 281–2.
75. Assam Legislative Assembly Proceedings of March 1946.
76. The following references are from the Assam Legislative Proceedings of 1946.
77. 'Ulster' in this context refers to the continuous rivalry between the Irish Catholics and the English Protestants in Northern Ireland, between those

who wished to join the Irish Republic and those who wanted to stay in the
United Kingdom. Das is here obviously referring to the growing state of
tension between the indigenes and the immigrants because of the government's immigration and land policies.

78. This clearly reveals the politics of census in Assam which continues till the
present day. It is to be noted that before and after every census there is a
hue and cry over the changing demography and the threat to the existence
of the indigenous population. In recent years the controversy centring
around census reports has gained serious dimensions and the Government
of India has often hesitated to come out with the language and religion
figures. On the eve of every census the Assamese population is gripped
by apprehension that their majority status might finally go and there have
been several instances when Assamese intellectuals have been appealing to
the immigrant population to return to Assamese as their mother tongue
so that the majority status of Assamese language was ensured. Initially, the
immigrant population decided to return Assamese as their mother tongue
in lieu of the protection that they got from the state government run mainly
by the Assamese. Moreover, returning Assamese as the first language also
brought these people into the broader fold of Assamese nationalism, with
Assamese organizations such as the Asom Sahitya Sabha welcoming the
immigrants as part of the Assamese 'nation' (jati).

79. It is interesting to read this argument because it presents a counterstory
to the oft-repeated argument that immigration from Bengal of Muslim
peasants has led to the province's prosperity.

80. It is interesting to note that most of the points raised by Beli Ram Das were
later echoed during the Assam Movement of 1979–83. The fear of being
turned into a minority in their own province has been at the heart of many
an identity movement in Assam.

81. Speech by Syed Abdur Rouf at the Assam Legislative Assembly, March 1946.

82. Shams, in his speech supporting immigration into Assam, said, 'If you really
want to consider the welfare of India as a whole, throw open all your waste
lands to all people and allow the immigrants to come as they came before
and thereby show your real sympathy for the Muslims.' Refer to Assam
Legislative Assembly proceedings of March 1946.

83. Speech by Mafiz Chaudhury at the Assam Legislative Assembly session of
March 1946.

84. Speech by Mayeen-uddin-Chaudhury at the Assam Legislative Assembly
session of March 1946. In the same speech, Chaudhury declared that no
'artificial barriers' such as the Line System would ever be able to protect
the Assamese and that they 'are bound to be extinct if they are not made
strong and industrious'.

85. Speech by Abdul Matin Chaudhury at the Assam Legislative Assembly session of March 1946. He justified the occupation of the reserves on the plea that more food crops needed to be produced and said: 'Sir, this state of things must cease. Call it Civil Disobedience, call it defiance of the law, call it by whatever name you please. Sir, we are determined that we shall spare no effort to see that food crop is produced.... Line system or no Line system, professional grazing reserves or no professional grazing reserves.' Matin Chaudhury's argument was refuted in a lengthy intervention by Congress member Omeo Kumar Das who pointed out that the immigrants from Bengal were not just grower of cereals and that they were more interested in growing cash crops. He pointed out that while the area for paddy had increased only 30 per cent over the years, the area under jute had gone up by a staggering 1,000 per cent in some districts. In the Assam Valley during 1920–46 paddy area increased from 20 lakh acres to 29 lakh acres, whereas the jute area increased from 50,000 acres to over 3 lakh acres.

86. One may refer to the Bodo–Immigrant Muslim clashes that started erupting from the early 1990s. Assamese villagers had long cultivated seasonal crops such as sesame and mustard on the alluvial sand banks of the Brahmaputra and other rivers that remained inundated during the monsoons and surfaced in the winter months. These low-lying lands, known as *da-mati*, on both sides of the river banks were used for what the Assamese called *paamkheti* (winter crops that were raised on such land once the river had retreated) and for grazing cattle. The immigrants who initially settled on the sandbanks in the midstreams of the Brahmaputra and its tributaries, known as *chars* or *chaporis*, often moved into the da-mati areas during floods and occupied those. This led to tension and conflict between the indigenous peasants and the immigrants. One of the worst conflicts that took place in recent years was the one at Chaolkhowa Chapori, during the height of the Assam Movement against foreigners, when in February 1983 both Assamese Hindu and Assamese Muslim villagers attacked the immigrant Muslims who had settled at the chapori that had been earlier used as a grazing reserve by the former. Refer to E.N. Rammohan, *Insurgent Frontiers* (New Delhi: India Research Press, 2005). That the struggle for control over riverine char areas still continues is evident from a report published in an Assamese daily of 14 January 2016, which referred to the occupation of some 800 bighas of riverine land in September 2015 by immigrant peasants in the Mangaldoi revenue circle of the Darrang district. This land had long been cultivated especially to raise winter crops by the Assamese villagers. The report was vindicated by Upamanyu Hazarika, the Supreme Court lawyer who

had been asked by the Supreme Court to submit a report on the state of infiltration into Assam. Refer to 'Oboidha Prabajankaarik Prasashan, Araakshie Rakshanabekshan Dise' (Illegal Immigrants being Protected by Administration and Police), by staff reporter, *Dainik Janambhumi*, Guwahati, 13 January 2016.

3

THE CRITICAL FORTIES II

In this chapter an attempt has been made to discuss the politics of the Muslim League in Assam and how it led to the communalization of politics in the province. It throws light on the Muslim League's strategy of linking up the immigration and land issue with that of Pakistan and how it consistently tried to disprove the fact that Assam was a Hindu-majority province. The Muslim League's movements in favour of immigration and against the Line System as well as its civil disobedience movement are also discussed. References to papers and documents of the Muslim League are made in this context. The chapter also takes up for a brief discussion the politics that took shape in Assam after the announcement of the Cabinet Mission's proposals and the way in which the Assam Congress put up a concerted fight against the grouping scheme of the Cabinet Mission with the support of Gandhi. It also highlights the fact that the issues of land, immigration, and language would find echoes several decades later in Assam in the form of populist agitations and land-related violence, particularly in plains tribal areas, and how these issues retain their relevance in present-day Assam politics.

Muslim League and the Communalization of Politics in Assam

Right from the beginning,[1] the politics of the Muslim League in Assam was inextricably linked with the land and immigration question. Unlike in other parts of India, the communal divide between Hindus and indigenous Muslims in the province was quite thin. Hence, the Muslim League strategy in Assam was to back the immigrant occupation of land

and at the same time prove that Assam was in essence not a Hindu-majority province. The period from the early 1940s is marked by a concerted attempt by the Muslim League to incorporate the province of Assam into the framework of Pakistan.[2] A common strain in the Muslim League position on the opening up of more and more reserves and tribal belts to the immigrants was (a) that there was enough land in the province and (b) that measures such as the Line System would never be able to protect the Assamese because they were 'inherently lazy' and could not do justice to whatever land they occupied. Both these arguments try to nullify the right of small communities and nationalities to defend their own lifestyle which, of course, included their relationship with land and cropping pattern. For instance, when the Nagas said that they be left to forge their destiny according to their way of life, they were not only stressing their distinctness as a people but also their right to not be sucked in by the wheel of 'prog-ress', which in this case meant more and better crops by making the maximum utilization of land. The immigrant leaders argued that since the Assamese could not do justice to their land, the former had every right to take over these lands and turn them 'prosperous'. In fact, this argument has also been accepted by a wide range of liberal scholars in recent times who try to justify that the flow of people from land-scarce East Bengal/East Pakistan/Bangladesh was inevitable because there was enough land in Assam and the local people were not adept at putting this land to good use. It was the immigrant Bengali Muslim peasant who turned the fallow land into lush green fields. The Muslim League doubled up its efforts to prove that Assam was in reality a Muslim-majority province since the hill and plains tribes along with the tea garden labour population could not be counted as Hindus. In order to further this argument, the Muslim League built up pressure on the governments led by Syed Muhammad Saadulla to step up immigration from East Bengal.[3] During the last days of the Congress coalition min-istry[4] headed by Gopinath Bardoloi it passed a resolution on the land question, which stated that occupation of professional reserves would not be permitted and all encroachers would henceforth be evicted. The resolution also affirmed the findings of the Line System committee and stated that indigenous interests in land would be protected through a planned settlement. The reaction to the above land resolution on the part of the newly formed Assam Provincial Muslim League was totally negative, and this was reflected in the very first session of the Assam Provincial Muslim League held in November 1937. The Provincial Muslim League upped its ante for the abolition of the Line System and this once again became a rallying point for the immigrant Muslim settlers. The Hindu–Muslim divide centred on land occupation was beginning to bring dividends for the Muslim League, despite Congress's attempts to prevent the communalization of the Assam Valley politics. For the rest of its term, the Congress coalition ministry faced consistent opposition from both the Muslim League and the Assam United Party.

Meanwhile, the politics of the AIML was taking new turns and the Lahore Resolution of 1940[5] pressed the panic button for all those small nationalities and communities in Assam, who were harbouring apprehensions that Muslim League politics in the province would ultimately veer towards the demand for the incorporation of the region in a future Muslim homeland. Politics in Assam was never the same after the Lahore Resolution, and swift religious and political and polarization took place. Every statement and every speech by Mohammad Ali Jinnah added to the anxiety of the non-Muslim population of Assam. Jinnah addressed scores of meetings in 1940–1 to underline that fact that Hindus and Muslims in India would never be able to forge a common Indian nation and that India did not constitute a united country and that Muslims must carve out their own homeland. In his speeches, he frequently referred to the 'Muslim-majority' states of Punjab, North-West Frontier Province, Sind, Baluchistan, Bengal, and Assam.[6] In his presidential address to the special Pakistan session of the Punjab Muslim Students' Federation at Lahore in March 1941, Jinnah declared:

> But it is as clear as daylight that we are not a minority. We are a nation. And a nation must have territory. What is the use of merely saying that we are a nation? Nation does not live in air. It lives on the land; it must govern land and it must have a territorial state and that is what you want to get.[7]

One can well imagine the impact of these speeches especially in a situation where the Muslim League in Assam was desperately trying to push its agenda of increasing immigration of Muslim peasants from Bengal, encouraging them to occupy government reserves and wastelands, and ultimately swinging the demographic balance in its favour to prove that

Assam was in reality a Muslim-majority province.[8] Political opinion
amongst the hill tribes had not yet consolidated and, with the large
Muslim population of the district of Sylhet, demographically it was a
major challenge for all those who wished to resist the League's politics.[9] As it was, when Saadulla returned to power in August 1942, the
Provincial Muslim League's clout in Assam politics had substantially
increased and it was under its pressure that the Saadulla government
initiated its new land settlement plans in the middle of 1943[10] under
the 'Grow More Food' programme, which clearly favoured the Bengali
Muslim immigrants.

Politics in Assam took a completely new turn when Maulana Bhasani
took over as the president of the Assam Provincial Muslim League in
1944. It was in the third session of the Provincial Muslim League held
in April of the same year that Bhasani made it clear that the Muslim
League's agenda in Assam could not be complete without a struggle for
achieving Pakistan. This is what he said before the conference began:
'The Muslim brethren of the twelve districts of Assam will assemble
together in the grand conference and will adopt the resolution to
establish Pakistan based on full independence. Except Pakistan, there is
no other means by which we can achieve our advancement. Be determined to achieve Pakistan by any means, even at the cost of sacrificing
your life and property.'[11]

In the same session Bhasani called upon the Assam Premier, Syed
Saadulla, to lead the movement in Assam for the establishment of
Pakistan. It was under the leadership of Bhasani that League activities
in the Assam Valley were geared up. Discussing this, Dev and Lahiri
comment:

> Under the direction of Bhasani the movement for inclusion of Assam in
> Pakistan acquired a new dimension. Thus, the problem of Muslim immi-
> grants in Assam hastened up the movement and intensified the hostil-
> ity towards the Line System as a part of the battle cry for Pakistan....
> The Assam Muslim Association of Calcutta and the East Pakistan
> Renaissance Society, Calcutta, also extended support to the Provincial
> League.[12]

The efforts of the Provincial Muslim League were supported in
no small measure by the League ministry of Bengal, but Saadulla
was clearly not being able to keep pace with the Provincial Muslim
League's demands and his political future was becoming uncertain. A

measure of self-survival, Saadulla worked out the Tripartite Agreement of March 1945 and reconstituted his ministry with Congress support from outside. The new ministry issued a new resolution on land settlement in July 1945 in the face of opposition from the Muslim League. This resolution tried to undo all the harm that had been done to the indigenes in the past and laid down provisions for the protection of land held by the tribals and for the eviction of illegal encroachers from the professional reserves, while at the same time providing for planned settlement of the tribals and indigenous Assamese peasants. The resolution also opened the way for the eviction of illegal settlers in some of the PGRs in the district of Kamrup, a clear setback for the League's agenda on Assam. The eviction plan of the Congress government led to massive protests from the Assam Provincial Muslim League, which worked out a series of protests. Eviction had by now become a major issue for the Assam Provincial Muslim League and it did its best to mobilize not only the immigrant peasants on this score but also Muslim public opinion throughout the province. Its efforts clearly bore fruit in the 1946 elections when the League captured all but three of the seats reserved for Muslims.[13] The election results demonstrated that the League had successfully expanded its base and had been able to secure substantial support even amongst the non-immigrant Muslims of the province. It was evident that the idea of Pakistan had caught the imagination even of a section of indigenous Assamese Muslims who, otherwise, had not been drawn into the earlier anti-eviction programmes of the League. But, its spectacular electoral success met with a roadblock because the Congress secured an absolute majority in the 108 member House. Now, with a Congress government in power, the League's problems started multiplying. The Bardoloi-led Congress government started its programme of evicting illegal encroachers from the PGRs. The eviction programme came under severe attack from the AIML[14] and the Muslim press. Even the premier of Bengal, H.S. Suhrawardy, sent a wire to the Assam premier, Bardoloi, asking him to stop the eviction process and begin negotiations. The Bengal Legislative Assembly also passed a resolution moved by the Muslim League minister Saiyed Hossain, which called for a stop to the evictions that were seen as a 'crime against humanity'.[15] The Assam Provincial Muslim League threatened that if the evictions continued, there could be outbreaks of communal violence in the province. The province, however, did not

see any instances of communal conflict, and even during the Direct
Action Day of 16 August 1946, which resulted in the Great Calcutta
Killings, there were no outbreaks of violence in Assam, barring a few
isolated incidents in the district of Sylhet. However, communal tension
ran quite high because of the League's slogans and leaflets endorsing
the demand for Pakistan and its call to the Muslims to achieve Pakistan
at all costs.[16]

Even as communal polarization was swiftly advancing in Assam,
and the Muslim League was achieving moderate successes in winning
over Muslim public opinion against the Bardoloi government's eviction
policy and in favour of Pakistan, the Cabinet Mission proposals were
announced in May 1946. The Cabinet Mission Plan[17] was easily the
most important political development in the year immediately preceding Partition. The moment the Cabinet Mission proposals were made
known, the Assam Congress leadership informed the Congress high
command that the groupings would not be acceptable to the people
of the province because Bengal, with its majority members, would
impose its will on Assam. As subsequent events proved it, the Assam
Congress leadership rightly anticipated that in the face of the League's
persistent demand for an independent Pakistan, the Cabinet Mission
might concede a Muslim-dominated zone within a united India.[18]
While mass protests took place in the state, the Assam Assembly in an
unprecedented move resolved against joining the Section and declared
that the provincial constitution could be framed only by Assam's own
representatives.[19] The Assembly asked all the ten representatives in
the Constituent Assembly to stay out of the Section when the provincial constitution would be drafted, but asked them to participate
in the framing of the Union Constitution. The Assam Congress leaders
pointed out to the central Congress leadership the vagueness in two of
the clauses of the Cabinet Mission's plan. While Clause 15(5) stated
that the provinces could be free to form Groups, clause 19(V) con-
tradicted this by directing the provinces to form Groups. Initially, the
central Congress leaders tried to assure the Congressmen from Assam
that the province could later opt out of the Sections if it so desired.
Meanwhile, Pethick-Lawrence declared at a press conference that the
provinces were actually not free to decide upon their own course of
action as mentioned in clause 15(5).

Initially, Jawaharlal Nehru and Maulana Azad too seemed quite sympathetic towards Assam's stand and Patel was unequivocal in his support to the Assam Congress leadership. According to the then Assam Congress president, Mohammad Tayyebulla, Nehru had said: 'Whereas no province could be compelled to go into the grouping, provinces unwilling to opt in will refuse to go. Who can force a constitution on Assam in Section C when Assam will not accept it at all?'[20] Nehru suggested that the Assam Assembly should adopt a resolution refusing to sit in the Group, and a clear directive should be given to the Assam representatives to the Constituent Assembly in this regard. Patel too told the Assam leaders that the Congress was opposed in principle to grouping and that he fully backed Assam's stand.[21] Finally when the Assam delegation met Gandhi, he categorically told them to stay out of the Group.[22] The Congress Working Committee headed by Azad expressed its support for the stand taken by the Assam Congress and endorsed Nehru's suggestion regarding a resolution by the Assam Assembly. But, when Azad and Nehru met the Cabinet Mission on 10 June 1946 they did not raise the issue of Assam's objection to the Group.[23] By the time the Assam Assembly passed the resolution against grouping, the attitude of the central Congress leaders had undergone a change. Nehru not only expressed his unhappiness at the wording of the resolution but viewed Assam's objection as an obstacle. On 10 August 1946, the Congress Working Committee accepted the Cabinet Mission Plan and Nehru declared: 'We are perfectly prepared to, and have accepted, the position of sitting in sections which will consider the question of formation of groups.'[24] Though Nehru soon wrote to Bardoloi saying that Assam would not be forced to do anything against its will, yet it became clear that the central leadership was about to go against the crucial resolution on the issue of grouping. The apprehensions of the members of the Assam Congress were further strengthened by the British government's statement of December 1946, which clearly favoured the Muslims League's position on the disputed clauses by declaring that issues in dispute could be resolved by a simple majority in the Sections. The provision for reference to the Federal Court appeared unconvincing to the Assam Congress, and Gandhi was soon to declare that it was a packed court. The die was finally cast and the Assam

Congress decided to stick to its earlier decision to stay away from the Groupings and fight the AICC if necessary.

It was at this moment of grave crisis that Gandhi came to Assam's assistance and told a delegation of Assam Congress leaders:

> If Assam keeps quiet it is finished. No one can force Assam to do what it does not want to do. It must stand independently as an autonomous unit. It is autonomous to a large extent today. It must become fully independent and autonomous.... As soon as the time comes for the Constituent Assembly to go into sections you will say, 'Gentlemen, Assam retires'. For the independence of India it is the only condition. Each Unit must decide and act for itself. I am hoping that in this, Assam will lead the way.... If Assam takes care of itself the rest of India will be able to look after itself. What have you got to do with the Constitution of the Union Government? You should form your own Constitution. That is enough. You have the basis of a constitution yourself.[25]

Gandhi exhorted the Assam Congress to revolt against the central Congress leadership if necessary, saying that, not to speak of a provincial committee, even an individual had the right to rebel against the Congress. Gandhi's stand changed the scales in favour of Assam. Azad and Nehru, however, continued to hold the view that Assam's stand was helping the Muslim League and also acting as an obstruction to freedom. Nehru is reported to have told a three-member delegation from Bengal, which asked him as to why Assam was being let down after being given such high hopes by him: 'Assam could not hold up the progress of the rest of India and support to Assam would mean refusal to accept the British Prime Minister's statement of December 6 and letting loose forces of chaos and civil war.' [26]

Nehru was not alone in holding such a view. Sardar Patel, known for his consistency of views, is reported to have said the following in reply to a question as to whether the Congress's change of stand was not a climbdown on its part:

> But for the good of the people of India principles have sometimes to be swallowed for the sake of expediency. In a political game compromises have to be made, and in India the Congress prestige will not suffer more than it has already suffered by entering the Interim Government.... Surely the whole of India cannot be plunged into a civil war for the sake of Assam.[27]

In the light of all this, it was but natural that at the AICC meeting held on 5 January 1947, Nehru's resolution accepting the general terms of the British statement of 6 December 1946, regarding the Cabinet Mission proposals, was accepted by 522–99 votes. Six of the eight members from Assam voted against the motion, while the Assam Congress chief, Tayyebulla, voted in favour of it and Fakhruddin Ali Ahmed abstained. Assam's demand for an outright rejection of the 6 December statement was supported by Jayaprakash Narayan, Saratchandra Bose, and several other leaders.[28] Nehru said that though he was 'alive to the danger that confronts Assam', he would still recommend the resolution for acceptance. Referring to Assam's uncompromising stand, Nehru stated:

> It is true that Assam has a mandate to oppose Sections and Groups and Assam can fight if it wants. But I would like to remind you that battles are won not by the personal courage of one or two but by the cooperation of many thousands and by mobilization and right use of resources. The time may come when Assam will have to fight; that fight will not be single handed but will be waged with the whole of India behind them.[29]

Nehru's rhetoric did not convince the Assam leaders, who felt let down by the central leadership.

Azad's views on the issue are recorded in his memoirs:

> Both Congress and the Muslim League had originally accepted the Cabinet Mission Plan which meant that both accepted the Constituent Assembly. So far as the Congress was concerned, it was still in favour of the Cabinet Mission Plan. The only objection raised from the Congress side was by certain leaders from Assam. They were possessed by an inexplicable fear of Bengalis. They said that if Bengal and Assam were grouped together, the whole region would be dominated by Muslims. Gandhiji had initially accepted the Cabinet Mission Plan ... however Gandhiji's views changed and he gave his support to Bardoloi. Jawaharlal agreed with me that the fears of the Assam leaders were unjustified and tried hard to impress them. Unfortunately, they did not listen to either Jawaharlal or me, especially since Gandhiji was now on their side and issued statements supporting their stand. Jawaharlal was however steadfast and gave me his full support.[30]

Azad's position on grouping was apparently similar to that held by the British government and the Muslim League. This is evident from his

statement as the Congress president after the Muslim League accused
the AICC of violating its pledge to adhere to the 6 December statement by adopting the 6 January resolution, which gave the provinces
the right to opt out of the Sections if they so desired. Azad, as president
of the Congress, issued a clarification saying that the doubts of the
AIML were unfounded. His statement ran thus:

> The Cabinet Mission's statement of 16 May made it clear that after
> the preliminary meeting of the Constituent Assembly, it would divide
> into three Sections. These Sections would decide whether there would
> be Grouping or not. Even if it was decided to form a Group and a
> Constitution formed for it, provinces would have the right to opt out
> of the Group after the first elections held under the new Constitution.
> The question then arose as to how the Section would arrive at a decision
> on the point. The Congress held that the representative of a province
> within the Section could act as a unit and decide whether the prov-
> ince should enter into the Group or not. The League and the Cabinet
> Mission, on the other hand, held that decision within the Section would
> be by simple majority and the province would exercise the right of opt-
> ing out only after the first elections. This made Assam nervous as Bengal
> has a majority in Section C. Assam fears that Bengal might so frame the
> Constitution of Assam as to make her right to opt out at a later stage a
> dead letter. Both the Secretary of State and Sir Stafford Cripps in their
> statements to Parliament made it perfectly clear that this right of the
> provinces to opt out must not be tempered with and any attempt to
> frame a provincial Constitution which prejudices such right of the prov-
> inces would be against the letter and spirit of the State Paper of 16 May.
> The Congress had in its resolution of 6 January, accepted the British
> Government's interpretation of the State Paper expounded in the state-
> ment of 6 December and thus agreed that decision in the Section will
> be by simple majority.[31]

But, even while saying this, Azad stressed that the crucial point
would be the manner in which the work in the Section is carried
out. He said that it was possible that Bengal could use its majority in
Section C to frame the constitution in such a manner as would prevent
Assam from opting out at a later stage. If this were to happen, Assam's
apprehensions would be fully justified and 'nobody can blame them if
her representatives walk out of the Section'. In this there seems to be a
slight change in Azad's position regarding Assam's views on grouping,
even though he is adhering to the official Congress position on simple

majority of the Sections. Could this be the result of Mahatma Gandhi's intervention through a telegram addressed to the Assam Congress president, Tayyebulla, wherein he urged the Assam representatives to virtually revolt against the AICC's stand on grouping?[32] It is possible that Azad was aware of the fact that on the Assam issue Gandhi was taking a position quite opposite to that of the AICC.

Though Azad says that Nehru was consistent in his stand, yet there is evidence to suggest that he was equivocating right from the start. For instance, just three months after the AICC resolution of 6 January 1947, Mountbatten records that when he asked Nehru whether the Congress had accepted the statement, he replied in the affirmative but added that 'if they were to be asked if whether they were going to force Assam and the Sikhs to abide by it they would have to admit that they were in no position to force any Province or section of a Province to comply with all the terms against their will and interest'.[33]

Jinnah had insisted that the provinces first join the Groups and later separate if they so wished. Though Azad had to go along with the Congress Working Committee's views broadly supporting Assam's stand, yet he comments:

> Looking back after ten years, I concede that there was force in what Jinnah said. The Congress and the League were both parties to the agreement, and it was on the basis of distribution among the Centre, the provinces and the Groups that the League had accepted the Plan. Congress was neither wise nor right in raising doubts. It should have accepted the Plan unequivocally if it stood for the unity of India. Vacillation would give Jinnah the opportunity to divide India.[34]

It is obvious from the above that the central leadership of the Congress did not share Assam's apprehensions about the Cabinet Mission Plan and, but for Gandhi's support for Bardoloi and the Assam Congress, would have gone ahead with its implementation. Assam's stand was one of the major reasons why the Cabinet Mission Plan ultimately fell through. But, it is interesting to note that the struggle against the Cabinet Mission Plan instead of strengthening centrifugal forces, helped the centripetal ones to consolidate. While discussing this critical juncture of Assam's history, one is naturally prompted to ask as to why those political forces who were in favour of Assam retaining its identity outside India did not take advantage of the equivocation and betrayal by the central Congress leadership to build up their case effectively

among the masses? An increasing apprehension of a possible separation
from India because of the politics of the Muslim League might have
been a reason for keeping separatist forces in abeyance for the time
being. These forces knew only too well that given the demographic
pattern of the province and its past experience with the Saadullah
ministries, a *Swadhin Asom* (sovereign Assam) would be even more
vulnerable to the political manoeuvres of Bengal, which might end up
as a part of Pakistan. The hill leaders too were aware of the need to stay
with India and Nichols Roy, a Khasi leader, articulated these complexi-
ties very powerfully:

> We know what the policy of the Muslim League is in Assam.... Now
> the Muslim League in Bengal wants to send thousands upon thousands
> of immigrants into Assam. That is feared by everyone. The people of
> the hills are afraid of that immigration and say they will fight it to the
> last. The people of the plains do not want to be swamped. They do not
> want Assam, which is a non-majority province now, to be turned into a
> Muslim-majority province. This is the crux of the whole fight between
> Assam and the Muslim League.[35]

All this had far-reaching consequences on the political scenario
of Assam, and acted as a catalyst in bringing together various ethnic
nationalities, communities, and groups in a joint struggle against the
grouping proposals as incorporated in the Cabinet Mission Plan and
the machinations of the Muslim League. This is an important mile-
stone in the story about Assam and Partition. Thus, even as the indigenous peoples of the region were grappling with the fear of being
turned into minorities in their own homeland, the Cabinet Mission
Plan acted as a sharp catalyst in polarizing opinion on communal
lines. The grouping of Assam with Muslim-majority Bengal aggravated ethnic fears and the Assam Congress, under Gopinth Bardoloi,
led a concerted struggle to stay out of the Cabinet Mission Plan. In
this it was supported by hill leaders such as J.J.M. Nichols Roy, among
others.[36] Ultimately, it was Gandhi's support to the Assam Congress's
stand that tilted the scales in their favour.[37] But the entire issue generated a lot of distrust and bitterness amongst the Assamese people over
the role of leaders such as Nehru and Azad and several ethnic organizations demanded independence for the region rather than becoming a part of Pakistan. Discussing this, Amalendu Guha writes: 'The
immigrant question quickly matured into a political crisis, in the last

pre-independence decade. During the controversy over "grouping" under the Cabinet Mission Plan, a demand for the self-determination of Assam was brought into the limelight to forestall its threatened inclusion in East Pakistan.'[38]

The success of the Assam Congress, backed by Gandhi, in scuttling the Cabinet Mission Plan came as a major setback for the Muslim League, which had initially opted for the Plan in the hope that provinces such as Assam would eventually become a part of a sovereign Pakistan.[39] But the fear of being grouped with Muslim-majority Bengal brought the non-Muslim population of the hills and the plains of Assam together on a common platform. Hill leaders like J.J.M. Nichols Roy played a leading role in building up opposition to the Cabinet Mission Plan, and the Muslim League's efforts to win over the hill tribes and other non-Hindu segments of the province's population suffered a setback. Nonetheless, the politics of the Muslim League did succeed in bringing about, perhaps for the first time, a clear divide between the province's Muslim and non-Muslim population.

Muslim League's Civil Disobedience Movement

The dropping of the Cabinet Mission proposals did not deter the Muslim League in its efforts to somehow include Assam into the scheme for Pakistan. This is clearly revealed in the League's efforts to launch a civil disobedience movement similar to its programme in Sind and the North-West Frontier Province. But, unlike in the Sind and the North-West Frontier Province, the Muslim League's civil disobedience programme in Assam was almost exclusively aimed at defending the interests of the immigrant Muslim peasants and their quest for land in the province. The struggle for Assam's inclusion in Pakistan was combined with the mobilization of public opinion throughout the country against the eviction measures in PGRs adopted by the Assam government led by Bardoloi. Not only were these eviction measures swiftly opposed by the Bengal Muslim League but influential newspapers such as the *Dawn*, which represented Muslim opinion to a very large extent, regularly commented on the 'fascist' measures of the Bardoloi government. In its editorial of 2 April 1947, the *Dawn* compared the Assam government's eviction measures with that of the persecution of the Jews in Nazi Germany and went on to say:

In sheer ruthlessness, hatred and violence the immigrant-baiting of
the Bardoloi Ministry of Assam can only be compared with the brutal
persecution of the Jews by the Nazis under the guidance of that mas-
ter Jew-baiter Julius Streicher, who has since paid for his crimes with
his life in the Nuremberg gallows. In both cases, the objective would
appear to be the same: Streicher exterminated the Jews from Germany
and other German-occupied areas in the heyday of Nazi power, while
Premier Bardoloi, especially power-drunk, has been waging an unholy
war against peaceful Muslim immigrants in Assam with a view to extir-
pation. The tragic irony of it, however, is that the engine of repression
has been set in full gear against those very persons who have enriched
the economic life of Assam by making wastelands bloom by the sweat
of their brows just as in Germany it was the hounded-out Jews who
enriched the cultural heritage of the country in every sphere of human
activity.[40]

The editorial rues the fact that although the Nazi dispensation
has ended, the tyranny in Assam continues. It, however, holds up a
ray of hope to the immigrants by saying that the civil disobedience
movement to be launched by the Assam Provincial Muslim League
against the Bardoloi ministry would surely bring succour. It refers to
the resolution adopted by the working committee of the Provincial
League that called upon every branch of the Muslim League organization throughout the province to immediately start a 'peaceful, non-
violent non-communal mass civil disobedience movement on a wide
scale to break the Government which has been unjust and unfair to the
Muslims'. The editorial ended with the hope that just as in the Punjab
the civil disobedience movement had led to the 'glorious victory of the
League', in Assam too the same would happen and it concluded by
saying: 'We have no doubt that the history of Northern Pakistan will
repeat itself in Eastern Pakistan.'[41] A few days later, the same paper
referred to the occupation of government reserves by the immigrants
and observed:

> At Barpeta there is not a single Reserve Area which people have not infil-
> trated and constructed their houses in spite of the authorities. Success
> at Barpeta has raised the morals of the immigrants at Mangaldoi. Those
> who left the place re-appeared and again started cultivating the land.
> The situation has become so desperate for the Congress Government
> that Mr. Gopinath Bardoloi, Premier was obliged to send an SOS to
> Sardar Baldev Singh, Defence Member, Interim Government, praying

for more troops to assist him in warding off what he calls a Muslim invasion.[42]

Though the response of the indigenous Assamese towards the programmes of the Muslim League was lukewarm, yet it succeeded in mobilizing Muslim opinion in its favour not only in the immigrant-majority areas of the province, but also in several pockets in eastern Assam, especially in the district of Sibsagar.[43] The main thrust to the Muslim League politics in Assam was provided by Bhasani,[44] with Saadulla providing the much-needed cementing force. Although Saadulla was quite often at odds with the politics of Bhasani, yet he was all along aware that it was men like Bhasani who were the main motivating force.[45]

The aim of the Muslim League was to have a civil disobedience movement in Assam in line with that of the North-West Frontier Province where too a Congress ministry, headed by Dr Khan Sahib, was in power. The AIML had already succeeded in dislodging the Khizar ministry in the Punjab through a civil disobedience movement,[46] which it had claimed was non-violent in nature. The plans and programmes of all the three civil disobedience movements of the Muslim League were essentially the same. While the aim was to build up a mass movement against the government in power, this was sought to be achieved by roping in the tribals and other non-Muslim marginalized sections into the struggle. The main target of the movements would obviously be the Congress governments then in power. While the civil disobedience movements in the Punjab[47] and the North-West Frontier Province succeeded in dislodging the governments in power, in Assam the Provincial Muslim League failed to receive the support of the tribals, of both the hills and the plains, as well as that of the large tea garden community, and the scheduled castes.[48]

In March 1947 the Assam Provincial Muslim League decided to launch a civil disobedience movement aimed against the Line System and the Bardoloi's government's eviction policy. The League called upon the Muslim peasants to start cultivation on all available government land, and thousands of immigrant peasants responded to the call throughout the province. The provincial assembly was boycotted by the League and it formed a Committee of Action comprising, among others, Bhasani, Abdul Matin Chaudhury, and Saadulla. Prior to the launch of the civil disobedience movement, the Assam Provincial

Muslim League had observed Black Flag Day on 3 January 1947 to be followed up by demonstrations throughout the immigrant pockets of the province. According to Dev and Lahiri, 'upto the middle of May [1947] the Provincial League with the help of borrowed elements in [from] Bengal held about 450 meetings, 180 processions and 30 hartals affecting a total audience [population] of 400,000 Muslims in both the valleys'.[49] However, unlike in the Surma Valley, it was in the Brahmaputra Valley that occupation of government land and resistance to evictions from illegally occupied reserves formed the main plank of the movement. During the said period the Provincial Muslim League tried to take out rallies in migrant-dominated areas of Nowgong, Barpeta, Darrang, and Goalpara and several persons lost their lives in police firing,[50] while the leaders of the agitation, including Bhasani, were put under arrest.

As the law and order situation was severely threatened by the disobedience movement, Bardoloi wrote to the central government for additional security forces. But the request was met with a qualified response from the Government of India. Referring to Bardoloi's request,[51] Patel wrote to Baldev Singh on 9 April 1947 that 'the intention clearly was that military aid should be given when civil forces are unable to cope with the situation, whether it arises out of the eviction policy of the Government of Assam or any other matter, but that it would not be given merely to evict immigrants'.[52] Two days later, Patel wrote to Bardoloi expressing his full support for the former's eviction policy and saying that 'not an inch of land should be surrendered to the illegal immigrants'.[53] Yet, in the same letter, he repeats his earlier argument that military aid could not be provided to help in the eviction process or to protect the reserves from being further occupied. Clearly, faced with a belligerent Provincial Muslim League set upon building up a mass movement, which had the inherent possibility of breaking into violence, Bardoloi was left with no option but to meet the situation with his own police force, which was clearly not equipped to deal with the situation.

Another interesting fact which surfaces when one goes into the correspondence that Gopinath Bardoloi was having with the central government during this period was that both the governor of the province, Sir Akbar Hydari,[54] as well as the army chiefs were unwilling to help Bardoloi. General Stuker of the Eastern Command came forward with a suggestion that the platoons placed in some grazing reserves be removed and deployed in areas where there could be trouble. Bardoloi wrote to Patel on 15 April 1947 that he was strongly opposed to the idea put forward by General Stuker, and repeated by General Renkin, that 'we had dissipated the provisional force, the railway force and the Assam Rifles by distributing them in weaker stations and thereby weakening the striking force of the army'. Bardoloi further added: 'To my great surprise, the Governor also joined with him [General Stuker] and thought that we should withdraw the few platoons placed in the grazing reserves and concentrate them in particular places.' Bardoloi also wanted additional forces for the defence of vulnerable points on the border. He says in the letter that after much argument, the general agreed to render 'whatever help was possible to be given to us'. Bardoloi further says:

> I wanted the Governor by an order to place our specific demands for a brigade; but neither did the Governor do so in our presence nor did the General agree that such a strength could be immediately made possible. As far as I know, it is the Governor who is to requisition, but if the Governor would not act according to the advice of the Ministry, what can we do.

Regarding the attitude of the Centre, Bardoloi writes to Patel: 'The friends who saw you report that you were considering us to be weak. I boldly say that we have been more than strong considering the forces at our disposal; but if the Government of India cannot have their orders enforced with regard to the requirements of the province, blame should not come to the provincial government.' These are strong lines indeed from the premier of a province who while being asked to defend the government land from encroachers is at the same time not being provided any assistance by the central government. Bardoloi ends his letter to Patel by reaffirming that his government was resolved not to give any extra land to the immigrants other than that which was stipulated in the Tripartite Agreement. He also adds as a footnote that though Baldev Singh had wanted the Assam government to use the entire Assam Rifles and wanted it replaced by other troops in the border areas, both the governor and the general opposed the idea.[55] All this shows the highly ambiguous role played by the central ministers, the province's governor, and the army officers[56] at a time when Assam was facing a grave crisis about her very future.

The civil disobedience movement continued till the announcement of the partition plan on 31 June 1947, when Jinnah asked for
the withdrawal of the movement in Assam. What is interesting is that
the civil disobedience movement in Assam received active support
from the Muslim League leadership of Bengal and the secretary of the
Bengal and Assam Joint Action Committee declared that 'Bengal will
do all that is possible to undo the cruel and inhuman eviction policy
of the Government of Assam'.[57] Referring to the claim of the Muslims,
Chaudhury Kahilique-uz-Zaman, a leading member of the Action
Committee set up by the Provincial Muslim League, questioned the
Assam Congress's politicization of the immigration issue and asserted
that by its very numbers the Muslims in Assam could demand the inclusion of Assam in the Eastern Zone of the proposed Pakistan. Referring
to the claim of the Muslims, he declared:

> Muslims are the largest single unit in Assam and they have the sympa
> thies of a large number of tribal people, including Khasis, Ahoms and
> Garos. The Caste Hindus in the province are only 24 lakhs.... Assam
> cannot for reasons economic, cultural linguistic and other allied con-
> siderations, join any other group except Bengal, which even now pro-
> vides Assam with a University, a High Court, Veterinary Department
> and similar other facilities to serve its economic and other interests in
> many ways.[58]

Trying to drive a wedge between the tribal and non-tribal sections of
the people of the province, the Muslim League leader said that 'the
leaders of the tribal people have been deeply shocked at the unfair
methods of the Congress Government' and that there was a strong
possibility of an open revolt against the Congress in tribal areas.[59] In a
similar vein, the League leader from Assam, Abdul Matin Chaudhury,
wrote to K.H. Khurshid in April 1947 claiming that

> obviously with [only] 2–10 per cent of the total population in the Hill
> districts, the Hindus have no right to claim domination over the hill
> tribes of the four hill districts forming 87 to 97 per cent of the popula-
> tion. On the other hand, Muslim Zones have a greater claim to these hill
> districts on the grounds of contiguity, commercial intercourse and stra-
> tegic defence. Lushai Hills have no physical contiguity with the remnant
> [sic] Assam. Access to the Lushai Hills[60] can be only through Pakistan
> Zones in Bengal and Assam. As the last War has shown, Lushai Hills and
> Naga Hills are a necessity to the Pakistan Zone for its strategic defence.

Garo Hills are surrounded practically on three sides by overwhelming Muslim Zones in Bengal and Assam, its main outlet to outside world lie through the predominantly Muslim areas in Bengal and Assam. Khasi and Jaintia Hills have close historical association with the predominantly Muslim district of Sylhet, the plain portion of the ancient kingdom of Jaintia forming even today a part of Sylhet district.[61]

The Muslim League had hoped that the hill tribes, the tea garden population, and the Ahoms, along with the plains tribes and scheduled castes, would all join in the struggle to oust the Congress ministry headed by Gopinath Bardoloi. Accordingly, plans were made. But the situation in Assam was quite different. The League not only failed to secure the support of the tea tribes, plains tribes, and the Ahom community but also from the majority of the indigenous Assamese Muslims, whose response to League's programmes was, at best, lukewarm. In a letter addressed to Jinnah within a month of the launching of the civil disobedience movement in Assam, Saadulla rued the fact that 'the *entire Assam Valley Hindus, Tribal people and also the Tea Garden labourers are dead set against the Muslim immigrants from Bengal*' (emphases mine). He added:

> We can expect no help, no sympathy from them in the Assam Valley in our Civil Disobedience Movement, and we are in a minority in the Assam Valley. Please, therefore, give your best thoughts to the situation in Assam and guide the Committee of Action, who is meeting you at your place on the 20th April, and give me directions [about] what to do. If a vigorous Civil Disobedience Movement is to be carried on, it will surely mean much loss of innocent lives and destruction of property. It is a moot point whether by launching such a movement we can dislodge the present ministry with our 31 Muslim League members in a House of 108—and yet 'Down with the Ministry' is the slogan at this moment.[62]

Saadulla here is clearly demolishing the argument put forward by his fellow Muslim League leader, Chaudhury Kahilique-uz-Zaman. It is interesting to note Saadulla's observation on the minority status of the Muslim community in the Assam Valley, especially when one takes into account the consistent attempt on the part of the Muslim League to prove that Assam was not a Hindu-majority province, once the plain tribes and the communities such as the Ahoms were not categorized as Hindus. For instance, in a detailed note prepared by Mohammad Afzal Hussain Qadri of the Aligarh Muslim University and sent to Jinnah on

18 April 1947, the author maintains that 'in the whole of Assam only three districts, namely Kamrup, Sibsagar and Lakhimpur have a Hindu majority. Furthermore, Assam is divided into three natural regions, namely the Brahmaputra Valley, Surma Valley and the Hills. In none of these natural divisions are the Hindus in a majority'. Qadri tries to prove his point by showing a break-up of the population that shows the Hindus in a minority in all three regions, especially with all non-caste Hindus shown as tribes in a separate grouping and only caste-Hindus shown as Hindus.[63] During his interview with Mountbatten on 26 April 1947, Jinnah had presented a note on Assam which stated that

> The total population of Assam, according to the 1941 Census is 1,02,04,600, of which 42,13,000 are Hindus (including Caste Hindus and Scheduled Castes); 34,42,560 are Muslims; 24,85,000 are Tribes and the rest are Others. Out of 14 districts only two (Lakhimpur and Sibsagar) are Hindu-majority districts while in the rest Muslims plus Tribes form a majority. In case the number of Scheduled Castes is taken out, the Caste Hindus will become a minority everywhere.[64]

In the same letter, Saadulla expressed his confidence that Assam had no option but to join Pakistan. He wrote:

> The Congress Government has raised the false cry that the Movement is specially designed to bring Assam into the Pakistan Zone. The varied geographical position of Assam will compel her ultimately to align herself with Bengal, for Assam has got no outlet to the outside world except through Bengal and an alienated Bengal can use the stranglehold on the economic life of Assam.... In the future Constitution of India, if Assam becomes an independent State or a part of Hindustan while Bengal enjoys [joins] Pakistan, Bengal will have the whip-hand over Assam to make Assam ask for grouping with Bengal.[65]

Saadulla's woes about the Muslim League's failure to kick-off its civil disobedience movement in true form was not shared by several other leaders of the AIML. For instance, Dr Emran Hussain Chaudhury, MLA and member of the Committee for Action of the Provincial Muslim League, claimed in June 1947 during a tour of Cachar that 'the Muslim League struggle in Assam had the full sympathy of 3 lakhs of Ahoms, 19 lakhs of tea garden labourers, 7 lakhs of Scheduled castes and 16 lakhs of tribals'.[66] He further added that 'the non-Hindus of Assam have sympathy for any struggle directed to overthrow the inefficient and oppressive Government full of corruption and nepotism'.[67] That there was a concerted attempt on the part of the League to carve out Muslim-majority districts in Assam and the northeastern region is borne out by the involvement of the League leadership in working out the possibility of creating such districts by encouraging the transfer of the Muslim population from one state to another. For instance, one may refer to the 'report on the Migration and Concentration of Muslims in India and a Note on Areas Where Caste Hindus and Sikhs Together are Not in a Majority' prepared by Abdul Rashid Khan. In the section dealing with the 'Assam States', the author works out the Muslim population of Manipur and Kasia (Khasi Hills) and suggests that if the 9.7 per cent Muslims of Manipur cross over to neighbouring Cachar district (where Muslims are in a majority) they would 'increase the strength of their brethren there from 2,49,310 to 2,80,982 against 2,41,310 Hindus there'. Similarly, it is suggested that the mere 2,200 Muslims of Kasia 'should cross over to Sylhet—another Muslim-majority district of Assam district of Assam—thereby increasing the Muslim strength there from 20,05,626 to 20,07,826 as against 12,18,470 Hindus'.[68]

Notwithstanding all these well-worked out arguments, the Muslim League campaign in Assam met with a number of roadblocks. While the League's politics met with success in Bengal because of distinct social and economic factors, in Assam the scenario was quite different. Not only did the League fail to draw the support of the large tribal population of the province, it could not achieve marked success even amongst the indigenous Assamese Muslims. While the League made capital out of the often intense class divide between the Hindus and the Muslims in East Bengal, in Assam such strong class divisions were absent. Unlike most of their East Bengal co-religionists whose status was miserable under the zamindari system, in Assam the Assamese Muslims did not face such problems. They were well integrated into Assamese society and were like any other Assamese peasant under the ryotwari system. During the Ahom rule, Assamese Muslims were treated at par with other peasant groups and often held privileges. Moreover, Assamese Muslims were free from many of the social inequalities that marked Muslim women elsewhere in India. This was applicable to all sections of Assamese Muslims, and was especially true of the middle classes. An illustration of this may be found in the resolution moved at the All India Muslim Students' Federation meeting at Calcutta in December

1937. In her resolution, Georgina Hazarika of Assam called for 'real-
izing the necessity for education amongst Muslim girls' and for rec-
ommending the authorities concerned to 'get co-education introduced
in all institutions of primary, post-graduate and technical studies'.[69]
The resolution was, of course, rejected. Nonetheless, it reflected the
very different perceptions of indigenous Assamese Muslim women
and that the class and gender divide that marked the Bengali Muslim,
particularly in East Bengal, was not as strong in Assam. These are
among the reasons why Bhasani's call to all the peasants of Assam to
occupy all fallow land received a response only from the immigrant
sections of the peasantry. This also explains the muted response that
the Muslim League's other programmes received from the Assamese
Muslims, a large section of which was with the Congress that was led
at a crucial period by Mohammad Tayyebulla.[70] It would, however, be
a simplification to state that Assamese Muslims were not influenced
by the ideology of the Muslim League. Since the main plank of the
Muslim League's civil disobedience movement in Assam was the securing of land and land rights for the immigrant Muslims, the indigenous
Assamese Muslims did not have much to share in this. But on the question of religious solidarity, the Muslim League's propaganda did have
quite some effect. Thus, the failure of the civil disobedience movement
was not necessarily reflected in the elections that followed. The League
had succeeded in drawing the support of a sizeable section of Assamese
Muslims and no one illustrates this better than Saadulla, who himself
was an Assamese Muslim.[71] That the Muslim League had succeeded
in polarizing the state along religious lines becomes evident in the
results of the January 1946 elections. In these elections, the Muslim
League in Assam secured as many as thirty-one out of the thirty-four
Muslim seats, and this despite the campaign conducted in favour of the
Congress by leaders such as Nehru. This is reflective of the fact that the
communal situation in the province had taken a sharp turn in 1946,
with many Assamese Muslims being convinced that Assam would/
should finally go to Pakistan.[72] And, one of the Muslim leaders who
steadfastly contributed towards changing the perception of a section of
Assamese Muslims was none other than Saadulla.

Saadulla was, right from the beginning of his political career, primarily a leader of the Muslims of Assam. Although at a later stage of
his career this leadership was effectively challenged by leaders such as

Bhasani, yet from all relevant records available, it appears that his support and sympathy for the immigrant Muslims from East Bengal was
never in doubt. At every stage, whether it be in his government's land
policy or his position on reservations for Muslims, Saadulla's loyalty to
the Muslim cause was quite clear. On the land question, Saadulla took
every measure possible to open up the PGRs to the immigrant peasants and he resolutely opposed the Bardoloi's government's attempts to
evict encroachers from government land. Whenever his ministry was in
power, he actively encouraged the settlement of immigrants on government land, although he sought to give the impression that his aim to
secure benefits for all landless peasants. While it is true that Saadulla
had reservations about Bhasani's programme of unchecked occupation of government land by the immigrants, and even warned Bhasani
about the negative consequences of such a course of action, at heart he
was for changing the demographic balance of the province in favour
of the Muslims. This is clearly illustrated in a letter Saadulla wrote to
Laiquat Ali Khan in March 1945. Justifying his stand regarding the
formation of a government with tacit Congress support from outside,
Saadulla reiterates his commitment to the cause of the Muslims of
Assam and states: 'After mature deliberation and prolonged discussion
and also the full approval of my party, I have now re-formed [sic] the
Ministry yesterday. In these negotiations I have been more than able to
safeguard the interest of the Moslem community and never have deviated from the creed and policy of the Moslem League.' He concludes
the letter by saying: 'I can assure all the Moslem Leaguers that the
interests of Moslem immigrants into Assam are safe in my hands and
settlement with them is going apace. In the lower districts of Assam
Valley these Bengali immigrant Moslems have quadrupled the Moslem
population during the last 20 years.'[73] Clearly, the Muslim League was
trying to hold on to the argument that Assam was a Muslim-majority
province and must go to Pakistan.[74] This stand of the AIML unnerved
the indigenes of Assam who seemed convinced that the manipulation
of demographic figures was part of the wider game of clubbing Assam
with Bengal, as a first step to the realization of a Pakistan that would
include Assam.

The Assam Provincial Muslim League's civil disobedience movement failed[75] because of a variety of reasons. First and foremost was
the weakness of its very premise that Assam was a Muslim-majority

province once the hill tribes and the tea garden labour population were counted separately. Second, it seemed to take for granted what it believed to be the antagonism of the hill tribes towards the Congress in Assam. The leadership of Bardoloi had added a new dimension to the Assamese–tribes relationship and this later found fruition in the enactment of the Sixth Schedule of the Constitution of India.[76] Moreover, the Assam Provincial Muslim League itself was a divided house when it came to launching the civil disobedience movement. The organizational wing of the Muslim League in Assam was at loggerheads with the political or legislative wing, many of its members not being in favour of any mass agitation on the land and eviction issue. Saadulla, in his letter to Jinnah, states that 'the Working Committee declared civil disobedience on the 9th of March [1947] without taking any steps to prepare the country for the move'. He further adds:

> They took no approval of their scheme from the Central Committee of Action as is necessary under the Muslim League Constitution.... For the prestige of the Muslim League organization, and as we are presented with a fait accompli by the President[77] of the Provincial Muslim League, *we are forced to* adopt the resolution of the civil disobedience movement.[78] (Emphases mine)

Saadulla informs Jinnah that except in one or two areas the response to the Muslim League's movement 'has been poor' and there are 'absolutely no funds' with the organization. Saadulla also mentions in his letter that 'the Muslims are not at all prepared to launch big civil disobedience movement' and that they were disorganized. This letter is significant in view of the fact that Saadulla himself was the chairman of the Action Committee for civil disobedience set up by the Assam Provincial Muslim League. It indicates the growing rift between Saadulla and the militant sections of the Muslim League led by Bhasani. Yet another factor which contributed to the failure of the civil disobedience movement in Assam was the pre-Partition complications that developed in Bengal. Enmeshed in its own problems, Bengal now had little time to spare for developments in neighbouring Assam and this came as a boon for the Congress. Finally, it was the firm but non-communal handling of the situation by the Congress government which prevented the outbreak of communal violence in the province. In conclusion, it may be said that although the Muslim League's civil disobedience movement in Assam failed to achieve its targeted goal, yet it instilled a strong sense of solidarity and unity of purpose among the immigrant Bengali Muslims, who emerged as a strong political force in several districts of the state. This consolidation of the immigrant Muslims would take on new sociopolitical dimensions in the years to follow.

Notes

1. The nucleus of the Muslim League in Assam was formed in the district of Sylhet in the 1930s but its presence in the Assam Valley was felt much later. Prior to this the Muslims of the Assam Valley had only one political organization, the Assam Valley Muslim Party, led by Tayyebulla, which later merged with the Congress. Prior to the 1937 elections, most of the Muslim leaders of the Brahmaputra Valley were elected as independent candidates. In the first cabinet headed by Saadulla (April 1937–February 1938) the Muslim League made its presence felt, and by the time he formed his second ministry (February–September 1938) Saadulla knew that he would not be able to survive without the support of the Muslim League, whose strength by then had increased to ten members in the assembly. This forced Saadulla to veer towards it. Jinnah appointed the organizing committee for the province of Assam on 14 June 1938 with Bhasani as its convener and Saadulla as one of its members. A year before, in 1937, Saadulla had joined the Muslim League. But throughout his career, Saadulla relied on the support of the Surma Valley United Muslim Party and the European group, and used this to counter his opponents within the Muslim League whenever needed.

2. Thus, the Muslim League politics may be said to have added to the communal polarization by the end of the 1930s. Reacting to Muslim League moves, Assamese organizations such as the Asamiya Sanrakshini Sabha, led by Ambikagiri Raychoudhury and Nilmoni Phukan, presented a memorandum to Nehru during his visit to Assam in November 1937, which alleged that the question of immigration has been given a communal colour by the League. The memorandum stated that 'as a means of saving the Assamese race from extinction, a considerable section of the Assamese intelligentsia has even expressed their minds in favour of the secession of Assam from India', and appealed to the National Congress to help the Assamese. Writers such as Jnananath Bora already tried to build up their thesis for an independent Assam in the late 1930s, and now the fear of the Assamese—of their province being included in

Pakistan—further spurred such concepts. It is interesting to note that even within Congressmen in Assam, the fear of Pakistan brought out autonomist and separatist demands and this can be seen in the writings of Assamese intellectuals such as Ambikagiri Roychoudhury. An ardent Congressman who nourished the idea of an autonomous Assam within the *mahajati* (greater nationality) of India, Ambikagiri, in his article, 'The Case of the Great Assamese People and their Homeland: Assam', spawned autonomist ideas which were taken up later on in the post-Independence period by organizations such as the Asom Jatiyatabadi Yuva Chatra Parishad. This memorandum was submitted by the Asom Jatiya Mahasabha to the AICC dated 9 June 1946. Refer to Girin Phukan, *Assam's Attitude to Federalism* (New Delhi: Sterling Publishers, 1984), pp. 79–80. Nirode K. Barooah refers to another memorandum submitted by Ambikagiri Raychoudhury and Nilmoni Phukan on behalf of the Asom Sanrakshini Sabha and Asomiya Deka Dal to Nehru in November 1937 in which they hinted that, if need be, Assam should separate from India. Refer to Nirode K. Barooah, *Gopinath Bardoloi: 'The Assam Problem' and Nehru's Centre* (Guwahati: Bhabani Print and Publications, 2010), p. 105.

3. Thus, in a span of just one year, 1939–40, the Saadulla government settled Bengali Muslim immigrants on 1,60,000 bighas of reserved land in the Brahmaputra Valley.

4. September 1938–November 1939.

5. Speaking on the Lahore Resolution of the Muslim League, Jinnah made his case clear for a separate homeland for Indian Muslims so that they 'have the opportunity to develop their spiritual, cultural, economic and political life in accordance with their own genius and shape their own future society'. (*Speeches, Statements and Messages of Quaid-i-Azam [1938–1941]*, vol. II, collected and edited by Khurshid Ahmed Khan Yusufi [Lahore: Bazm-e-Iqbal, 1996], pp. 1190–1.)

6. *Speeches, Statements and Messages of Quaid-i-Azam*, vol. II, p. 1181.

7. *Speeches, Statements and Messages of Quaid-i-Azam*, vol. II, pp. 1327–8.

8. The occupation of government reserves and grazings came to be inextricably linked with the League's demand for a separate Muslim nation state.

9. The total population of Assam in 1941 was about 100 lakhs of which some 34 lakhs or 34 per cent were Muslims. Minus Sylhet, the province's Muslim population was around 18 per cent or some 14 lakhs only. Refer to Bimal J. Dev and Dilip Kumar Lahiri, *Assam Muslims: Politics and Cohesion* (Delhi: Mittal Publications, 1985), p. 75.

10. By April 1943 the Muslim League had formed ministries in Bengal, Punjab, and Sind. Refer to Dev and Lahiri, *Assam Muslims*, p. 131.

11. Refer to Dev and Lahiri, *Assam Muslims*, p. 74. This quote is from the first day's proceedings of the third annual session of the Assam Provincial Muslim League held at Barpeta on 7 April 1944.

12. Dev and Lahiri, *Assam Muslims*, p. 75.

13. The Muslim League captured 31 of the 34 Muslim seats, while the Congress secured all the general seats having won 58 of the total 108 seats.

14. The working committee of the AIML met in February 1947 and condemned the evictions of immigrants.

15. Dev and Lahiri, *Assam Muslims*, p. 102.

16. Bhasani's slogan was 'Pakistan is our only demand/History justifies it/ Numbers confirm it/Justice claims it/Destiny demands it'. Quoted by Dev and Lahiri from the leaflet 'Achieve Pakistan or Perish', issued by Maulana Bhasani on 16 August 1947. See Dev and Lahiri, *Assam Muslims*, p. 86.

17. The Cabinet Mission Plan provided for the division of the different provinces into three Sections: A, B, and C. Section C was to consist of Bengal and Assam. The provinces were free to form Groups with executives and legislatures. Each Group could determine the provincial subjects to be taken in common. In Section C, Assam would have had seven general members and three Muslim members, whereas Bengal would have had twenty-seven general members and thirty-three Muslim members.

18. A.C. Bhuyan (ed.), *Political History of Assam*, vol. III (Guwahati: Government of Assam, 1968), p. 342.

19. Amalendu Guha, *Planter Raj to Swaraj: Freedom Struggle and Electoral Politics in Assam 1826–1947* (New Delhi: ICHR, 1977), p. 311.

20. Bhuyan, *Political History of Assam*, vol. III, p. 360.

21. Bhuyan, *Political History of Assam*, vol. III, p. 361.

22. Bhuyan, *Political History of Assam*, vol. III, p. 361.

23. Bhuyan, *Political History of Assam*, vol. III, p. 364.

24. Tara Chand, *History of the Freedom Movement in India*, vol. III (New Delhi: Ministry of Information and Broadcasting, Government of India, 1972), pp. 485–6.

25. Nicholas Mansergh and Panderlal Moon (eds), *The Transfer of Power: 1942–47, The Mountbatten Plan, Viceroyalty, Princes, Partition and Independence, July–August 15 1947–8*, vol. IX (London: Her Majesty's Stationery Office, 1983), pp. 403–5.

26. Nicholas and Moon, *The Transfer of Power*, vol. IX, p. 510.

27. Nicholas and Moon, *The Transfer of Power*, vol. IX, p. 509.

28. Bhuyan, *Political History of Assam*, vol. III, p. 85.

29. *Selected Works of Nehru*, vol. I, edited by Gopal Sarvepalli (New Delhi: Jawaharlal Nehru Memorial Fund, 1984), p. 42.

30. Maulana Abul Kalam Azad, *India Wins Freedom* (New Delhi: Orient Longman, 1988), pp. 184–5.
31. Sucheta Mahajan (ed.), *Towards Freedom: Documents on the Movement for Independence in India, 1947*, part 1 (New Delhi: Oxford University Press, 2013), pp. 111–13.
32. Gandhi's telegram to Tayyebulla, 26 January 1947, *Collected Works of Mahatma Gandhi*, vol. LXXXVI, pp. 392–3. Gandhi's telegram was sent on 26 January 1947 and Azad's statement was carried in the *Hindustan Times* of 27 January 1947.
33. Nicholas Mansergh and Panderlal Moon (eds), *The Transfer of Power: 1942–47*, vol. X (London: Her Majesty's Stationery Office, 1983), p. 623.
34. Azad, *India Wins Freedom*, p. 185
35. Bhuyan, *Political History of Assam*, vol. III, p. 384.
36. Referring to the Cabinet Mission proposals, Nichols Roy specifically pointed out to Section C, which he saw as being totally unjust and unacceptable for Assam since it would have given Muslim-majority Bengal the right to dictate the terms of the proposed Constitution. Assam, he declared, was a non-Muslim province with seven non-Muslim and three Muslim representatives to the Constituent Assembly. But if it was included in the Section, then the fate of Assam would be decided by Bengal which had twenty-seven non-Muslims and thirty-three Muslim members. Nichols Roy accused the Cabinet Mission of having changed its initial stand relating to the autonomy given to the provinces to decide their future. He argued that, once back in England, the Cabinet Mission had come under the influence of the Conservative Party and had been pressurized by Mohammad Ali Jinnah and the Muslim League to change its earlier position. Nichols Roy summed up his speech at the Constituent Assembly with the following words:

> The principle of driving by force a non-Muslim Province to come under a Muslim province is absolutely wrong. Mr Jinnah has forced His Majesty's Government to commit this great injustice to our Province.... We are an autonomous province and a non-Muslim Province. Why should we be forced to go to that kind of a Section which could outvote the Province of Assam [to] frame the Constitution according to the desire of the majority.

(Sumit Sarkar [ed.], *Towards Freedom: Documents on the Movement for Independence in India 1946*, part 1 [New Delhi: ICHR and Oxford University Press, 2008], pp. 2444–6.)
37. For details about the Cabinet Mission and Assam's fight against it, refer to Udayon Misra, *The Periphery Strikes Back: Challenges to the Nation State in Assam and Nagaland* (Shimla: Indian Institute of Advanced Study, 2000), pp. 104–9.
38. Guha, *Planter Raj to Swaraj*, p. 337.

39. The AIML in its resolution of 6 June 1946 had declared its acceptance of the Cabinet Mission Plan in the following words:

> Inasmuch as the basis and the foundation of Pakistan are inherent in the Mission's Plan by virtue of the compulsory grouping of the six Muslim provinces in Section B and C, the Muslim League is willing to co-operate with the constitution-making machinery proposed in the scheme outlined by the Mission, in the hope that it would ultimately result in the establishment of a complete, sovereign Pakistan.

(Dev and Lahiri, *Assam Muslims*, p. 84.)

40. Editorial of *Dawn*, 2 April 1947. Refer to Mahajan, *Towards Freedom*, pp. 1048–9.

41. Mahajan, *Towards Freedom*, p. 1049.

42. Mahajan, *Towards Freedom*, pp. 1049–50.

43. For instance, Mujib Ahmed Moti, president of the Sibsagar Muslim Federation, had drawn Jinnah's attention to the 'almost defunct' state of the Assam Provincial Muslim League under Saadulla, and wrote how the Muslim Students' Federation had been 'celebrating Pakistan Day and distributing Pakistan pamphlets and was trying to get Arabic/Persian introduced in the girls' schools of Assam'. Jinnah in his letter thanked Muhib Ahmed for his good work. Letter dated 20 May 1944, Doc. 138, S.M. Zaman (ed.), *Quaid-i-Azam and Education* (Islamabad: National Institute of Historical and Cultural Research, 1995), p. 326.

44. Bhasani was right from the beginning the undisputed leader of the Muslim League in Assam. His politics veered round the demands of the Muslim immigrant peasants for more and more of government land and reserves. Though he tried to win the support of the immigrant peasants on the question of eviction from government reserves, he was quite clear in his aim of incorporating Assam in Pakistan.

45. As early as 1938, Jinnah, as president of the AIML, had appointed the organizing committee of the League for the province of Assam. Among other members were Saadulla and Bhasani. Bhasani was appointed as the convener of the said committee.

46. During the civil disobedience movement in the Punjab, the AIML had succeeded in enlisting the support of a section of the scheduled caste Sikhs. Z.H. Zaidi (editor-in-chief), *Quaid-i-Azam Mohammad Ali Jinnah Papers: Prelude to Pakistan*, vol. I, part 2 (Lahore: National Archives of Lahore, 1998), p. 319.

47. The Muslim League's victory in the Punjab encouraged it to launch the civil disobedience movement in the North-West Frontier Province. Refer to *Jinnah Papers*, vol. I, part 2, p. 322.

48. By contrast, the Muslim League had quite succeeded in drawing in the support of a section of the castes in Bengal. The Communal Award of

1932 helped the rise of Scheduled Caste politics in Bengal, with leaders such as Jogendra Nath Mondal, who tried to mobilize Scheduled Caste support for Pakistan during the Sylhet referendum. Mondal became the chairman of the Pakistan Constituent Assembly and the Minister of Law in the Liaquat Ali government. By contrast, in Assam the Scheduled Castes were all along with the Congress, with leaders such as Ram Nath Das and Jogendra Nath Hazarika from the Brahmaputra Valley and Akshay Kumar Das from the Surma Valley. Refer to K.S. Chalam, 'Dalit Muslim Relations in Pre-Partition Bengal: Paradigm Shift in Dalit Discourse', *Mainstream*, vol. LI, no. 22 (18 May 2013). Also refer to Joya Chatterji, *Bengal Divided: Hindu Communalism and Partition, 1932–1947* (Cambridge: Cambridge University Press, 1994).

49. Dev and Lahiri, *Assam Muslims*, p. 105.
50. A total of some forty people were killed in police firings during the Muslim League's programmes of occupation of government grazing reserves.
51. Bardoloi had written to the Government of India on 31 March 1947 about

> the reservation that has been put to it [military assistance] that it could not be applied for eviction purposes will create certain difficulties. The trouble will arise out of the Government's policy of maintaining the inviolability of the grazing reserves which was agreed to by all parties, including the Muslim League.... It is not known how the maintenance of law and order of the province as a whole could be distinguished from maintenance of law and order in the grazing reserves and waste lands where law and order are proposed to be infringed.

(Mahajan, *Towards Freedom*, p. 1030.)

52. *Sardar Patel's Correspondence*, vol. V, quoted in Mahajan, *Towards Freedom*, pp. 1048–9.
53. Interestingly, Patel is here using the term 'illegal immigrants' when these immigrants were clearly Indian citizens who were trying to forcibly occupy government land.
54. Akbar Hydari had proposed that Muslim immigrants be settled in the north bank areas of the Brahmaputra and this move was opposed by the Assam Congress, led by Bardoloi, as a move which would do great harm to the interests of the indigenous people of the region.
55. Mahajan, *Towards Freedom*, pp. 1054–5.
56. That the sympathies of the British officials were with the League rather than with the Congress, as far as the case of Assam was concerned, is evident from the correspondence between them and the viceroy, especially on the issue of Grouping. For instance, Wavell wrote to A. Clow on 13 January 1947 that the 'fears of Assam that the Muslim League might abuse their majority in Section C to reduce the Caste Hindus to a position of permanent subordination ... has been one of the main difficulties in the way of the Congress

acceptance of HMG's statement of 6th December'. In reply, Clow refers to the 'many groups in Assam-hill tribes, people from the plains, Ahoms, and so on and if they all got separate electorates then there would be no unity' and sees this as 'a tacit admission to Saadulla's claim that a plebiscite in Assam would record a vote in favour of Grouping' and that 'the unity of Assam is an aberration and not a fact'. (Nicholas and Moon, *Transfer of Power*, vol. IX, p. 512; Mahajan, *Towards Freedom*, p. 103.) It is clear from this that, by and large, British officials accepted the Muslim League's position that Assam was essentially not a Hindu-majority province and the resistance to Grouping was primarily led by the Caste Hindu Assamese. This discounts the fact that the resistance to Grouping in Assam came from all sections of the indigenous people, both from the plains as well as the hills.

57. As reported in the *Pakistan Times* of 21 March 1947; refer to *Jinnah Papers*, appendix IX.7.

58. *Jinnah Papers*, appendix IX.24.

59. *Jinnah Papers*, appendix IX.24.

60. Present-day Mizoram.

61. Letter from Abdul Matin Chaudhury to K.H. Khurshid, 28 April 1947, *Jinnah Papers*, vol. I, part 1, pp. 617–21; Mahajan, *Towards Freedom*, pp. 1065–9. Chaudhury in his letter enclosed a detailed note on Assam's demographic break-up along with maps. He wrote to Khurshid that he had 'promised to send an important Note about Assam with maps to Mr. Jinnah' and asked Khurshid to hand these over to the Quaid-i-Azam.

62. Saadulla's letter to Jinnah, dated Shillong, 16 April 1947, sub-file no. 7, Saadulla Papers, NMML, New Delhi.

63. Mohamad Afzal Husain Qadri to M.A. Jinnah, F. 410/3, no. 328, *Jinnah Papers*, first series, vol. I, part 1, p. 565.

64. Record of interview between Louis Mountbatten and M.A. Jinnah, *Jinnah Papers*, appendix XIV.20.

65. Syed M. Saadullah to M.A. Jinnah, F. 455/1-4, no. 323, *Jinnah Papers*, first series, vol. I, part 1, pp. 555–6.

66. *Jinnah Papers*, first series, vol. I, appendix IX.43, p. 478.

67. *Jinnah Papers*, vol. I, part 2, appendix VI and VI.I, pp. 130, 197.

68. *Jinnah Papers*, vol. I, part 2, appendix VI and VI.I, pp. 130, 197.

69. Zaman, *Quaid-i-Azam and Education*, p. 184.

70. Tayyebulla headed the Assam Congress during the tumultuous days of the grouping scheme and he supported the position taken by Congress leaders such as Azad on the issue. He was against the formation of a Congress-backed ministry headed by Saadulla just prior to Independence.

71. That the Muslim League has succeeded in establishing its pockets even in upper Assam is borne by the correspondence which the president of the

Sibsagar Muslim Students' Federation had with Jinnah, who paid a lot of attention to the League's activities in Assam. In his letter to Jinnah, the League leader from Sibsagar draws Jinnah's attention to the near-defunct state of the Assam Provincial Muslim League under Saadulla. Refer to Zaman, *Quaid-i-Azam and Education*, p. 326.

72. Once the Cabinet Mission proposals were dropped and the possibility of Assam being grouped with Bengal receded, the Muslim League lost steam in Assam and many of its leaders, including Saadulla, ended up joining the Congress while others such as Bhasani left for East Pakistan. Several of the League leaders finally secured berths in the Congress ministry in Assam and these included ones such as Moinul Haque Chaudhury, who was a secretary to Jinnah. In post-Independence Assam, Saadulla continued to play his role in securing benefits for the Muslim community and continued to exert quite some influence in Congress quarters.

73. Saadulla's letter to Liaquat Ali Khan, dated Shillong, 25 March 1945, Saadulla Papers. After the Independence, Saadulla represented Assam in the Constituent Assembly. Here too he pleaded for reservations for Muslims. Saadulla was quite clear on the position of reservations for Muslims. This is amply revealed in his arguments during the debate on separate electorates for Muslim in the Constituent Assembly. Refuting the argument of Begum Aizaz Rasul, a member from the United Provinces, Saadulla declared:

> The previous speaker, my honourable friend Begum Aizaz Rasul said that reservation will not benefit the community in any way. I quite agree with her that without the help of the majority community's votes, the Muslims will not be able to return any one in whom they have confidence; the candidates must enjoy the confidence of both the Hindus and Muslims, yet reservation will have tremendous psychological effect upon the Muslim community. They at least will secure that one of them is in the legislature and will speak on their behalf, to safeguard their interests. Why deny this bit of charity to the Muslims? Rise up to the occasion and show mercy; as the great English poet said 'mercy is twice blessed.

74. In his first public speech after the launch of the League's civil disobedience movement in Guwahati on 11 April 1947, Saadulla dwelt on the question of Assam's inclusion in Pakistan and reiterated that Assam was a Musim-majority province if the tribals and the Scheduled Caste people were excluded from the Hindu fold. In the same speech he completely backtracked on his earlier commitment to the 1946 Tripartite Agreement and declared that the Bardoloi government had adopted an entirely new policy, although in 1939 the Congress had 'virtually accepted the abolition of the Line System', which was certainly not the case. Refer to Saadulla's

speech reported in the *Dawn*, Karachi, 11 April 1947 and quoted in Mahajan, *Towards Freedom*, p. 1052.

75. The civil disobedience movement continued till the announcement of the Partition plan on 31 June 1947, when Jinnah asked for its withdrawal.

76. It is, however, a different matter that eventually the hill tribes demanded separation from Assam. The Assam Congress's equations with the hill tribes started changing after leaders such as Bishnuram Medhi took over and Assamese hegemonistic aspirations developed.

77. Reference to Maulana Bhasani.

78. Saadulla's letter to Jinnah, Saadulla Papers.

4

THE QUESTION OF SYLHET AND THE ASSAMESE–BENGALI DIVIDE

This chapter focuses on the Referendum in the Bengali-speaking district of Sylhet and how the Assamese–Bengali animosity in post-Partition Assam was considerably aggravated owing to it. An attempt is made to show how the question of status of the Assamese language was closely linked with the question of Sylhet, which tilted the scales against an Assamese linguistic majority in the province. The chapter traces the history of Sylhet's incorporation into Assam and how this had all along been resisted by the Assamese, who wished to see a homogenous Assamese homeland. It analyses how Bengali perceptions about the Assamese 'betrayal' of Sylhet are not based on historical facts and that such assumptions have flourished and found their way into scholarly works; that though the Assamese did want Sylhet to be separated and they had strong reasons for it, yet the Assamese middle-class leadership represented by the Assam Congress was neither in a position to influence nor did it have any direct hand in influencing the outcome of the Referendum in favour of Pakistan. The chapter also takes up for discussion the language issue and concludes on a positive note by referring to the dissipation of Assamese–Bengali rivalry and the emergence of greater understanding and cooperation between the Brahmaputra and Barak Valleys.

Rivalry of the Valleys

Partition politics in Assam came to be dominated in the months immediately preceding Independence by the question of Sylhet. The question of the separation of the district of Sylhet from Assam through the Referendum of 1947 has always been a contentious issue for both the Assamese and the Bengali Hindu population of the state. While the latter has been assiduously maintaining that but for Assamese eagerness to see the district go to Pakistan, Sylhet would have remained in post-Partition India, the former welcomed the results of the Referendum because they never accepted the overwhelmingly Bengali-speaking populous district of Sylhet, which was incorporated in Assam in 1874, as a part of their province. In order to understand the issue of Sylhet and its ramifications in post-Partition Assam politics, it would perhaps be necessary to go back a bit in history when boundaries were drawn and redrawn to accommodate the administrative needs of colonial rule. Only then would it be possible for one to understand why the question of Sylhet still continues to be a major point of contention between the Bengali Hindus of Assam and the Assamese. Assamese political opinion had always favoured the separation of the district of Sylhet from Assam. There was also substantial political opinion in Sylhet itself favouring its reunion with Bengal. Apart from the all-important fact that the Assamese middle-class elite believed that the separation of the populous Bengali-speaking district from Assam would pave the way for a more or less homogenous Assamese homeland, economic consider-ations too played a role in this, primarily because Sylhet was a revenue-deficit district.[1] From 1826, when Assam came under British rule, the province was tagged with Bengal as an administrative adjunct. It was in 1874 that the province was placed under a chief commissioner and three districts of Bengal, namely Sylhet, Goalpara, and Cachar, were added to it. In 1905 when Bengal was partitioned by Lord Curzon, the Chief Commissioner's province of Assam was joined with a part of Eastern Bengal and it was named Eastern Bengal and Assam, with its capital at Dhaka. It was only in 1912 that Assam became a separate province together with Sylhet,[2] Goalpara, and Cachar. While the incor-poration of Cachar and Goalpara[3] was viewed as normal, these areas being a part of pre-British kingdoms, the addition of Sylhet was always seen as an anachronism not only by the Assamese middle class but also by several British administrators.[4]

Addressing an all-party meeting in October 1935, Mohammad Tayyebulla declared: 'Sylhet is a permanently deficit district of Assam. The average deficit from the year 1930–31 up to 1934–35 stood at 18.5

lakhs. Poor Assam is bled white.' He was of the view that the district was 'alien' to the people of Assam and it was needless to keep it in Assam.[5] Historians writing on the region have held contrary positions regarding this contentious history. Amalendu Guha says that Sylhet 'historically, as well as ethnically, was an integral part of Bengal'.[6] But a recent work on the subject insists that despite this, Bengal was largely indifferent to the fate of the Sylhetis during the Referendum and argues that 'the transfer of Sylhet to Assam in the formative years of national spatial imagination removed Sylhet from the territorial imagination of Bengal'.[7]

The separation of Sylhet from Assam has occupied a central position in the discourse of Assamese–Bengali relations in Assam right from the early decades of the twentieth century. There was a consistent demand in Sylhet that the district should be reunited with Bengal because Assam was a 'backward' province. In a letter dated 11 August 1925, the officiating chief secretary to the government of Assam, in reply to the Government of India's directive to find out the opinion of the people of the Sylhet regarding reunion with Bengal, writes:

> The subject has been extensively discussed in the press and on the platform, and unquestionably the bulk of the educated Hindu opinion in the Sylhet district favoured re-union with Bengal.... The desire for unification is based on sentiment. The Bengali Hindu of Sylhet feels that he is looked down upon by his brothers in Bengal owing to his being included in a province inhabited by semi-civilised tribes and by the Assamese whom he considers to belong to a lower standard of civilisation than he does, and he feels keenly that he is not appreciated if indeed he is not actively disliked by the Assamese who in his estimation is inferior. The leading Hindus of the Assam valley if they do not actively dislike the Hindus of Sylhet at least disown any kinship with them and regard them with feelings of jealousy.... The fact that the administration of Sylhet is carried on at a loss gives them an additional reason for desiring that the district of Sylhet should go to Bengal But it was undoubtedly these feelings of jealousy that led the Assam Valley members of the Legislative Council to support the resolution adopted in July 1924.[8]

Referring to the debate in the legislative council in January 1925 about the status of the Jaintia Parganas, the official says that they are indeed temporarily settled, that they were under the Jainta Rajas, and that 'there is considerable feeling in these Parganas against transfer to Bengal'. About Cachar, the memo states that 'while there may be something to be said for the transfer of Sylhet, the transfer of Cachar is hardly a practical proposition.... Cachar has always been intimately associated with Assam, to which it gave a Kachari dynasty and in almost every district of which small bodies of its original inhabitants are to be found to this day.' Referring to the argument that the region is inhabited predominantly by Bengali settlers, the memo adds:

> The Bengalis now inhabiting the district of Cachar, while forming the majority of the population are mere settlers there and can hardly claim that they have annexed the district and have right to demand its transfer to Bengal. Arguments based solely on numerical strength and linguistic affinity, if admitted, would at the present rate at which immigration from Mymensingh into several districts of the Assam valley is going on, entitle Bengali settlers in these districts after a few years to assert that they were in the majority and that therefore the districts in which they had settled should go to Bengal. [9]

The memo refers to the legislative assembly resolution on the transfer of Sylhet and says that Cachar was added 'as an afterthought'. The memo also states:

> The resolution recommending the transfer of Sylhet Cachar [meaning South Cachar] was carried with the aid of votes of the members representing the Assam Valley constituencies. The case of Cachar was really not discussed, and if the Assamese members considered the matter at all, they were so anxious to get rid of Sylhet and the Sylhetis that they were prepared to let Cachar go as well if that was the only way of getting rid of Sylhet. Since then there has been a pronounced change of feeling and several of the members who supported the resolution now admit that they made a mistake about Cachar. The Governor in Council does think it necessary to discuss the case of Cachar further.

The letter was written to 'comply with the instructions of the Government of India and to find out the real wishes of the people concerned'.

In reply to the above letter, H. Tonkinson, joint secretary to the Government of India, stated that unlike the status of Sylhet, Cachar was an integral part of the province of Assam and the Government of India did not favour its inclusion in Bengal. The joint secretary observed in the following manner:

In the first place the Govt. of India consider that the question of the transfer of the district of Cachar from Assam to Bengal need not continue to complicate the main issue of whether the district of Sylhet should be transferred or not. They observe that the original motion of the Assam Council merely recommended the transfer of Sylhet, and that at a later stage an amendment was moved on Cachar. In the Bengal Council an amendment urging the transfer of Cachar was lost.[10] The Govt. of India are of the opinion that Cachar is an essentially Assam district and, that moreover, its transfer to Bengal would mean the isolation of the Lushai Hills district.[11]

In the same letter the Government of India stated that the Jaintia Parganas, then a part of the Sylhet district, historically belonged to Assam.[12] From this, it appears that the stand taken by the Assam Congress regarding Cachar was actually endorsed by the Government of India's position on the matter concerned. Thus, the colonial administration too favoured the transfer of Sylhet from Assam, while accepting that Cachar was an integral part of Assam.[13] This was much before any idea of the country's division on religious lines had taken shape.

Ever since the annulment of the partition of Bengal in 1912 and the amalgamation of the Surma Valley, made up of the district of Sylhet and the plains of Cachar, with the newly constituted Commissioner's province of Assam, civil society moves were afoot among the inhabitants of Sylhet and the Surma Valley for its reunion with Bengal. Initially, the Muslim intelligentsia supported the separation of Sylhet from 'backward' Assam. Representations were made to the government by the Sylhet-Bengal Reunion League, which was made up of leading Muslims and Hindus of the Surma Valley.[14] The Bengal Legislative Council passed a resolution, moved by A.K. Chanda, in 1918 asking for the transfer of Sylhet to Bengal.[15]

However, in the course of time a large segment of the Muslim leadership started opposing the separation of the region from Assam, and linguistic and cultural considerations for uniting with Bengal were 'gradually' subsumed by religious factors. This, as has been pointed out by some scholars, became even more apparent after the chief commissioner initiated the policy of proportional representation of different communities in government jobs on the basis of population. This policy was instrumental to a certain extent in pushing the question of linguistic and cultural solidarity of the Sylheti Hindus and Muslims to the backseat and bringing to the fore the argument that Muslims as a whole had more to gain by Sylhet being with Assam rather than uniting with Bengal.[16] This change in the Muslim position was also because of the pressure being mounted by Brahmaputra Valley Muslim leaders such as Syed Muhammad Saadulla, who believed that the transfer of Sylhet would endanger the interests of the Muslims of the state as a whole. Polarization on religious lines started to gain pace by the late 1920s, and many see this as a direct fallout of the Khilafat movement when Muslim religious leaders took a prominent and often deciding role. Despite all this, Muslim public opinion was still quite divided, as may be seen in the voting pattern, on the resolution moved by Brojendra Narayan Choudhury in 1924 in the provincial legislative council. While the Hindu members of both the Brahmaputra and Surma Valleys voted for the transfer, five Muslim members voted against and six voted for the motion, while all the European members opposed the transfer.[17] Another resolution for Sylhet's transfer was moved in the Assam Legislative Council by Sadananda Dowerah in 1926. This process of the polarization of opinion on religious lines continued throughout the 1930s.

It was the Lahore Resolution of the AIML that put a final seal to the Hindu–Muslim divide in the Surma Valley over the question of re-union or otherwise with Bengal. Muslims now supported Sylhet's retention in Assam and Hindus still insisted on reunion with Bengal.[18] But the prospect of Partition once again changed the equation, with the Hindus now wanting to stay in Assam (India) and the Muslims opting for Surma Valley as a part of Pakistan. The Muslim leadership had initially thought that Sylhet's Muslim population was crucial to make Assam a part of the proposed Pakistan as a Muslim-majority province. But the dropping of the Cabinet Mission proposals on grouping brought forth the idea of a referendum in Sylhet. Thus, while Assamese Hindu opinion on Sylhet's transfer was consistent right from the beginning, it was the Hindus and the Muslims of Sylhet and the Surma Valley who kept changing their positions in line with political developments.

The Assam Pradesh Congress Committee (APCC) and Cachar

Within the APCC there was a continuous tussle over the question of Sylhet and Cachar between the members from Cachar and those

from the Brahmaputra Valley. The Assam Congress always seemed to
be in a dilemma when it came to Cachar. About the status of Sylhet
it was quite unambiguous in that it should be separated from Assam.
But the APCC's position on Cachar, especially Bengali-speaking
southern Cachar, kept changing. The acrimony between the APCC
and the Congressmen from Cachar was also aggravated when the
Shillong District Committee of the Congress[19] initiated a move to
get itself affiliated to the Surma Valley District Congress,[20] which,
in turn, meant that it would be under the Bengal Congress. When
the controversy arose as to whether the Shillong District Congress
Committee should be allowed to become a part of the Surma Valley
Congress, the APCC stated in no uncertain terms that since it was
against Sylhet and south Cachar forming a part of Assam province,
the Shillong District Congress Committee could never go to the
Surma Valley District Congress and must remain with the APCC.
The APCC, in its letter dated 15 April 1938, requested the AICC to
direct the Shillong District Congress Committee to function under
the APCC: 'We further desire to point out that one of the items of the
Congress Programme of the Congress Party in the Assam Assembly,
is to separate Sylhet and the Bengali speaking portion of the Cachar
District from the Province of Assam.'[21] This goes against the argument of those who argue that the separation of Sylhet was not part of
the Assam Congress's agenda. In fact this letter shows that the Assam
Congress was also in favour of separating the Bengali-speaking part
of south Cachar, which meant broadly the Silchar and Hailakandi
subdivisions.

But barely five months later the APCC changed its position on
Cachar, which it now claimed as an integral part of the province of
Assam. This change of position was brought about by the Surma Valley
Congress's demand that entire Cachar (both south and north Cachar)
be brought under its jurisdiction which, in effect, would mean that
it would be under the Bengal Provincial Congress. Reacting to the
demand, the APCC shot off a lengthy letter to the AICC. Stating that
the APCC had decided to transfer the south Cachar plains, comprising
the Silchar and Hailakandi subdivisions, to the Surma Valley District
Congress 'for the sake of convenience and on mutual understanding', it
decried the Surma Valley Congress's move to bring entire Cachar under
its control.[22] The APCC stated that 'Cachar has ever been an integral

part of Assam unlike the neighbouring district of Sylhet (excluding Jaintia Hills)' and wrote: 'It is somewhat surprising to see the South Cachar Plains having cut all connections with the A.P.C.C. now claim the whole of Cachar District to be ceded to Bengal Congress Province through the Surma Valley D.C.C.'

The Assam Congress Legislature Party's decision to place south Cachar under the jurisdiction of the Surma Valley Congress Committee was soon followed by moves on the part of the latter to bring the whole of Cachar district, including north Cachar, consisting mainly of the hill region, within its fold. At this, the APCC panicked and in its long letter addressed to the AICC, dated 15 September 1938, it put forward the claim to north Cachar which, according to it, was 'linked up with Assam as flesh and blood from time immemorial'. It also drew the attention of the AICC to the need for inducting into APCC members from the hills and tribal areas. It is interesting that the Surma Valley Congress Committee based their claim to north Cachar on the plea that the people of south Cachar would need these undeveloped regions for future expansion. Refuting this argument, the APCC writes:

> The virgin soil of waste tracts or the reserves of forest wealth offer sufficient temptations to the people of South Cachar but that cannot be a plea for annexing the ancient home of tribal people who would not part with their kindred of Assam. The argument that the people of South Cachar plains will require these undeveloped regions for their future expansion seems quite irrelevant on the issue of transferring North Cachar Hills to the Bengal Provincial Congress Committee. Moreover, such argument is sure to lead to unhappy complications as that will entitle the natives of Maimensingh districts of Bengal to cede the whole of Lower Assam valley as they too are in great need of waste lands available in Assam for their immediate expansion.

Referring to the continued influx of people from Bengal, the letter says: 'It is a matter of common occurrence in Assam that large hordes of landless and unemployed fortune seekers are incessantly flowing into Assam from Bengal and other provinces and occupying and utilising the reserves of this province without any appreciable hindrance.' Refuting the argument that compared to its population it had large reserves of available land, the letter continues, 'One important factor to be considered in this connection is that Assam has a fast growing population not only by influx of immigrants, but also largely by her own production. In Assam Valley variation of population during the last 50 years shows an increase by 90%.... These results indicate the urgent necessity for reserving waste lands for future expansion of the people of Assam as well.'[23]

From this, it is clear that there has been a change in the APCC's position regarding Cachar.

Referring to Assamese public opinion on the question of Sylhet, the historian Amalendu Guha observes:

On the Sylhet question, the Assamese opinion, too, remained understandably cold, but consistent with its earlier stand. The APCC election manifesto had pledged to the electorate in 1945–46 that the party would work for separating Sylhet from Assam. 'Maulana Sahib (i.e. Azad) seemed to come to the conclusion that the only alternative to this state of things is' wrote Bardoloi to Patel in February 1946, 'to separate the Bengali district of Sylhet and a portion of Cachar from Assam to join these to Bengal—a consummation to which the Assamese people are looking forward for the last 70 years...' Bardoloi led the Cabinet Mission to understand in April that Assam would be quite prepared to hand over Sylhet to Eastern Bengal.[24]

Guha further adds:

It was indeed a life-time's opportunity for the Assamese leadership 'to get rid of Sylhet'[25] and carve out a linguistically more homogeneous province. When the results of the referendum were declared, there was a feeling of relief in the Brahmaputra Valley.... The Boundary Commission, presided by Cyril Radcliffe, published its award three days after independence. Only the three thanas of Patharkandi, Ratabari, and Badarpur and about one half of the thana of Karimganj were to remain in Assam, as per terms of the award and the rest of the district went to Pakistan. Sylhet, 'the golden calf' which was sacrificed in 1874 to usher in a new province, was now once more sacrificed at the altar of the new state.[26]

Here Guha seems to apportion blame on the Assamese middle-class leadership for having desired that the Bengali-speaking plains portion of Cachar district should have gone to Pakistan and for discouraging the Sylhet leaders 'when they tried to salvage a portion of the district through an effective representation to the Boundary Commission'. However, it is a known fact that Assamese middle-class opinion was always in favour of Sylhet's separation from the province but there was no unanimity of view on the separation of Cachar. Even Guha admits that the Hindus of Sylhet, ever since the district's incorporation with Assam in 1874, had all along clamoured for union with Bengal. It is significant that one year before the Referendum, on 27 June 1946, the influential Sylhet Bar Association, which represented a substantial measure of the intellectual opinion of the Surma Valley, put on record its opposition towards the movement against the grouping plan led by the Assam Congress and stated that 'it would be inappropriate for the Surma Valley to support the movement launched by the Assam Valley in respect of the proposed grouping of Assam with Bengal'. The Bar Association further requested 'all the Surma Valley members of the Assam legislature' to support its views. The Sylhet Bar Association's views were communicated to the Assam premier, Gopinath Bardoloi, through a telegram sent to him by Labanya Chandra Goswami, who chaired the meeting where the said resolution was passed.[27] Yet, it was this same Sylhet District Bar Association that sent a telegram in May 1947 to the president of the Indian National Congress stating the following: 'Sylhet District Bar Association records emphatic unequivocal opposition to transfer of Sylhet district to East Bengal Province in event Bengal Partition as such step disastrous ruinous to people's welfare and against declared will demonstrated in last provincial election.'[28] Referring to the change of stand of the Sylheti Hindus just prior to the Referendum, Guha says: 'Sylheti Hindus who had for decades agitated for a re-union with Bengal, now clung to Assam. On the other hand, Sylhet Muslims who were, on political considerations consistently opposed to the move since 1928, now reversed their position.'[29] Obviously, the 'political considerations' because of which the League initially wanted Sylhet to be in Assam were based on the hope that Sylhet would substantially add to the Muslim population of Assam, thereby bolstering the League's demand for the province to be included in Pakistan.

Writing in a similar vein, Anindita Dasgupta says:

Sylhet, a Bengali-speaking district historically a part of East Bengal, was joined with its Assamese-speaking neighbour Assam in 1874 by the British who wanted to make the latter province 'economically viable' and self-sustaining. For several years afterwards, the Hindus of Sylhet demanded for a return to the more 'advanced' Bengal, whereas the Muslims of Sylhet by and large preferred to remain in Assam where

its leaders, along with the Assamese Muslims, found a more powerful
political voice than they would have had if they returned to a Muslim
majority East Bengal.[30]

It was through Saadulla's efforts in the early 1940s that Muslim opinion in the Brahmaputra Valley veered towards retaining the district of
Sylhet in Assam. Saadulla was aware of the fact that minus Sylhet, the
proportion of Muslims in Assam would drastically go down and this
would affect the position of the Muslims in both the valleys.[31] Hence,
in the first session of the Assam Provincial Muslim League the consen-
sus was that the separation of Sylhet from Assam would weaken the
Muslim population of Assam by some 16 lakhs and that this would be
a retrogressive step as far as the Muslim community was concerned.[32]
Referring to the attitude of the indigenous Assamese elite regarding
Sylhet, Dasgupta writes:

> The indigenous Assamese too supported the separation of Sylhet from
> Assam for the entire period from 1874–1947 as the Sylhetis— or inhab-
> itants of Sylhet—with their earlier access to English education were
> seen as competitors for jobs, and as exercising a cultural hegemony over
> an incipient Assamese middle class trying to come into its own under
> the aegis of British colonialism since 1826. Ironically, when the oppor-
> tunity for a return to East Bengal (later East Pakistan) came in 1947,
> the Sylheti Hindus defended their right to remain in Assam/India while
> many Sylheti Muslims wanted to separate. When the referendum was
> held on July 6 and 7, the outcome was by and large consistent with the
> demographic composition of the district where Muslims had a numeri-
> cal edge: 56.6 per cent of Sylhetis voted for joining East Pakistan and
> 43.3 per cent voted for remaining in Assam/India. Following this out-
> come, most of the Sylhet district was ceded to East Pakistan. Over the
> next few years, large numbers of Sylheti Hindus from the ceded parts of
> Sylhet district began to relocate to the Indian north-east, particularly to
> southern Assam, where they had established considerable economic and
> social networks in the period 1874–1947.[33]

Other scholars from the region have also expressed their anger at
what they have seen as 'Assamese machinations' at getting Sylhet into
Pakistan. For instance, referring to the 'loss' of Sylhet to Pakistan, Sujit
Chaudhuri writes:

> The Assamese people in general greeted this loss and the Assam press
> projected it as a gain. This attitude, somewhat unusual in the context of

the national aspiration of the period, has its origins in what can be called the long-cherished quest of the Assamese–carving out a homogenous province for themselves. The Assamese perceived the partition of 1947 as a god-sent opportunity to attain that goal.[34]

He refers to Bardoloi's letter to Sardar Patel[35] and also to the APCC's election manifesto of 1945, which called for the reorganization of the province of Assam by separating the 'Bengali-speaking Sylhet',[36] and says that 'to the Assam Congress it did not matter whether Sylhet went to Pakistan or remained in India' for 'the Bengali speaking district Sylhet was regarded as an ulcer hindering the emergence of a unilingual Assam'.[37] Chaudhuri is not stating anything new about the position adopted by the Assam Congress in relation to Sylhet. For, all along, the Assam Congress had asked for the separation of this district from Assam. What, however, Chaudhuri seems to overlook is the fact that Bengali Muslims in Sylhet had voted in favour of Pakistan and that the result of the Referendum was accepted by both nations; that the Referendum was based not on language but on religion. Also he himself states that the Assam Congress's election manifesto of 1945 calling for a reorganization of the province of Assam 'on the basis of Assamese language and culture' must have had the approval of the AICC. Referring to the said manifesto, Chaudhuri writes, 'Of course, the parti-tion of India was yet a far cry in 1946 and *the Congress high command allowed the Assam Congress to air the proposal for the transfer of Sylhet to Bengal* only as a part of a futuristic plan for reorganisation of prov-inces within undivided India' (emphasis mine). In the latter part of the same article, Chaudhuri states even though Nehru was not impressed by arguments that favoured a stop to continuous Muslim immigration into Assam affecting a change in the province's religious and linguis-tic profile, the central command of the Congress 'allowed the Assam Pradesh Congress Committee to pose as the saviour of the Assamese nationality and the election manifesto of the Pradesh Congress in 1945 incorporated a pledge to this effect'. According to him, in doing so the provincial unit of the Indian National Congress had 'put aside its national commitment'.[38] What the author seems to overlook is that the decision for a referendum was not taken by the Assam Congress but by the Government of India as part of the Mountbatten Plan for division of the country on religious and communal basis prior to transfer of power. The Assamese certainly wanted the separation of Sylhet from

Assam but that does not mean that they were instrumental in any way in making Sylhet a part of Pakistan. The erroneous argument that the Sylhet Referendum was based on two factors, the religious and the linguistic, has been picked up by other scholars writing on the Sylhet Referendum. For instance, Anindita Dasgupta writes: 'While Punjab and Bengal were divided on the basis of religion, the Sylhet referendum was a vote not on one, but on two concentric issues of the reorganisation of India on a communal basis and of Assam on a linguistic basis.'[39] She repeats the arguments forwarded by Guha[40] and Chaudhuri to buttress her point. But the terms of reference of the Sylhet Referendum clearly referred to a choice of the population on religious grounds for India or Pakistan. The question of reorganization of Assam on a linguistic basis did not figure in the Referendum.[41]

If the separation of Sylhet from Assam helped the Assamese in their quest of a more homogenous homeland, it was an entirely different matter. While the Assamese leadership was quite unanimous about the separation of Sylhet from Assam, opinion regarding Cachar was divided. In fact, Bardoloi and his cabinet strongly advocated the retention of Cachar in Assam. Central Congress leaders such as Sardar Patel were, however, not impressed by the arguments put forward by Bardoloi and insisted that the Assam Congress should try to ensure Sylhet's retention in Assam.[42]

The feeling seems to have persisted that the 'Assamese government' of Bardoloi did not exert itself to prevent the Sylhet Referendum going in favour of Pakistan. For instance, in a memorandum submitted by the Cachar States Reorganisation Committee to the States Reorganisation Commission of India in April 1954 it is stated: 'At the time of partition in 1947, it is well known that Assam made no serious effort to win the plebiscite in Sylhet and even allowed propagandists from the Punjab to preach in favour of Pakistan while it harassed the men sent from Calcutta to speak in favour of its retention in the Indian Union.'[43] The same memorandum says that the 'Muslim Superintendent of the Government Press of Assam, where ballot papers were printed, printed false ballot papers and issued them to the members of the Muslim League, these being actually used during the plebiscite'.[44] While there is no ostensible proof about these allegations, they helped to strengthen the perception that the government of Assam helped the results of the Referendum to go in favour of Pakistan. But there were certainly some grave allegations that the Hindus were restrained from exercising their franchise in certain pockets of Sylhet district.[45] Some of the allegations were of quite a serious nature and Nehru found them to be 'gravely disturbing', a fact which he communicated to Lord Mountbatten in his letter dated 13 July 1947.[46]

One of the major allegations was that the entire tea garden labour population of the district had been excluded from the Referendum.[47] There was also the allegation that some 50,000 non-Muslim voters were excluded from the rolls.[48] As for the tea garden workers being excluded from the exercise of their franchise, it has been argued by a set of scholars that these labourers were part of a floating population and were ineligible to vote in the Referendum. Referring to this, Ashaque Hussain cites the letter that Liaquat Ali Khan sent to Lord Mountbatten wherein he sought an assurance from the latter that the electorates of 'special constituencies', such as tea labour, would not participate in the Referendum. Mountbatten is said to have agreed to the request. Hussain also refers to the rule that according to law in the 1940s, only those people who had paid 9 *annas* (1 anna equals one-sixteenth of a rupee) rent to the government were eligible to vote; that the requisite qualification was that the voter should have been working as a permanent employee in one or more qualifying tea gardens for not less than 180 days; and that all permanent tea labourers had cast their vote in the 1946 election. He argues that it would be wrong to overlook the historical trajectory of labour migration into the Surma Valley and the floating nature of the tea labour force that did not have any 'stakes in the district'. He also argues that by not taking this fact into account 'many post-colonial Hindus' have been misled into distorting 'what had actually happened'. Thus, Hussain accepts the British administration's view that there was no strong reason as to why plantation labour should have been given a special voice when other agricultural and industrial labour were left out, and concludes that 'the polemics around the tea labourers' votes is mostly a product of post-partition imagination'. All these technicalities apart, it is difficult to accept the argument about the question of the denial of franchise to the large tea labour force during the Sylhet Referendum as a mere post-Partition polemic.[49] This certainly appears to be a weak argument, especially when one takes into account the fact that most of the tea labour population of Sylhet district and the Surma Valley were working in the different plantations for several decades and their floating character and impermanent status were actually forced upon them to meet the convenience of the tea industry and the planters. To justify the denial of franchise to the tea labourers on the plea that they did not have any stakes in the district is surely not doing them justice. Therefore, the contention that the denial of voting rights of the tea labourers did tilt the scales in favour of the Muslim League and Pakistan cannot be summarily dismissed.

However, allegations were also made by the Muslim League about the administration's attempts to tilt the scales against the League. For instance, the *Dawn* of Karachi published a report a month before the Referendum in Sylhet where it stated:

> The June 3 Statement specifically provided that the Referendum in Sylhet, like that in the North West frontier Province (N.W.F.P.) would be held under the aegis of the Governor-General. Lord Mountbatten elucidated this further by saying that British officers of the Indian army would supervise the proceedings. This has not been done in Sylhet where, according to our information, no such military officer has been deputed. Instead, matters appear to have been left in the hands of the Provincial Government which means a Congress Ministry[50] interested in the Referendum and a Governor[51] notorious for his anti-Muslim League views and also for his anxiety to placate the Congress.[52]

The same report questions the neutrality of the British ICS officer appointed as the referendum commissioner. It refers to his aversion to the 'Turkish cap' and says that 'there is no denying that the Muslims of Assam regard him with distrust'.[53] Further, it accuses Lord Mountbatten of not 'living either up to his reputation or his own standard of fairness' ever since the Sylhet Referendum was announced and says that the governor has been creating various new 'offences' in connection with the Referendum.[54]

Whatever the accusations from the two sides about the lack of transparency of the Referendum, ultimately for historians this was just a yes or no for Pakistan. Once the votes were counted and the majority secured for Sylhet's integration with Pakistan, the matter seemed closed to politicians and bureaucrats alike of both the nations. But, if one goes deeper into the human issues involved and the rights of those people who were against amalgamation with Pakistan and who commanded a majority in their own areas, it cannot be said that the Referendum was a fair one. This is revealed in the numerous memoranda that the non-Muslim people of the different parts of Sylhet district sent to the Government of India and to leaders of the Congress and the Hindu Mahasabha.[55] Representations were also made for the retention of the six Hindu-majority thanas of Ratabari, Patharkandi, Barlekha, Sirimangal, Kamalganj, and Kulaura. Similarly, the Hindu-majority thanas of Fulla and Ajmirganj of Sunamganj and Habiganj subdivisions that had voted overwhelmingly for retention in Assam were awarded to Pakistan. The Sunamganj and Habiganj Congress Committees petitioned the Central Congress leadership about the injustice meted out to the people of these two thanas but to no avail.[56] Several non-Muslim majority areas that had voted against merger with Pakistan were included in Pakistan on the plea that railway communications would otherwise be disrupted. So, reasons other than demographic also played a leading role in determining the future of the inhabitants of the Surma Valley. For instance, the non-Muslim inhabitants of the south Sylhet subdivision, which had a non-Muslim majority (having voted against merger with Pakistan during the Referendum), demanded that their subdivision be included in India as it was contiguous with the 'non-Muslim areas composed of the thanas of Barlekha, Patharkandi and Ratabari of the Karimganj Subdivision which enjoin the Cachar District within the Indian Union'. In fact Cyril Radcliffe admitted that 'South Sylhet comprising a population of over 5,15,000, has a non-Muslim majority of some 40,000'. Yet he included this region in Pakistan because he felt that its inclusion in India would lead 'to the awkward severance of the railway line through Sylhet so that the junction (Kulaura) for the town of Sylhet itself … will lie in Assam and not in East Bengal'. If disruption of road/railway links were indeed the prime consideration in deciding the fate of particular regions, then this could have been applicable in dozens of other cases in the subcontinent. The resolutions adopted at a meeting of the non-Muslim inhabitants of the south Sylhet division held on 28 August 1947 pointed out that the inclusion of the railway junction of Kulaura in India would not have disrupted links with Sylhet town because there was a motorable road connecting it with the railway junction at Shaistagaon. The reason put forward by Radcliffe clearly went against the parameters of the Referendum because the fate of the majority of the non-Muslim population of the south Sylhet subdivision was decided not on the number of votes cast in favour of or against Pakistan, but on connectivity issues.[57]

Referring to all these representations as also to allegations of rigging by the Muslim League supporters, Mountbatten records in the Viceroy's Personal Report No. 13 of 18 July 1947: 'As I had complaints from both Nehru and Jinnah about the handling of the Referendum, I came to the conclusion there could not have been much wrong with it, and, in spite of Nehru's request for an investigation, I decided the result must stand, particularly as Hydari[58] expressed himself as quite satisfied. I wrote to inform both leaders accordingly.'[59]

The strength of these accusations of bias against Radcliffe notwithstanding, there is no evidence to suggest that there was any intervention by the Assam government to influence the results of the Referendum. It is, however, a different matter if the Assam government or the Assamese middle-class leadership did not cry foul over what may be termed as 'Radcliffe's manipulations'. The Assamese position on Sylhet needs to be seen against the backdrop of increasing consolidation of Bengali political opinion in favour of a province where the Bengalis would be in majority, once the hill tribes and the non-Assamese of the Brahmaputra Valley were accepted as separate entities. In the immediate pre-Partition period, Assamese fears of losing their identity were strengthened by a development that added to apprehensions of Assam being made a part of Muslim-majority Bengal. This development was the demand for a sovereign united Bengal put forward by Sarat Chandra Bose and Kiran Shankar Ray of the Bengal Congress. The scheme that envisaged a united sovereign Bengal of both Hindus and Muslims was supported by S. Suhrawardy, leader of the Muslim League and the then prime minister of Bengal. On 3 May 1947 the Working Committee of the provincial Muslim League of Bengal set up a subcommittee of six members to carry forward discussions with Hindu leaders on the future constitutional status of Bengal.[60] Stanley Wolpert, in his book on Jinnah, argues that Jinnah's hopes of a united Bengal as part of Pakistan were shared by leaders such as Liaquat Ali Khan. Wolpert suggests that Jinnah knew that a Muslim-majority Bengal would decide, by referendum or otherwise, to eventually join Pakistan and that the Bengal Provincial Muslim League's strategy of keeping Bengal unified was part of a greater game plan.[61] Rejecting the Mountbatten Plan, Jinnah wrote to Mountbatten:

> The Muslim League cannot agree to the partition of Bengal and Punjab.... It cannot be justified historically, economically, politically or

morally. These provinces have built up their respective lives for nearly a century … and the only ground for the partition is that the areas where Hindus and Sikhs are in a majority should be separated from the provinces…. The results will be disastrous for the life of these provinces and all the communities concerned … if you take the decision—which in my opinion will be a fateful one—Calcutta should not be torn away from Eastern Bengal … if the worst comes to worst, Calcutta should be made a free port.[62]

Suhrawardy proposed a coalition government to his Congress and Forward Bloc opponents while advocating an independent national status for Bengal. He declared: 'We Bengalis have a common mother tongue and common economic interests. Bengal has very little affinity with the Punjab. Bengal will be an independent state and decide for herself later whether she should link up with Pakistan.'[63]

This point about the Muslim League's insistence on an undivided Bengal on the basis of Bengali linguistic nationalism needs to be discussed against the background of developments in Assam around that period. Ever since the Lahore Resolution of the Muslim League, the provincial Muslim League in Assam had stepped up efforts to build up the case for the inclusion of Assam in Pakistan. In the second session of the Assam Provincial Muslim League held on 30–1 January 1941, Saadulla had declared: 'If Muslims be a majority in Assam, then Bengal and Assam can form one Pakistan State.'[64] It may be mentioned that as early as April 1944, the Assam Provincial Muslim League in its Barpeta session has passed a resolution asking for constituting Bengal and Assam into a sovereign state of Eastern Pakistan. It was in this meeting that Maulana Bhasani was elected the president of the Provincial Muslim League. In the same year Humayun Kabir[65] observed:

One can easily visualise a Bengali State, comprised of about ten million people and living in a compact area. Such a state would include the present administrative province of Bengal and some of the outlying districts of Assam and Bihar. In fact, the province of Assam may be wholly incorporated in it. Cachar and Sylhet in the Surma Valley and Nowgong and Goalpara in the Assam Valley are Bengali-majority districts. There can hardly be an Assam if these districts join Bengal.[66]

Statements such as these, made by leading leaders of Bengal, plus the resolutions adopted Muslim League in favour of a union with Bengal added to Assamese apprehensions about preserving their identity.

Moreover, the announcement of the Cabinet Mission proposals and the grouping scheme further added to the atmosphere of uncertainty as far as the status of Assam as a separate province was concerned. As such, it was but natural that such a proposal put forward by the Bengal leaders would send shock waves in the Assamese mind, which was aware of attempts being made to include Assam within a greater Bengal and, finally, incorporate it in Pakistan. Jinnah and the Muslim League had been assiduously building up the argument that Assam was, after all, not a Hindu-majority province and the Muslim League was reaching out to certain segments of the province's population so as to win over their support. Although ostensibly the Muslim League's civil disobedience movement was aimed against the eviction policy of the Bardoloi government, the real purpose was to push forward the agenda of Pakistan.

To add to all this, there had been an earlier move by a section of Bengali politicians of the state to do away with the very name of the province itself. This naturally further added to Assamese apprehensions about losing their identity. For instance, in the early 1930s, a member of the Central Legislative Assembly, Basanta Kumar Das,[67] moved a resolution for changing the name of the province of Assam because he felt it was a misnomer, especially since the Assamese did not constitute a majority.[68] Yet another factor which added to Assamese antagonism against Sylhet and its Bengali population was the resistance to the idea of setting up a university in Assam. The Bengali middle-class leadership felt that there was no bona fide need for a university in Assam and the move was being initiated by the Assamese middle class to strengthen their hegemonic intentions. It was also argued that the population of Assam and its educational scene did not justify a separate university for the province.[69] The Calcutta press too echoed such opinions, which obviously added to the Assamese–Bengali divide.

The incorporation of the district of Sylhet in Assam had given a demographic advantage to the Bengali-speaking population of the province because at the time of its incorporation into Assam, the population of Sylhet was almost equal to the population of the Brahmaputra Valley districts and the hill districts.[70] Thus, from the early decades of the twentieth century, Assamese public opinion led by the Assam Congress leaders particularly of the Brahmaputra Valley was in favour of Sylhet's separation from Assam. Bardoloi and his team were consistent on this point from the beginning. This is clearly evident from Bardoloi's meetings with Wavell and Mountbatten as also in his jail diaries.[71] As already stated, the Assamese urge for a province minus Sylhet seemed quite justified. They had all along wanted to see Sylhet as a part of Bengal; it was a mere coincidence of history that the Referendum resulted in Sylhet becoming a part of Pakistan. Despite all this, it is difficult to understand why certain historians have attempted to show that Bardoloi had a 'complete change of heart over Sylhet'[72] following the transfer of power announcement of 3 June 1947. Referring to this Barooah writes:

> As for Bardoloi, he was very relieved at the demise of the imposed Grouping Plan. But, at the same time, he could not be complacent about the forthcoming referendum in Sylhet which might impose Pakistan on a large number of unwilling people, mostly Hindus, but some Muslims as well. Moreover, many of them had been his loyal Congress friends since 1937. There had, no doubt, been bitterness produced by the 'valleyism' in the past, but, for Bardoloi, it was past history and he had a complete change of heart over Sylhet.

Barooah refers to a meeting at Guwahati in the second half of June 1947 where Bardoloi declared that he was in favour of the retention of Sylhet in Assam. It is not at all plausible that Bardoloi, after consistently calling for the separation of Sylhet from Assam, justifying it on a variety of grounds and making it a part of the agenda of the Assam Congress, should suddenly have a change of heart.

It is obvious that, against the backdrop of the proposed Referendum and the possibility of Sylhet going to Pakistan, Bardoloi was trying to placate his Bengali cabinet colleagues from the Surma Valley, who had time and again supported him on several contentious and difficult issues. For instance, in the resolution passed by the Assam Assembly on 16 July 1946[73] finally rejecting the grouping scheme of the Cabinet Mission, Bardoloi was fully supported by the Bengali Congress members from the Surma Valley.[74] Referring to this, Barooah tries to downplay this support from the Surma Valley members and instead says that 'it was *to Bardoloi's great credit* that he obtained the support for the resolution from the Surma Valley Congressmen as well as from the Hill Representatives' (emphasis mine).[75] Barooah further tries to build up the argument that Bardoloi's demand for a separate boundary commission to demarcate the borders between Sylhet and Assam and his insistence that the Hindu-majority Ratabari, Kulaura, Kamalganj, and Srimangal thanas of Sylhet should not go to Pakistan was proof enough of his sympathy and concern for 'the Bengali Hindus of Sylhet and the surrounding areas of Assam proper'.[76] He says that 'it was probably due to the efforts of Bardoloi that the four thanas of Patharkandi, Ratabari, Badarpur and half of Karimganj remained in Assam' and 'the fact that the Bardoloi Government of Assam did not assert the right to exclude Sylhet from Assam was itself a great gesture'.[77] All this is not borne out by historical facts and there is enough evidence to suggest that, following the announcement to the results of the Referendum, a lot of public mobilization took place in the Hindu-majority thanas for their retention in Assam. Despite this, the Hindu-majority thanas of Kalaura, Kamalganj, and Srimangal went to Pakistan because Radcliffe had his own considerations about communication links and railway connectivity for East Pakistan.[78]

That Sylhet with its Muslim majority[79] would in all probability go to Pakistan appeared like an accepted fact once the Referendum was announced. Hence, for Bardoloi and the Congressmen from the Brahmaputra Valley it mattered little whether four of their cabinet colleagues from the Surma Valley tried to influence the Referendum in India's favour or whether one felt great concern for the fate of more than 40 per cent of Sylheti Hindus who might go to Pakistan. Moreover, public opinion in the Brahmaputra Valley led by the Assam Congress was clearly in favour of Sylhet's separation from Assam. Also, till the question of a referendum arose, Bengali Hindu opinion in the Surma Valley was also in favour of Sylhet's amalgamation with Bengal. Therefore, it would certainly be wrong to ascribe the separation of Sylhet from Assam through the Referendum to the wiles and conspiracy of the Assam Congress and the Assamese people. It would also be unwise to try to project Bardoloi and the Assam Congress from the Brahmaputra Valley as having attempted to influence the results of the Referendum in India's favour and also doing Sylhet a 'great favour' by forgoing the right of exclusion. When, after the Sylhet Referendum, Bardoloi met Gandhi, the latter pointedly asked him: 'I have heard all about your attitude regarding the separation of Sylhet. Why did you agree to the Referendum?' When Bardoloi told Gandhi that he was 'no party to it', the latter retorted, 'Can anything happen without its Prime Minister becoming a party to it?' To this Bardoloi replied that while it was true that 'a large number of people of the Assam Valley wanted Sylhet to be separated and, at one time, even the Hindus of Sylhet wanted the same', 'the Congressmen of both the places wanted to live together as they fought a common fight together for ten long years under my leadership for weal or woe'.

What is significant is that Gandhi was not at all prepared to listen to Bardoloi's part of the story and virtually condemned him even without giving him a chance to place his views. Bardoloi did try to put up a defence by saying that even the Surma Valley leader, Basanta Kumar Das as home minister of Assam, had agreed to the Referendum at a garden party with Mountbatten. Moreover, the Working Committee of the Congress had also approved of the Referendum. But Gandhi remained unconvinced.[80] This was a totally different Gandhi from the one who had spurred on the Assam Congress to go against all odds, including the Congress High Command, in its fight against the grouping scheme. It is clear from the account left by Bardoloi about his meeting with Gandhi that the latter's views on the Sylhet Referendum had been deeply influenced by what he had heard from those quarters that believed that Bardoloi was squarely responsible for the Sylhet Referendum and the merger of Sylhet with Pakistan. This view continues to persist today and is reflected in many writings on the Referendum. A section of scholars have consistently maintained that the APCC was not in favour of retaining even the four thanas that were awarded to Assam by the Radcliffe Commission, and that the Assam government was in such a great hurry to 'get rid of Sylhet' that it also forgot to lay claim to some 17 lakh rupees, which was its due as India's share of certain property in Sylhet.[81] For instance, Anindita Dasgupta says that the Assam government withdrew from 'the entire district of Sylhet even before the decision of the Boundary Commission was made known', and though it subsequently 're-occupied only a portion of the territory allotted to India/Assam' it failed to take 'possession of the 12 thanas'.[82] Dasgupta overlooks the fact that the four thanas[83] were awarded to India/ Assam by the Boundary Commission and hence the question of the Assam government reoccupying the twelve thanas, she mentions, does not arise. It is true that a section of the nationalist Assamese opinion was not in favour of these thanas being included in Assam because of their overwhelming Bengali population. But this cannot be seen as the unanimous view of the Assam government headed by Bardoloi. Even granting the fact that Assamese middle-class opinion was in favour of separation of Sylhet and that the Assam government displayed a sense of haste in accepting the Boundary Commission's verdict, yet it would not perhaps be correct to suggest that it willingly gave up to Pakistan areas that were given to India/Assam by the Commission. Nonetheless, such positions, which took shape in the years immediately preceding Partition, unfortunately continue to colour Assamese–Bengali relations to a certain extent even today. The Sylheti Hindus who were forced into second-class citizenship in East Pakistan and who were forced to leave their homeland in overwhelmingly large numbers were naturally burdened by a sense of victimhood. This sense of victimhood grew partly out of West Bengal's indifference to their plight combined with the aggressive nationalism they faced in Assam. It was quite natural in such a situation to view the Assamese as being mainly responsible for their plight.

In the years immediately following the separation of Sylhet from Assam, there seemed to be a resurgence of Assamese nationalism with the growing feeling that the Assamese were finally approaching their goal of a homogenous homeland.[84] But Assamese nationalism failed to move out of its narrow linguistic groove and reach out to all the other linguistic and ethnic/cultural groups of the state—something for which it had to pay the price of Balkanization of the state. Certain leading Assamese nationalists refused to acknowledge the fact that post-Independence Assam, made up of the Brahmaputra, Barak Valleys, and the hill regions, was essentially a bilingual state and that efforts to impose the Assamese language throughout the state could lead to a break-up. Instead, led by the Asom Sahitya Sabha, this section of Assamese nationalists succeeded in bringing pressure on the government to make Assamese the official language. This process, which proved to be a self-defeating one for the Assamese, was initiated in 1951 when the Asom Sahitya Sabha declared State Language Day on 16 July 1950 to press for the making of Assamese as the official language of the state. This resulted in strained relations between the Assamese and the Bengali communities in the Brahmaputra Valley and sectarian demands were raised. Demands supporting Assamese as the official language of the state were subsequently a part of the Asom Sahitya Sabha's agenda and ultimately it was ten years later, in 1960, that the Assam Assembly passed the Official Language Bill, which made Assamese the official language of the state,[85] thereby putting into motion the fragmentation of Assam.[86] Resistance to the Official Language Act climaxed in the Cachar district when on 19 May 1961 as many as eleven persons, mainly students, were killed in police firing while agitating against the Language Act. Although the movement in Cachar continued for some time, it eventually died out primarily because the Language Act had in reality provided for a bilingual state.

Quest for Separate Statehood in Cachar

The Assamese–Bengali divide, which found its most strident expression in the rivalry of the Brahmaputra and Barak Valleys in the years immediately following Partition, gave rise to a strong movement for a separate state of Cachar. This was clearly a fallout of what was perceived by most Bengalis as Assam's 'betrayal' of Sylhet, the Assam government's stand on refugees, the move to make Assamese the official language of the state, and the alleged policy of discrimination against Sylheti Bengalis being pursued by the state administration. Moreover, there was a sizable opinion among the Assamese middle class that Cachar should be separated from Assam. This demand had a long history and was part of the agenda of several Assamese nationalist organizations such as the Asom Sanrakshini Sabha led by Ambikagiri Roy Chaudhury.[87] In reaction to such demands, as also the feeling that Cachar would be better off outside Assam, the movement for separate union territory/ statehood was born. Beginning with the 'Sangram Samiti', set up in Cachar to oppose the Assam Official Language Act, in 1967 the Jana Mangal Parishad was formed to push forward the demand that Cachar be either made into a 'federating unit' with Meghalaya and Mizoram or be turned into a union territory. This was followed by the formation of the Union Territory Demand Committee, with a focus on securing union territory status for the district.[88] Though the movement for union territory status did succeed in creating a popular base among certain sections of the people of Cachar and received the support of a section of Assam government's Bengali bureaucrats working in Cachar, yet it could not make much headway because the national parties, including the Congress, stayed away from it.[89]

Those who advocated separate statehood or union territory status for Cachar maintained that historically Cachar was never a part of Assam and that the area was 'completely separate from Assam, culturally or linguistically'.[90] The Union Territory Demand Committee, in its 'Memorandum Demanding Union Territory Status for Cachar', submitted to Mrs Indira Gandhi, prime minister of India, on 15 July 1986, also asserted that a separate Cachar would be of benefit to the Assamese of the Brahmaputra Valley.[91] The union territory movement, which was all along led primarily by the Bengali Hindu leadership of Cachar,[92] continued till the 1980s when it finally petered out. It was in July 1986 that the last memorandum on the issue was submitted to Prime Minister Rajiv Gandhi by the Union Territory Demand Committee. Apart from distinct geographical factors which stood in the way of the union territory demand, change in demographic equations, the failure of regional political groups to make a dent in Cachar politics, and the attitudinal change that occurred amongst the young generations of both the Assamese and Bengali communities were other factors. Subsequently, although other organizations such as the Cachar Gana Parishad Union Territory Demand Committee were formed, they could not make much headway. The sociopolitical situation in the region was changing fast and the middle-class leadership of Cachar started facing new challenges. The complex issues thrown up by the Assam Movement (1789–95), the increasing polarization along religious lines in both the Barak and Brahmaputra Valleys, the weakening of regional-linguistic forces, new economic compulsions, and the growing relevance of national political parties have all contributed towards new and positive equations emerging between the Barak and the Brahmaputra Valleys.

Notes

1. Sylhet was always a revenue-deficit district and this was one of the reasons why despite its eagerness to join Bengal, the latter was not willing. When the question of Sylhet being separated from Assam and joined to Bengal arose, the government of Bengal, in its telegram dated 28 August 1925, raised the question of the financial effect of such a transfer. It claimed a contribution from the government of Assam as a set-off against the deficit of the Sylhet district. In reply to this demand, the joint secretary of the Government of India (Home) wrote: 'The Government of India are of the opinion that although Assam will be better off financially after the transfer of the district of Sylhet, after that transfer the district will form part of the Bengal Presidency and there will be no reason why the Government of

Assam should pay any contribution on account of it to the Government of Bengal.' (Letter from the Joint Secretary of Government of India, Home Division, to Chief Secretary of the Government of Assam, AICC Papers, P-4, 1938, NMML, New Delhi.)

2. At the time of its incorporation into Assam, Sylhet had a population of approximately 1.72 lakhs. The total population of Assam minus Sylhet at that time was some 2.5 lakhs. At the time of Partition, out of the fourteen districts and frontier tracts of Assam, the Sylhet district alone had about 31 per cent of the total population of Assam and it had a Muslim majority of about 61 per cent. Assam's population at the time of Partition included 35 lakh Hindus, 34 lakh Muslims, 7 lakh Scheduled Castes, and 26 lakh tribes.

3. For a detailed discussion on Goalpara's status, refer to Sanghamitra Misra, *Becoming a Borderland: The Politics of Space and Identity in Colonial Northeastern India* (New Delhi: Routledge, 2011).

> Between 1765 and 1822, following the imposition of the East India Company's rule in Bengal, the permanently settled parts of Goalpara were included within the district of Rangpur. In 1822, Goalpara was formed into a separate district of northeast Rangpur, also in Bengal. In 1826, the year of the beginning of formal colonial intervention in Assam, northeast Rangpur was separated from Bengal and included within the Assam Valley Division. In 1867 northeast Rangpur became a part of the newly formed Chief Commissionership of Cooch Behar. The following year it was placed under the jurisdiction of the Judicial Commissioner of Assam. In 1874, Goalpara was included as a district under the new province of Assam but was transferred to Bengal after the Partition of 1905. In 1912, Goalpara was once again included within the administration of Assam.

(Misra, *Becoming a Borderland*, p. 16fn1).

4. Nirode Kumar Barooah, *Gopinath Bardoloi: 'The Assam Problem' and Nehru's Centre* (Guwahati: Bhabani Print and Publications, 2010), p. 36.

5. A.C. Bhuyan and S. De (eds), *Political History of Assam 1920–1939*, vol. II (Guwahati: Government of Assam, 1978), p. 294, quoted by Barooah, *'The Assam Problem' and Nehru's Centre*, p. 105.

6. Amalendu Guha, *Planter Raj to Swaraj: Freedom Struggle and Electoral Politics in Assam 1826–1947* (New Delhi: ICHR, 1977), p. 27.

7. Saptarshi Deb, 'The Construction of the Sylheti Identity in Assam', thesis, submitted to the University of Hyderabad, 2015, p. 109. Deb goes on to add that 'Sylhet's extreme north-eastern location and by virtue of its being placed with "backward" Assam, amidst "wild aboriginal races", coupled with its peculiar speech raised doubts about its "Bengaliness"' .

8. Letter from the officiating Chief Secretary to the Government of Assam, no. 1573-Pol-3860-AP, dated Shillong, 11 August 1925, to the Government of India, AICC Papers, P-4.

9. Letter from the officiating Chief Secretary to the Government of Assam, no.1573-Pol-3860-AP, dated Shillong, 11 August 1925, to the Government of India, AICC Papers, P-4.

10. It was such moves that accentuated Assamese fears of a 'Greater Bengal'.

11. Letter from the Joint Secretary to the Government of India, Home Department, no. F 81-25-Public, dated Simla, 24 October 1925, to the Chief Secretary to the Government of Assam, *The Assam Gazette*, 20 January 1926, part VI, AICC Papers.

12. Letter from the Joint Secretary to the Government of India, Home Department, no. F 81-25-Public, dated Simla, 24 October 1925, to the Chief Secretary to the Government of Assam, *The Assam Gazette*, 20 January 1926, part VI, AICC Papers.

13. The Sylhet issue was debated in the Indian Legislative Assembly in January 1926 when a member moved a resolution for the transfer of Sylhet and Cachar to the Bengal Presidency because 'a great wrong had been done to these districts' by joining them to Assam. No decision was, however, taken on this resolution. But the Assam council debated the transfer issue once again in its special session of January 1926 when a member, Sadananda Dowersh, moved a resolution for the transfer of Sylhet to Bengal. The Assamese member argued that such a transfer would finally put an end to the rivalry between the two valleys. Interestingly, this motion was opposed by a Sylheti Bengali member from Sylhet who insisted that the district had made rapid strides after its amalgamation with Assam and that 'bar, benches and subordinate services', which were once dominated by the Bengalees, were now being manned by the Sylhetis. For details, refer to Bhuyan et al., *Political History of Assam*, vol. II, pp. 287–8.

14. In 1917 several deputations from the Surma Valley made up of both Hindus and Muslims demanded the transfer of Sylhet to Bengal. Brahmaputra Valley Muslims opposed the transfer. Saadulla, while opposing the transfer, suggested that in case it was given effect to, then the entire Brahmaputra Valley be transferred to Bengal and adequate measures be incorporated for the 'preservation of the Assamese nationality, culture and language'. Refer to M. Kar, *Muslims in Assam Politics* (New Delhi: Omsons Publications, 1990), p. 114.

15. Kar, *Muslims in Assam Politics*, pp. 113–14.

16. Deb, 'The Construction of the Sylheti Identity', p. 70.

17. The motion was carried by twenty-two votes against eighteen. Assamese leaders such as Rohini Kanta Hati Baruah supported the transfer on the ground that the Sylhetis were never a part of the Assamese nationality. Taraprasad Chaliha had reservations about the transfer because he felt that this could affect the status of the Governor's Province but eventually gave

in to what he believed to be the overwhelming sentiment in the Surma Valley, which favoured a reunion with Bengal. Nilmoni Phukan favoured Sylhet's reunion with Bengal but opposed the transfer of Cachar. Refer to Kar, *Muslims in Assam Politics*, pp. 116–22.

18. Saadulla made it clear that the demand for transfer of Sylhet was primarily a demand of the educated Hindus of the Surma Valley.

19. In the Shillong District Committee of the Congress, which was formed in 1938, the overwhelming majority of the members were from Sylhet and other provincial committees of the Barak Valley and there was not a single member from the Brahmaputra Valley. The Shillong Committee expressed its willingness to be under the Surma Valley District Congress. Refer to the letter from Secretary, Shillong District Congress Committee, C.S. Joshi, to the Secretary of the Provincial Congress Committee (Assam), where he writes: 'Please note that there is none even primary Congress members from the Assam valley in this committee. All are Sylhet and other provincial members in the committee. They are willing to join with the Bengal and Surma Valley Congress Committee.' (AICC Papers P-4, 1938.)

20. The Assam Congress Legislature Party in April 1938 decided to transfer the area known as south Cachar and constituting the Silchar and Hailakandi subdivisions to the jurisdiction of the Surma Valley District Congress Committee which was under the Bengal Provincial Congress Committee.

21. Letter dated 15 April 1938, from the Secretary of the APCC, Siddhinath Sarma, to the General Secretary of the AICC. The 'Bengali-speaking portion' of the Cachar district refers to the Silchar and Hailakandi subdivisions.

22. This meant that the entire Cachar region, including the North Cachar Hill region, would also have come under the jurisdiction of the Surma Valley Congress.

23. AICC Papers, P-4, 1938.

24. Guha, *Planter Raj to Swaraj*, p. 319.

25. In a later article Guha, while discussing the rise of Assamese 'chauvinism', says: 'As the Assamese middle class emerged stronger and more ambitious than ever after *Sylhet was shaken off its back*, its little nationalism started degenerating into chauvinism and minority-baiting' (emphasis mine). ('Little Nationalism Turned Chauvinist: Assam's Anti-Foreigner Upsurge, 1979–80', *Economic and Political Weekly*, vol. XV, no. 41–3, special number [October 1980]: 1699–1720).

26. Guha, *Planter Raj to Swaraj*, p. 320.

27. Barooah *'The Assam Problem' and Nehru's Centre*, p. 268, p. 296fn4.

28. Telegram sent by Secretary, Sylhet Bar Association, to the President of the Indian National Congress, May 1947, AICC Papers.

29. Guha, *Planter Raj to Swaraj*, p. 319.

30. Anindita Dasgupta, 'Remembering Sylhet: A Forgotten Story of India's 1947 Partition', *Economic and Political Weekly*, vol. XLIII, no. 31 (2 August 2008): 18–19.

31. As early as 1925, Saadulla had written to the chief secretary, government of Assam: 'Though some persons in the Assam Valley seem to think that the transfer of Sylhet to Bengal will be a good riddance in view of its being a deficit district, but the long view of the matter will convince them that it will not be an unmixed blessing'. Saadulla further insisted that the transfer of Sylhet would be disastrous to the Muslims in Assam as their proportionate share in representation in self-government would substantially go down. For Saadulla, the combined strength of the Muslims of both the Brahmaputra and Surma Valleys would be of great advantage to Muslim politics in the state. Refer to Bhuyan et al., *Political History of Assam*, vol. II, pp. 285–6.

32. Bimal J. Dev and Dilip Kumar Lahiri, *Assam Muslims: Politics and Cohesion* (Delhi: Mittal Publications, 1985), pp. 82–3.

33. Dasgupta, 'Remembering Sylhet', 18–22.

34. Sujit Chaudhuri, 'A God-Sent Opportunity', *Seminar* (2 February 2002)

35. Bardoloi wrote to Sardar Patel: 'Maulana Sahib seemed to come to the conclusion that the only alternative to this state of things is to separate the Bengali district of Sylhet and a portion of Cachar from Assam and join these with Bengal—a consummation to which the Assamese people are looking forward for the last 70 years.' (Durga Das [ed.], *Sardar Patel's Correspondence 1945–50*, vols I, III [Ahmedabad: Navjivan Publishers, 1972], p. 194.)

36. Das, *Sardar Patel's Correspondence*, vols I, III, p. 194.

37. Chaudhuri, 'A God-Sent Opportunity'.

38. Interestingly, the Assam Congress's stand against Muslim immigration into the province was supported by the central Congress command in the years following Independence, as may be seen in the different legislations and administrative decrees that were passed even though these were not of much avail.

39. Dasgupta, 'Remembering Sylhet', 18–22.

40. Guha writes: 'The Sylhet referendum was held in July 1947. It was virtually on the twin issues of the re-organisation of India on a communal, and of the province of Assam on a linguistic basis.' (*Planter Raj to Swaraj*, p. 319.)

41. The terms of reference of the Radcliffe Award, following the Referendum, were quite clear and stated that the Boundary Commission 'will also demarcate the Muslim majority areas of Sylhet district and the contiguous

majority areas of the adjoining districts of Assam'. Refer to Nicholas ergh and Panderlal Moon (eds), *The Transfer of Power 1942–47 (The ntbatten Plan, Viceroyalty, Princes, Partition and Independence July–gust 15, 1948)*, vol. XII (New Delhi: 1983), cited by L.A. Sherwani, in *The Partition of India and Mountbatten* (Karachi: Council for Pakistan Studies, 1986), pp. 164–6.

42. See M. Kar for an elaboration of Sardar Patel's views on this matter. Kar, *Muslims in Assam Politics*, p. 330. Kar refers to Durga Das (ed.), *Sardar Patel's Correspondence*, vol. V (Ahmedabad: Navjivan Publishers, 1972), p. 40

43. 'Purbachal Reconsidered, Being a Revised Version of the Memorandum', submitted by the Cachar States Reorganisation Committee to the States Reorganisation Commission of India in April 1954, with a supplement in May 1954 (based on 'A Plan For Purbachal' [1948] by Sri J. K. Chaudhury and published by The Cachar States Reorganisation Committee, Silchar, November 1954, p. 350). For full document, see P. S. Datta (ed.), *Autonomy Movements in Assam* (New Delhi: Omsons Publications, 1993), pp. 337–85.

44. Purbachal Demand Reconsidered, in Datta, *Autonomy Movements in Assam*, p. 350.

45. There were allegations from the Sylheti Hindus that at many places Hindu voters were not allowed to exercise their franchise because of the militant opposition put up by the Muslim national guards. The Referendum saw a voting percentage of 77.3 per cent and a total of 2,39,619 votes were cast for joining Pakistan, while 1,84,041 for remaining in Assam. The difference was just 55,578 votes. Following the results of the Referendum, there were several representations from the Hindu inhabitants of Hindu-majority areas. For instance, one may refer to the proceedings of a meeting of non-Muslim inhabitants of the south Sylhet subdivision, which was held on the 28 August 1947. The meeting protested the 'arbitrary amalgamation of the South-Sylhet Subdivision with East Bengal' that had a non-Muslim majority and was contiguous with the non-Muslim areas composed of the thanas of Barlekha, Patharkandi, and Ratabari of Karimganj subdivision, which adjoin Cachar district with the Indian Union. It accused Radcliffe of wrongly integrating south Sylhet area with Pakistan because he was of the view that if this was not done it would lead to the 'awkward severance of the railway line through Sylhet so that, for instance, the Junction (Kulaura) for the town of Sylhet itself, the capital of the district, will lie in Assam and not in East Bengal'. The meeting demanded the review of the question of south Sylhet subdivision by the Boundary Commission. (AICC Papers, F. No. CL-2-1 /MI/1946–47.)

46. Mansergh and Moon, *Transfer of Power*, vol. XII, pp. 140–1.

47. Referring to this, a scholar working on the Partition says: 'Exclusion of the entire labour population from the referendum was the most glaring deviation from the fundamental principle on which the country was divided. If this were to be accepted, then the entire valley, i.e., both Sylhet and Cachar as well as the adjoining hills would be a Muslim majority area.' (Kar, *Muslims in Assam Politics*, p. 336.) It was alleged that out of 166,750 labourers at least 50,000 were eligible to vote and were left out. But it has also been pointed out that these labourers were part of a floating population and were ineligible to exercise their franchise. This, however, appears to be a weak argument.

48. Refer to the telegram dated 4 July 1947 from Basanta Kumar Das (speaker of the Assam Assembly) and others to Lord Atlee. (Kar, *Muslims in Assam Politics*, p. 328.)

49. Ashfaque Hussain, 'The Making and Unmaking of Assam–Bengal Borders and the Sylhet Referendum', *Modern Asian Studies*, vol. XLVII, no. 1 (2012): 272–4.

50. Headed by Gopinath Bardoloi.

51. Sir Akbar Hydari.

52. Z.H. Zaidi (ed.), *Quaid-I-Azam Mohammad Ali Jinnah Papers: Pakistan in the Making, 3 June–30 June 1947*, first series, vol. II, annex to no. 335 (National Archives of Lahore, 1998), p. 636.

53. Zaidi, *Jinnah Papers*, p. 637.

54. Zaidi, *Jinnah Papers*, p. 637.

55. Memo submitted to S.P. Mookerjee by non-Muslim inhabitants of the southern part of Habiganj subdivision of Sylhet district, dated 30 July 1947. Also refer to memo submitted on behalf of Nikhil Cachar Haidimba Barma Samiti to the Chairman, Sylhet Boundary Commission, dated 21 July 1947, *S.P. Mookerjee Papers*.

56. Telegram from Sunamganj and Habiganj Congress Committees to Jawaharlal Nehru and Vallabhbhai Patel, dated 4 August 1947.

57. By the same logic, Radcliffe virtually gifted away the Chittagong Hill Tracts to Pakistan despite the fact that it had an overwhelmingly non-Muslim majority. His argument was that without the Chittagong Hill Tracts, the Chittagong port would be deprived of a hinterland.

58. Sir Akbar Hydari, the then governor of Assam. While the Muslim League accused Hydari of being partisan towards India, a section of Bengali Hindu opinion felt that he did not exert himself enough to keep Sylhet in India and wished that it should go to Pakistan.

59. Mansergh and Moon, *The Transfer of Power*, vol. XII, p. 227.

60. Sailesh Kumar Bandopadhyaya, *Quaid-i-Azam Mohammad Ali Jinnah and the Creation of Pakistan* (New Delhi: Sterling Publishers, 1991).

61. Stanley Wolpert, *Jinnah of Pakistan* (New York: Oxford University Press, 1984), pp. 322–4.
62. Wolpert, *Jinnah of Pakistan*, p. 325.
63. Wolpert, *Jinnah of Pakistan*, p. 320. Jinnah welcomed the move. But Nehru, Patel, and Shyama Prasad Mookerjee feared that a unified 'Bangladesh' led by a Muslim premier would form closer ties with Pakistan than with India.
64. Dev and Lahiri, *Assam Muslims*, p. 71.
65. Prof. Humayun Kabir was a well-known intellectual and Congress leader from Bengal. He was the private secretary to Maulana Azad and became a central minister in India after Independence.
66. Quoted by Barooah in *The 'Assam Problem' and Nehru's Centre*, p. 41. Barooah refers to the news report published in *India*, September 1944, Delhi. Also refer to Girin Phukan, *Assam's Attitude to Federalism* (New Delhi: Mittal Publications, 1984), p. 23.
67. Basanta Kumar Das was later elected a member of the Assam Legislative Assembly in 1937 and became its speaker. He was the home minister in the second Bardoloi cabinet (1946–50).
68. Barooah, *The 'Assam Problem' and Nehru's Centre*, pp. 37–8. There was a consistent attempt on the part of a section of Bengali intellectuals and politicians to prove that the name 'Assam' was a misnomer, given the linguistic plurality of the state. For instance, as late as November 1954, the Cachar States Reorganisation Committee of Silchar submitted a memorandum for a separate 'Purbachal' wherein one of the points was that Assam was a 'hotch-potch and a misnomer'. Refer to Document no. 2, Purbachal Reconsidered, in Datta, *Autonomy Movements in Assam*, pp. 347–8.
69. Assam was then under Calcutta University. The Silchar Bar Association in response to a government of Assam circular soliciting views on the setting up of a university in Assam had expressed its reservations. This report was published in *The Statesman* of 13 January 1936. Refer to Barooah, *The 'Assam Problem' and Nehru's Centre*, pp. 106, 566 (Appendix 2).
70. The incorporation of Sylhet into Assam had radically altered the demographic balance in favour of the Bengali-speaking population. At the time of Partition, out of the fourteen districts and frontier tracts of Assam, Sylhet district alone had about 31 per cent of the total population of Assam and it had a Muslim majority of about 61 per cent. Assam's population as per the 1941 Census (the last census before Partition) stood at some 1,04,18,000. Of this some 35 lakhs were Hindus and 34 lakhs were Muslims. The rest of the population was made up of tribes and Scheduled Castes.
71. In his recording of the proceedings of a meeting of the Congress prisoner group held in Jorhat Jail, on 24 December 1940, with Gauri Kanta Talukdar

in the chair, Bordoloi records, in his own handwriting, the decisions in the following manner:

> Sylhet should go to Bengal excluding Jaintia Pargannah. (i) Historical background: Sylhet was a part of Bengal Suba all along, while Jaintia Hills, as subject sometimes and always an ally of the Ahom Kings of Assam (including even Jaintia Pargannahs); (ii) Linguistic ... Bengalee for Sylhet; (iii) Tradition and culture are different; (iv) Sylhet was only added in 1874 for administrative convenience. The administrative convenience should point the way.

In the same meeting Bardoloi recorded the following about the status of Cachar:

> (i) Historically Cachar was a part of Assam and never a part of Bengal. Traditionally and culturally the bulk of the population is Assamese. (ii) The main home of the Population is Assam in as much they are Manipuris, Kacharis and other Assamese migrating owing to the Burmese invasion; (iii) Cachar was never part of Bengal. North Cachar hills can never go to Bengal; (iv) Land tenure is temporary settlement; (v) Geographically it forms a part of the compact area of Assam with the hills.

(Gopinath Bardoloi Papers, Misc. S. No. 1 [New Delhi: NMML.])

72. Barooah, The 'Assam Problem' and Nehru's Centre, p. 271.
73. It has been presumed Sarat Chandra Bose, who was strongly opposed to Assam accepting the grouping proposals, had a major say in the drafting of the resolution. Refer to Barooah, The 'Assam Problem' and Nehru's Centre, p. 243fn50. The resolution bound the ten representatives to the Constitution, including the three Muslim League members, to take part only in the framing of Assam's constitutions and to abstain from attending any meeting of the 'section' or the 'group' as envisaged in the Cabinet Mission Plan.
74. Prominent among them was the speaker of the Assam Legislative Assembly and later the home minister of Assam, Basanta Kumar Das, and tea planter and Cachar Congress leader, Baidyanath Mukherjee. Bardoloi also received support from the Surma Valley legislators (both Hindu and non-Muslim League) when he formed his coalition ministry in September 1938.
75. Barooah, The 'Assam Problem' and Nehru's Centre, p. 222.
76. Barooah, The 'Assam Problem' and Nehru's Centre, pp. 277–8.
77. Barooah, The 'Assam Problem' and Nehru's Centre, p. 278.
78. There remained a confusion regarding the Karimganj subdivision even after the Referendum. Six thanas of Karimganj and south Sylhet subdivision, Ratabari, Patharkandi, Barlekha, Kulaura, Kamalganj, and Srimangal, were Hindu-majority areas. On the extreme west of the district, two Hindu-majority thanas of Ajmirganj and Sulla as well as the Moulavibazar subdivision also fell within Hindu-majority areas. The Assam government submitted a memorandum to the Boundary Commission for the division

of Sylhet after the Referendum. The memorandum called for the river Kusiara to be the natural boundary of the two parts of divided Sylhet and claimed portions of Karimganj and Moulavibazar subdivisions up to the river Kusiara for India. But the Boundary Commission finally decided the three thanas of Patharkandi, Ratabari, and Badarpur and about a half of the Karimganj thana should be in India.

79. Muslims made up 60.7 per cent of the district's population and Hindus constituted 54.27 per cent.

80. Refer to 'A Meeting with Mahatma', in Lily Mazinder Baruah, *Lokopriya Gopinath Bardoloi: An Architect of Modern India* (New Delhi: Gyan Publishing House,, 1992), pp. 28–30.

81. Assam chief minister, Bishnuram Medhi, admitted in the Assam assembly in April 1954 that his government did forgo the claim but did not give any reasons for it.

82. Anindita Dasgupta, 'Partition Migration in Assam: The Case of the Bengali Bhadralok' in Imtiaz Ahmed, Abhijit Dasgupta, and Kathinka Sinha (eds), *State, Society and Displaced People in South Asia* (Dhaka: The University Press Limited, 2004), p. 132.

83. The Boundary Commission awarded the thanas of Ratabari, Patharkandi, Hailakandi, and half of Karimganj to Assam.

84. The separation of the populous Bengali-speaking district of Sylhet along with the decision of a substantial number of Muslim immigrants to return Assamese as their 'mother tongue' in the 1951 Census gave the Assamese-speaking people a clear majority for the first time in the Assam Valley districts. Refer to Udayon Misra, 'Little Nationalism Turned Chauvinist: A Comment', *Economic and Political Weekly*, vol. XVI, no. 8 (21 February 1981): 290–2.

85. For all practical purposes, the Official Language Bill provided for a bilingual state since Section 5 read as follows: 'The Bengali language shall be used for administrative and other official purposes up to and including the district level in the district of Cachar until the Mohkuma Parishads and Municipal Boards of the district, in a joint meeting of not less than two-thirds of the members present and voting, decide in favour of adoption of the official language for use in the district for the aforesaid purposes.' Following popular resistance to the Official Language Act in Cachar district, which claimed eleven lives in police firing in May 1961, Section 5 of the Act, pertaining to the use of Bengali in Cachar district, was amended 1961 and it read: 'The Bengali language shall be used for administrative and other official purposes up to and including the district level in the district of Cachar.' The clause referring to the possibility of Cachar at some future date opting for the Assamese language was dropped.

86. Once Assamese was made the official language with a provision for the use of Bengali in Cachar, demands for separate statehood were raised by

the Khasis, Jaintias, and Garos, and the stage was set for the emergence of Meghalaya and Mizoram as separate states. The joint struggle of the Khasis, Jaintias, and Garos was led by the All Party Hill Leaders' Conference (APHLC). The largely Hinduised Mikirs (Karbis) and the Dimasas, however, did not join the movement for a separate state. In subsequent years, plains tribal communities such as the Bodos as also the Karbis and Dimasas have expressed their unhappiness at what they saw as Assamese hegemony and started demanding separate statehood. For details about representations made by Karbi and Dimasa organizations, refer to Datta, *Autonomy Movements in Assam*.

87. During the Assam Movement (1979–85) on the foreigners' issue, the demand for the separation of Cachar was raised by several Assamese leaders. Fortunately, this did not work out and today the demand has virtually died down. Though the two valleys of the Brahmaputra and the Barak have come much closer, yet communication hurdles still stand in the way of faster and greater interaction between the peoples of the two regions. It is hoped that the completion of the East West Corridor and the upgradation of the railway line connecting Lumding with Silchar to broad gauge will further help the two valleys to come closer. The introduction of fast trains between Silchar and New Delhi via Guwahati is bound to make connectivity between the two valleys much easier, thereby putting an end to the isolation of the Cachar and the Barak Valley.

88. Subsequently other organizations such as the Cachar Gana Parishad Union Territory Demand Committee were formed.

89. Refer to Datta, *Autonomy Movements in Assam*, pp. 55–62, 415–47.

90. Refer to Datta, *Autonomy Movements in Assam*, p. 447.

91. Refer to Datta, *Autonomy Movements in Assam*, p. 447.

92. The overwhelming number of signatories to the different memoranda submitted to the Government of India on the issue of a separate union territory were Bengali Hindus.

5

UNRESOLVED ISSUES OF PARTITION POLITICS

The concluding chapter, apart from summing up the central arguments of the preceding chapters, takes up what it sees to be some of the major unresolved issues of Partition politics. While it tries to trace the roots of the violence centred around land in several areas of Assam, especially in the Bodo-inhabited region, it shows how issues such as the controversy over the cut-off year for immigrants to acquire citizenship are carry-overs from Partition days. Other major issues that the chapter takes up for discussion include the status of Hindu refugees/displaced persons in the state, the National Register of Citizens, and the larger question of language and Assamese identity. It shows how with the new wave of immigrants being assimilated into the Assamese nationality, its transformation is underway and how this transformation itself throws up new challenges and equations. Finally, it shows how in matters relating to immigration, identity, and language Assam seems to be in a time warp with these issues still occupying the major portion of public space—just as they did in the pre-Partition days.

It has been seen in the preceding chapters how the issues of land, immigration, identity, and language, which were thrown up in the pre-Partition years, continued to cast their shadow in the post-Partition political and social scenario of Assam. In the post-Independence years, the issue of land took on new dimensions especially in plains tribal areas where, in the 1930s and 1940s, areas reserved for the tribal people had already been encroached upon by the immigrants. Therefore, to understand

the dynamics of many of the identity movements and their relationship to the land factor, it is inevitable that one must return to the
decades before Independence and pre-Partition politics. The debates
centred around immigration and land, which dominated the 1940s and
stretched well into the 1950s and 1960s, took on new dimensions by
the 1970s when the Assam Movement (1979–85) started. Though the
agitation began on the plank of anti-outsider sentiments, it soon became
a movement aimed at throwing out from the state people categorized
as 'foreigners'.[1] Organizations from the other states of the northeastern
region extended their support to the anti-foreigner upsurge, and the
movement took on the characteristics of a mass upsurge.[2] The wide
support that the movement received during its initial stages from
different ethnic groups within the state, including the Bodos, can be
explained only from the land angle. But when the Assam Accord failed
to address the land question, these ethnic communities started etch-
ing out their own programmes of autonomy because they felt that the
Assam Movement had not been able to resolve the question of land
identity of the tribal nationalities.[3] Attempts by certain ethnic groups
to resolve the issue of land and identity through ethnic cleansing has
obviously proved counterproductive.

The genesis of the Bodo movement[4] for greater autonomy/separate
statehood, which eventually took on violent overtones, may be directly
traced to this alienation of tribal land that occurred in the wake of gov-
ernment-sponsored immigration and occupation of tribal reserves in
the 1930s and 1940s. But the very trend of developments suggest that
the burden of history is proving rather heavy for the small tribal communities, some of whom like the Bodos are desperately trying to put
the clock back. There seems to be no quick resolution of the land issue
even in areas where ethnic homelands have been created, for instance,
the Bodoland Territorial Autonomous District (BTAD). Efforts to create a Bodo-majority homeland are bound to meet with failure given the
fact that the Bodos constitute just 30 per cent of the total population.
Though figures relating to land ownership are not readily available, the
fact remains that much of the cultivable land of the BTAD continues
to be in the hands of the non-Bodos, with a substantial share being
taken by the Muslim immigrant population. Though there seems to
be no immediate solution to the Bodo imbroglio, palliative steps such
as stringent measures to prevent the further alienation of tribal-held

land and preserving whatever is left of the tribal belts and blocks could perhaps contribute to ease the present situation.

The question of the cut-off date for accepting immigrants from East Pakistan/Bangladesh became a central issue of the Assam Movement and finally, following the Assam Accord of August 1985, it was decided that 25 March 1971 would be the cut-off date. This too was opposed by several nationalist Assamese organizations that felt that the cut-off date should be according to the commencement of the Citizenship Act. It was insisted that there could not be two rules for citizenship, one for Assam and one for the rest of India, and that measures such as the Illegal Migrants (Determination by Tribunals) (IMDT) Act of 1983,[5] which was later struck down by the Supreme Court,[6] were meant to provide a safe haven in Assam for the hundreds of thousands of illegal immigrants from East Pakistan/Bangladesh, who had come over the years, occupied cultivable government land, and changed the demographic balance of the state. It is interesting to note that the debate over the cut-off date for immigrants stretches back to the 1930s and figures in all the discussions held in the elected legislature as well as in public space. Just as in the 1930s and 1940s the question of the post-1938 immigrants figured in the government resolutions on land, similarly today the question of the post-1971 immigrants is a much battered one defying any solution. While both the parties to the Assam Accord, the central government and the All Assam Students' Union–All Assam Gana Sangram Parishad, still swear by the Assam Accord and countless rounds of talks have been held on the issue of implementation of its different clauses, there seems to be a permanent roadblock when it comes to identifying the post-1971 immigrants. In the thirty odd years that have passed since the signing of the Assam Accord, one may safely add that no tangible progress has been made in the matter of detection of illegal immigrants and the deletion of their names from the electoral rolls, not to speak of deportation that is an extremely unlikely proposition given the lack of relevant treaties between India and Bangladesh and the sensitive humanitarian nature of the problem involved. This is where the important issue of land and immigration, which was thrown up by the pre-Partition politics of Assam, continues to exercise the public mind even today. The debate on the immigration issue continues to occupy central space in the state's politics and is bound to do so in the years to come. One has only to go through reports and editorials in the regional press in present-day Assam to realize how heavily the immigration issue continues to weigh on the Assamese mind.For instance, the editorial of 28 November 2014 in the leading English daily of the state, *The Assam Tribune*, commented:

> The entire process of detection and deportation of illegal Bangladeshi migrants continues to be clumsy, allowing enough time for the infiltrators to disappear during the lengthy proceedings.... Influx from Bangladesh is a danger not just for Assam or the Northeast, rather it is replete with sinister implications for the entire nation's integrity and sovereignty. Given the growing number of the infiltrators and their easy access to the voter's list, they stand a good chance of wresting political power in Assam in the near future.[7]

The paper urges the Centre to expedite the detection and deportation process and convince the Government of Bangladesh to take back the 'illegally detected migrants'. This is just one example to show how relevant the immigration issue remains in the context of Assam's present sociopolitical scenario.

The issue of illegal immigration from Bangladesh also figured in several judgment of the Supreme Court as well as the High Court of Guwahati in recent years. The latest in the series is the report to the Supreme Court by senior advocate Upamanyu Hazarika, which brought added focus to the issue of illegal immigration, land, and demographic change. A one-man fact finding commission was appointed by the Supreme Court in May 2015 to report on the ground situation along the Indo–Bangla border and the state of infiltration in Assam. The commission submitted its report in October 2015. The report stated that immigration from Bangladesh posed a major threat to the state's indigenous population that could be reduced to a minority by the year 2047, and suggested the setting up of a high-power enquiry commission by the Supreme Court to go into the entire issue of illegal immigration in Assam from Bangladesh. The report also referred to the laxity in the Indian judicial and administrative systems and stated, 'there is one significant fact which emerges from the fact finding undertaken since May 2015 and resulting in four reports, including the recent one, and which is that there is an established institutional mechanism which enables a Bangladeshi national to freely come into the country, acquire citizenship rights and more importantly voting rights, which is where their strength lies'. In this connection it referred to the judgments delivered by the Gauhati High Court. But the most significant observation of the Hazarika Commission has been on the land situation in Assam. The report stated that since land was the primary reason for illegal immigration, strict restrictions should be imposed on the transfer of land by sale, purchase, gift, or any other transaction. Referring to the restrictions on transfer of land to non-tribals in the tribal belts and blocks in Assam, the report recommended that these restrictions should also be made applicable in non-tribal areas. Thus, by once again linking the issue of illegal immigration with the land question, the Hazarika report has added to growing demands by indigenous organizations for restrictions on land transfer and the need for an Inner Line Permit to restrict the flow of 'outsiders' into the state. In the neighbouring state of Manipur, popular agitations have forced the government to enact several legislation aimed at protecting indigenous rights over land.[8] Similar demands for an Inner Line, which is believed would protect the land rights of the people, are also being raised in states such as Meghalaya.

The Supreme Court has also intervened several times regarding the updating of the National Register of Citizens (NRC) in the state. In one of its judgment, the highest court ordered that the updated NRC be published by January 2016.[9] This massive exercise, which initially met with resistance from certain minority groups, is nearing completion. But certain hiccups continue, the one relating to forged documents being the major one. The difficulties that the government is facing in updating the NRC in Assam are linked to the lack of unanimity regarding the cut-off date for foreign immigrants, with some organizations representing Assamese nationalistic feelings insisting that the NRC be updated on the voters' rolls of 1951. The Supreme Court directed the state coordinator for the NRC to work out the logistic arrangements for publishing the updated NRC in the state by the end of January 2016. Earlier the Supreme Court had given two weeks' time to the Centre to furnish an action plan on illegal infiltration, deportation of illegal migrants, sealing of the India–Bangladesh border, and the updating of the NRC. A two-judge bench of the Supreme Court referred the case of illegal migrants in Assam to a constitution bench in response to a petition that has challenged Section 6A of the Citizenship Act[10] as well as the cut-off date of 24 March 1971. The newspaper report continued: 'The Court also observed that "political expediency" had "taken over" in Assam, where "mess had been created" as people were granted citizenship even when they did not come within the protection of Section 6 A of the Citizenship Act. They could be given refugee status instead of granting them citizenship right ... they are not only aliens but enemy aliens.'[11] Thus, the petitions before the highest court of the country challenging the cut-off date set by the Assam Accord have naturally further complicated the process of updating the NRC in Assam. Then here is also the demand from certain minority organizations that 'D' voters be also included in the NRC.[12] Despite all these hurdles, the process of updating the NRC seems nearing completion. However, there is a section of public opinion that feels that the inclusion of names of illegal immigrants in the NRC would only help to legalize their status as Indian citizens. These quarters hold the view that unless the land question is seriously addressed and until swift measures are implemented to detect and deport the illegal immigrants by working out a treaty with neighbouring Bangladesh, the demographic change that is underway is bound to reduce the indigenes to a minority status in their own homeland.

Recently, two important developments have taken place in Assam, both having a serious impact on the society and politics of the state. Once again there appears to be a return to the language and identity debate of the 1940s and 1950s. The first such development has been a notification issued by the central government on the status of 'minority' refugees from Pakistan and Bangladesh who have come to India up to December 2014 and who have been living here without valid documents.[13] The notification stated that it would be applicable only to the Hindus, Sikhs, Christians, Jains, Parsis, and the Buddhists who crossed over to India from Bangladesh and Pakistan on or before 31 December 2014. This meant the granting of citizenship to thousands of Bengali Hindu refugees who have been staying in the state for decades and also all to those who came to Assam in the post-1971 period because of religious persecution in Bangladesh or for other reasons. Even though approximate figures about this population are still not available, yet conservative estimates put this number at several lakhs. The move is bound to help these people whose status as Indian citizens has been doubted time and again, especially in the case of those who did not provide valid documents to prove their citizenship. However, different ethnic organizations of the state[14] have unequivocally demanded that the notification be withdrawn because it went against the provisions of the 1975 Assam Accord, which fixed the date for identification of illegal migrants at 24 March 1971. These organizations asserted that if the post-1971 Hindu migrants were given citizenship on the plea that these people fled religious persecution, then the demographic balance would shift against the indigenous Assamese, who would eventually be turned into a minority. The actual fear of the Assamese was that if the number of Bengali speakers increased in the state, a section of Bengali-speaking Muslims who had earlier returned Assamese as their mother tongue may decide to return Bengali, and this would further reduce the number of Assamese speakers in the state and adversely affect the status of Assamese as the official language of the state. It is also being feared that any threat, imagined or otherwise, to the status of the Assamese language, which has always been a highly contentious issue in Assam, is bound to create major social and political tension. With both the Congress and Bharatiya Janata Party (BJP) leadership expressing themselves in favour of accommodating the post-1971 Bengali Hindu migrants within the state, the entire issue has been heating up since the early part of 2014. This was reflected in the editorials carried by the regional press and English dailies[15] published from the state on the issue of granting 'refugee' status to Bengali Hindu immigrants, which read very much like those published in the 1940s when the struggle for the supremacy of the Assamese language had reached its peak.

The central government's decision has been received with *bandhs* (a general strike) and protest demonstrations throughout the state. Apart from the core Assamese organizations such as the All Assam Students' Union and the Asom Sahitya Sabha, almost all the ethnic organizations covering the different plains tribes of the Brahmaputra Valley as well as those belonging to the tea tribes and Assamese indigenous Muslims have expressed their strong opposition to the Centre's move of granting citizenship status to post-2014 Bengali Hindus. Significantly, the move has also faced resistance from organizations of immigrant Muslims who have settled in Assam prior to 1971, many of whom consider themselves part of the broader Assamese nationality. It is interesting to note that some seventy years ago, similar sentiments were echoed in the regional Assamese press about the entry and settlement of Hindu refugees in Assam following Partition. The settlement of Hindu refugees in Assam was a major point of dissension between the Centre and the Bardoloi-led Assam government, and Nehru even threatened to cut off economic assistance to the state if it did not accommodate enough refugees.[16] It may also be recalled that Sardar Patel, who was otherwise sensitive to the issue of immigration into Assam, expressed his ire against the finance and revenue minister in Bardoloi's government, Bishnuram Medhi, for his refusal to accommodate any further refugees after the number had crossed some 3 lakhs in the years immediately following Partition. Patel also intervened to get the then chief secretary, S. P. Desai, removed because of the latter's contention that there was not any more land available in Assam for the rehabilitation of refugees.[17]

More than seventy years later, the issue of Bengali Hindu refugees in Assam has once again come to occupy centre stage. The same comments and observations that were made in the Assamese press in the 1940s can be seen being repeated today. The point made at the beginning of the book that Assam has been caught in a time warp has been effectively proved by this sequence of events. Once again, the contemporary political scenario of Assam sees the issue of settlement of Hindu refugees as a major challenge to the future of Assamese nationality, one of the major issues of post-Partition politics that remains unresolved. There seems to be an eerie similarity in the language of the editorials published in the 1940s on the issue of Bengali Hindu refugees and those published as recently as 2015. Commenting on the inflow of Bengali refugees into Assam following the Partition, *The Assam Tribune* of 2 June 1949, stated: 'The Centre must not be blind to Assam's interest and must not adopt any policy which will ultimately lead to the annihilation of Assam. The danger point has almost been reached, and the Centre should not expect Assam to commit suicide wither eyes wide open.' The same paper commented that it was beyond Assam's capacity to accommodate more refugees and asked: 'Has Assam no right to exist as a land of the Assamese people? Is it the intention of the Government to turn the Assamese people into a minority community in their own province and jeopardize their language, culture and their very existence?'[18] Almost seventy years later, the same paper again editorially commented:

> The Centre's decision to regularize the entry and stay of the Hindu migrants from Bangladesh in India has expectedly stirred a hornet's nest in Assam, with many organisations and political parties registering mass protests against the move.... The visible demographic changes in terms of the growing Muslim populace as also the growing Bengali-speaking

populace are matters that do not augur well for the sociopolitical interests of the indigenous people…. While the humanitarian aspect behind the move to grant refugee status to Hindu migrants cannot be ignored, it must be ensured that Assam is not further burdened by influx of refugees. The State has already had more than its fair share of legal and illegal migrants from East Pakistan and Bangladesh and under no circumstances should it be made to bear the burden of more migrants.[19]

Yet another newspaper, the *Dainik Asom*, in its editorial of 8 September 2015, titled 'Dustbin', stated that Assam was in no position to accommodate more Bengali Hindu refugees and that these should be distributed in the other states of the country.[20] Thus, the entire issue of Bengali Hindu refugees in Assam has once again been linked with the future status of Assamese language and culture.

However, it is to be noted that in the different movements over language and identity that have occurred in the Brahmaputra Valley beginning with the second decade after Independence, the land factor has always been a principal motive force. For instance, the language movement of 1960 or the movement aimed at making Assamese the medium of instruction in the universities and colleges that occurred in the 1970s were both related in some sense or other with the land factor.[21] There is no denying the fact that the increasing landlessness of the Assamese and other plains tribal communities gave a thrust to these movements, which on some occasions took on chauvinistic overtones. The debate over securing land for the landless indigenous population, which started in the 1930s and 1940s and spilled over to the 1950s, seems to retain its relevance even today. In this case too one may refer to recent newspaper reports on encroachments on grazing reserves that point to the fact that the issue is still to be resolved and continues to hold relevance in present-day Assam politics. For instance, a leading local English daily in its issue of 7 June 2014, reporting on encroachment upon grazing reserves, stated: 'People of Sarukhetri Mouza in Barpeta district have demanded immediate eviction of the encroachers from the grazing reserve in and around Kapala Beel under the Sarthebari revenue circle. Government should ensure eviction from Kaladi Grazing Reserve and ensure safety of indigenous people from the onslaught of encroachers.'[22] It may be recalled here that seventy-two years ago in March 1945, Gopinath Bardoloi, the then leader of the opposition in the Assam Assembly, while referring to encroachments on grazing reserves

had said: 'I only want to add this much that till now all actions that
have been taken by the government have gone in favour of the immigrants and aimed at throwing out the graziers and indigenous people
out of their soil.'[23] The land question remains as relevant today as it
was in the 1940s when safeguards for the land held by the indigenous
people occupied central space in the public discourse. The situation
today has assumed alarming proportions and unless stringent steps are
taken to prevent further alienation of indigenous land, measures aimed
at preventing further infiltration from across the Indo–Bangla border
will remain, at best, cosmetic. With plenty of loopholes in the present
land regulations, the indigenous peasant is clearly fighting a lost battle.
It is a significant aspect of the sociopolitical scenario of the state that
issues of language and identity far outweigh those of land, even though
the land question is inextricably bound up with the former.

Even though the rivalry of the valleys seem to have subsided and
earlier antagonism between the Assamese Hindus and the Bengali
Hindus have given place to greater understanding and cooperation and
also to some degree of assimilation, yet the issue of language continues to occupy central space. Assamese nationalism, which is primarily
language-based and which has been largely dependent on the Bengali
Muslim immigrants' acceptance of the Assamese language for the
survival of its majority status, still occasionally has anxieties about its
continued hegemony and this explains its reaction towards the Bengali
language.[24] Though the issue regarding the status of the Assamese language as the official language of the Brahmaputra Valley area appears
to be a settled one, given the clear majority that Assamese speakers
possess over other communities, yet there seems to be a lurking fear in
the Assamese mind that the present situation could change radically if,
in some future census, a substantial section of the immigrant Muslims
decide to return Bengali as their mother tongue. Hence, on the eve of
every census enumeration there is invariably a public debate on this
issue and appeals are often made to the immigrant Muslim community continue their 'support' for the Assamese language.[25] In the final
analysis it may be said that the status of the Assamese language remains
an unresolved issue, despite the fact that the pre-Partition politics was
centred on the idea of a linguistically homogenous Assamese homeland.[26] With the number of Assamese speakers coming down with
every census, the crisis centred on linguistic identity of the Assamese

is certainly going to become deeper and language politics, which has always superseded religious politics in the state, is bound to take on a new edge.

Another major unresolved issue from the pre-Partition days is that of Assamese identity. Just as in the 1940s, in the last two decades or so there have been acrimonious debates both in the state's public space as well as in the legislature over the parameters defining Assamese identity. That the issue of Assamese identity is getting more complicated with increasing demographic change affecting the composition of the people of the state has become evident in exchanges between members of the Legislative Assembly since the 1990s till the present day. Not only is the question of 'infiltrants' being staunchly denied by a section of the members representing immigrant interests, the very term 'Assamese people' has also become controversial and debatable. It may be recalled that the debate over identity took on a more focused turn after the signing of the Assam Accord, which, in one of its clauses, referred to steps calling for the preservation of the identity of the 'Assamese people'.[27] Different plains tribal communities of Assam, beginning with the Bodos,[28] raised questions about the definition of the 'Assamese people' and insisted that they did not come under that purview. Other plains tribal communities followed suit and soon the definition 'Assamese people' became clouded in controversy. The controversy was reflected in the Legislative Assembly debates, and the government of Assam even had to set up a committee to determine who really constituted the Assamese people! The Asom Sahitya Sabha was finally given the responsibility of fixing the definition as to who really was an Assamese.[29] The definition provided by the Asom Sahitya Sabha, in consultation with the Sanmilita Sahitya Manch, made up of several ethnic literary organizations, did not help in resolving the problem because several of the ethnic groups refused to accept it, while some Assamese nationalist organizations felt that by fixing the cut-off date for defining the Assamese, the Sabha had included all the immigrants who had gained citizenship up to March 1971. This, many observers felt, distorted the definition of 'indigenous' in the context of the Assam Accord. Moreover, a debate started over an identification of authentic 'indigenous' languages. But, whatever the ambiguities and the confusions centred on the Sabha's definition,[30] the fact emerged that, in any attempt to define who is an Assamese, the stage had been reached when the immigrant neo-Assamese could not be left out of the ambit—even if this meant alienating the ethnic/plains tribal nationalities. The Sabha was merely accepting the transformation that was taking place within the Assamese nationality.[31] This matter also came to occupy central place in the negotiations between the All Assam Students' Union and the Centre over the implementation of the Assam Accord.[32]

In the Assam Assembly debates of the 1940s, immigrant leaders had claimed that the immigrants,[33] through hard toil and cultivation of wastelands and riverine belts, had become as much Assamese as the indigenous people. Similar sentiments are often echoed by immigrant leaders in present-day Assam, though with much greater confidence. This confidence stems from the fact that, over the years since the 1940s and 1950s, the process of 'Assamisation' of a large section of immigrant Muslims had begun. The point that the neo-Assamese make to prove their Assamese credentials is that while the other communities such as the Marwaris, Beharis, and Bengali Hindus have stuck to their language and culture, it is the Muslim immigrants who have given up their language and also part of their culture and adopted the Assamese culture. The argument is also made by neo-Assamese Muslim intellectuals that even though large sections of these immigrant-Bengali Muslim–turned–neo-Assamese are still bilingual, and speak Bengali at home and Assamese otherwise, this should not be an obstacle of any sort in the evolving of their Assamese identity. In this, they refer to the plains tribes who form part of the Assamese nationality and still speak in their own languages at home. Thus, it is being pointed out that the neo-Assamese Muslims are as 'indigenous' to the region as the other indigenes.[34] Their contribution to the economy of Assam is also pointed out as a strong point in their indigenization. Referring to the immigrant-turned Assamese in one of his articles, Homen Borgohain, a leading Assamese intellectual, writes:

> Those who came from eastern Bengal some thirty, forty or fifty years ago, now number not just thousands but lakhs. These lakhs of people have totally given up their previous cultural and linguistic identity and are trying to newly identify themselves as Assamese…. Not only have the immigrants from East Bengal come to settle in Assam. From the Marwaris of Rajasthan to the Bengali Hindus, people from different parts of India have come and settled here. But none of these have come forward to accept the Assamese language and give their identity

as neo-Assamese. On the contrary, we see that they have set up Marwari Hindi high schools and Bengali schools in every town (and now even in the villages). Yet their numbers are much smaller than those of the neo-Assamese Muslim. The very fact that lakhs of people have given up their linguistic and cultural identity and merged themselves with the language and culture of another community may indeed be said to be a rare happening in the history of the entire world. (Translation mine)[35]

Borgohain, like many other Assamese intellectuals, seems happy over the fact that the future status of the Assamese language (read Assamese identity), has been ensured by the support it has received from the new entrants into the Assamese nationality. But this certainty about the status of the Assamese language may not hold for too long. There is always the possibility that some sections of the immigrant Muslims who continue to speak their mother tongue may, because of changing sociopolitical equations, eventually return Bengali as their main language in succeeding census enumerations. Added to this is the growing apprehension created by demands made by organizations such as the Bodo Sahitya Sabha that the word 'Assamese' in Clause 6 of the Assam Accord be replaced by the term 'indigenous people of Assam'.[36]

In conclusion, it may be said that while the parameters of the Assamese nationality have certainly expanded in such a manner that an overwhelmingly large section of immigrant Muslims are no longer considered even as neo-Assamese or Na-Asamiya but as Assamese or Asamiya,[37] this has also thrown up a lot of new issues. There is no doubt that the process of the transformation of Assamese identity is still on, with the large tea garden population also being accommodated within its ranks. What, however, is ironic is that the plains tribal communities, whose language and culture were an integral part of the Assamese nationality, seem to have drifted apart and have been claiming their own social and political spaces.[38] But there is a possibility of this alienation of the plains tribal communities being checked and even reversed as they perceived a threat to their identity from the increasing strength of the neo-Assamese Muslims.[39] This applies not only to the plains tribal communities but also to small communities such as the indigenous Assamese Muslims who have, in recent years, formed their own sociopolitical organization[40] and have been demanding special privileges for the community that they feel are being denied to them because they are being increasingly lumped with the immigrant neo-Assamese

Muslims.[41] Similarly, it is seen that even the Bodos who had been part of a violent agitation for separation from Assam are gradually trying to build bridges with the indigenous Assamese in their struggle against the immigrant Muslims in Bodoland. In the context of the growing sense of conflict between certain plains tribal communities desperately trying to hold on to their land and culture and the immigrant population, the question would naturally arise as to whether the indigenous Assamese would side with the plains tribal communities (some of which are integral parts of the Assamese nationality) or with the neo-Assamese immigrant Muslims who are now part and parcel of the Assamese nationality. This seems to be a major contradiction within the Assamese nationality, which is bound to assume challenging proportions in the years to come. There are other issues too. For instance, how would the cultural base of the Assamese society made out of an amalgam of folk traditions and tribal practices and belief with broad pan-Hindu forms, strengthened over the centuries by Sankardeva's school of liberal neo-Vaishanvism, be affected by induction of the immigrant neo-Assamese immigrants into the fold of Assamese nationality?[42] Added to all this, is the overarching question of the increasing political power of the immigrant neo-Assamese, who now form the largest group in the state assembly and who are very much in a position to influence state policy. Moreover, the rise of immigrant Muslim political organizations such as the All India United Democratic Front is bound to lead to further polarization along religious lines, with linguistic and cultural factors being pushed to the margins. As it is, Assamese indigenous Muslims are facing an increasing threat to their identity and have been voicing their concerns in different forums. The fault lines within the edifice of Assamese linguistic nationalism are clearly beginning to show. At the same time, a process of coming together of the different indigenous communities under a common platform of a broad Assamese identity also seems to be under way. The cementing force of such a combined force would obviously be the issues of land and identity in the face of swift demographic change.

Notes

1. 'Foreigners' in this context generally applied to Bengali Muslim migrants from East Pakistan/Bangladesh who came and settled in Assam in the 1960s

and 1970s onwards. The early settlers, which included Bengali Muslim migrants from East Bengal as also those who came from East Pakistan within the first few years of Partition, were excluded from the category of foreigners.

2. Given the number of people who participated in the different forms of protests worked out during the Assam Movement, it was easily the largest populist upsurge of post-Independence India.

3. The Assam Accord (15 August 1985) was a Memorandum of Settlement arrived at between the Government of India and the All Assam Students' Union and the All Assam Gana Sangram Parishad, the two organizations that had been spearheading a six-year movement (1979–85) for the detection, disenfranchisement, and deportation of foreign nationals in Assam. The accord, which was signed in the presence of the then prime minister, Rajiv Gandhi, stated, among other clauses, that 'foreigners who came to Assam on or after March 25, 1971 shall continue to be detected, deleted and expelled in accordance with the law'. It also stated that 'relevant laws for the protection of encroachment of government lands in tribal belts and blocks [be] strictly enforced and unauthorised encroachers evicted as laid down under such laws'. But more than thirty years after the accord, most of its clauses remain unimplemented.

4. Refer to 'The Bodo Movement', in Udayon Misra, *India's North East: Identity Movements, State and Civil Society* (New Delhi: Oxford University Press, 2014), pp. 228–58.

5. The IMDT Act of 1983 put the onus of proving whether someone is an illegal migrant not on the person concerned but on any Indian citizen residing within 3 kilometres of the place of residence of the person against whom the allegation has been made. Moreover, the application made to the tribunal would have to be accompanied by two affidavits sworn by two persons residing within the 3 kilometre limit, and there would also be a fee ranging from Rs 25 to Rs 100. This provision made the detection of illegal immigrants virtually impossible.

6. The Supreme Court struck down the IMDT Act in July 2005 as ultra vires of the Constitution of India. A report published in *The Hindu* of 14 July 2005, New Delhi, stated: 'The Supreme Court held that the Illegal Migrants (Determination by Tribunals) Act, 1983 and Rules "has created the biggest hurdle and is the main impediment or barrier in the identification and deportation of illegal migrants."'

A three-judge bench comprising Chief Justice R.C. Lahoti, Justice G.P. Mathur, and Justice P.K. Balasubramanyan, which struck down the IMDT Act as unconstitutional, observed: 'The presence of such a large number of illegal migrants from Bangladesh, which runs into millions, is in fact an aggression on the State of Assam and has also contributed significantly in causing serious internal disturbances in the shape of insurgency of alarming proportions.'

The court, in its 114-page judgment, noted that this 'aggression' had made the life of the people of Assam 'wholly insecure and the panic generated thereby had created fear psychosis'. The bench said this hampered the growth of Assam though it had vast natural resources. The rest of the country viewed it as a disturbed area and hence there were no investments or employment opportunities, giving rise to insurgency.

Justice Mathur, writing the judgment for the bench, pointed out that the IMDT Act and Rules had been so made that innumerable and insurmountable difficulties were created in identification and deportation of illegal migrants. The bench noted that though enquiries were initiated in 3,10,759 cases under the IMDT Act, only 10,015 persons were declared illegal migrants and only 1,481 illegal migrants were physically expelled up to 30 April 2000.

This, the bench said, 'comes to less than half per cent of the cases initiated'. On the contrary in West Bengal, where Foreigners Act was applicable, 4,89,046 persons were deported between 1983 and November 1998 in a shorter period of time. Thus, the IMDT Act 'is coming to the advantage of such illegal migrants as any proceedings initiated against them almost entirely ends in their favour, enables them to have a document having official sanctity to the effect that they are not illegal migrants'.

The bench said that 'the IMDT Act and the Rules clearly negate the constitutional mandate contained in Article 355 of the Constitution, where a duty has been cast upon the Union of India to protect every State against external aggression and internal disturbance. The IMDT Act, which contravenes Article 355 of the Constitution is, therefore, wholly unconstitutional and must be struck down'.

The judgment observed that the impact of such large-scale illegal migrants not only affected Assam but also other northeastern states as the route to these places passed through Assam. The bench said that the influx of Bangladeshi nationals into Assam posed a threat to the integrity and security of the northeastern region and their presence had changed the demographic character of the region, and the local people of Assam had been reduced to a status of minority in certain districts. The bench further added that the enforcement of the IMDT Act had helped the illegal migrants to stay in Assam. The illegal migrants had affected the language, script, and culture of the local people. The bench directed constitution of fresh tribunals under the Foreigner (Tribunals) Order, 1964.

7. 'Seal the Border', *The Assam Tribune*, Guwahati, 28 November 2014.

8. The Manipur Assembly passed three bills in 2015, namely the Manipur People's Bill, 2015, Manipur Land Revenue and Land Reforms (Seventh Amendment) Bill, and Manipur Shops and Establishment (Second Amendment) Bill. These three measures effectively put in place an Inner Line Permit without actually saying so.

9. Refer to the Supreme Court judgment on the writ petition filed by the Assam Sanmilita Mahasangha and two other organizations dated 17 December 2014. In this judgment, the Supreme Court began by saying: 'A prophet is without honour in his own country. Substitute "citizen" for "prophet" and you will get the gist of the various writ petitions filed under Article 32 of the Constitution of India assailing Section 6A of the Citizenship Act.' In a significant observation the Court stated: 'On 14th July, 2004 in response to an unstarred question pertaining to deportation of illegal Bangladeshi migrants, The Minister of State, Home Affairs, submitted a statement in Parliament indicating therein that the estimated number of illegal Bangladeshi immigrants into India as on 31st December, 2001 was 1.20 crores, out of which 50 lakhs were in Assam.' The Court also stated that 'the petitioners in the various writ petitions represent the entire people—the tribal and non-tribal population of the state of Assam'.

10. The Centre had inserted Section 6A in the Indian Citizenship Act following the signing of the Assam Accord. This amendment stated that migrants entering India after 25 March 1971 would be detected and deported back to Bangladesh. Refer to report by Kalyan Barooah in the *Assam Tribune*, Guwahati, 15 November 2014.

11. Report by Kalyan Barooah in the *Assam Tribune*, Guwahati, 15 November 2014.

12. 'D' voters are those individuals whose claim to Indian citizenship has been doubted by the Election Commission and hence the 'D' against their names. The matter went up to the Supreme Court, which ruled against such inclusion.

13. The union government through two gazette notifications under the Passport (Entry into India) Act, 1920, and Foreigners Act, 1946, on 7 September 2015 allowed Bangladeshi and Pakistani nationals who had entered India on or before 31 December 2014, without proper documents or after the expiry of relevant documents, to stay in India on humanitarian grounds. The full transcript of the Union Home Ministry statement runs as follows:

> The Central Government has decided, on humanitarian considerations, to exempt Bangladeshi and Pakistani nationals belonging to minority communities who have entered into India on or before 31st December 2014 from the relevant provisions of rules and order made under the Passport

(Entry into India) Act, 1920 and the Foreigners Act, 1946, in respect of their entry and stay in India without such documents or after the expiry of those documents, as the case may be. This notification was later replaced by the Citizenship (Amendment) Bill of 2016.

14. These include not only bodies such as the All Assam Students' Union and the Asom Jatiyatabadi Yuva Chatra Parishad, but also all other ethnic organizations covering the plains tribal groups of the state as also those belonging to the Assamese indigenous Muslims and tea tribes.

15. Commenting on the granting of citizenship to Hindu refugees from East Pakistan/Bangladesh, the *Assam Tribune* wrote in its editorial entitled 'Bangladeshi Infiltration' of 7 June 2014:

> The recent utterances on the part of both the Congress and the BJP to con-sider the case of the Hindu migrants on humanitarian grounds also smacks of such vested political agendas. Illegal migrants should be shown the door irrespective of their religious affiliation, as was agreed in the Assam Accord of 1985. And, if at all the Hindu refugees are to be accepted, the burden should be shared by the other states and not Assam which has already borne the brunt of cross-border influx.

In yet another editorial published within a month, on 19 July 2014, the paper said:

> The contention of the indigenous people has been that Assam should not be converted into a dumping ground for citizens from other nations.... If the Government of India does agree to waive the cut off dates in case of Hindus, it would do well to resettle these people in other states, for justice demands that Assam must not be made to bear the entire weight of the burden.

16. In his letter to Gopinath Bardoloi, chief minister of Assam, Nehru wrote in May 1949: 'Assam is getting a bad name for its narrow approach to the refugee problem. You say that there is no further land available in Assam.... If Assam adopts such a policy of incapacity to help solve the refugee problem, then *the claims of Assam for financial help would obviously suffer*' (emphasis mine). ('The Growing Hiatus: Tracing Some of the Early Causes', in Misra, *India's North East*, pp. 21–4.)

17. As the special officer given the responsibility of ascertaining the surplus land in the PGRs, S.P. Desai had submitted a report to the Saadulla gov-ernment in 1943 where he had stated that forcible occupation of graz-ing lands by the immigrants had already taken place on a large scale and this covered both tribal and Assamese areas. He concluded that there was no surplus land available for new settlements. But the Saadulla government ignored the report and went ahead with its policy of opening up the grazing reserves to the immigrants. Refer to Amalendu

Guha, *Planter Raj to Swaraj: Freedom Struggle and Electoral Politics in Assam 1826–1947* (New Delhi: ICHR, 1977), p. 281. Also see Rajendra Prasad, *India Divided*, (Bombay: Hind Kitabs, 1946), p. 247. Prasad quotes from S.P. Desai's report which, while referring to the state of the Assamese and tribal peasants, states:

> The Assam Land Revenue Regulation is, so far the immigrant encroachers are concerned, virtually non-existent. The immigrants openly claim to have short-circuited the local staff and officers.... Verily the cup of humiliation for the Assamese is full. They feel that the Government which is the custodian and trustee of their interests has failed them.'

Prasad refers to Desai as an 'experienced I.C.S. officer'. But Rajendra Prasad was also the author of a controversial scheme of settling Bihari Hindus in Assam so as to counter the immigration of people from Mymensingh. Refer to Rajendra Prasad, *Autobiography* (Bombay: Asia Publishing House, 1957), pp. 259–60 and also *India Divided*, pp. 246–8. For Amalendu Guha's comments, see *Planter Raj to Swaraj*, pp. 258–9.

18. *The Assam Tribune*, Guwahati, 2 June 1949 cited by Girin Phukan in *Assam's Attitude to Federalism* (New Delhi: Sterling, 1984), pp. 29–30.
19. 'Hindu Migrants', editorial, *The Assam Tribune*, 18 September 2015, Guwahati.
20. 'Dustbin', editorial, *Dainik Asom* (Assamese), Guwahati, 8 September 2015.
21. In both these identity movements, mainly Bengali Hindu immigrants, also generally known as 'refugees' owning land were targeted in different parts of the state. This was also true of the Assam Movement.
22. As many as forty-nine tribal belts and blocks in the state have been encroached upon. The newspaper *Dainik Janambhumi* (Assamese) of 14 January 2016 reported that on 15 September 2016 some 300–400 immigrants forcibly occupied more than 800 bighas of riverine land in circle no. 2 of the Hetow Chakra of Darrang district. This land was being cultivated for decades by Assamese farmers to raise winter crops. The newspaper quoted Supreme Court advocate Upamanyu Hazarika as saying that while states such as Manipur have passed legislation to defend indigenous interests in land, in Assam no such meaningful step has been taken. Refer to 'Aboidha Prabajankarik Prashasan, Arakshie Rakshanabakhan Dise' (Illegal Immigrants Being Protected by Administration and Police), *Dainik Janambhumi* (Assamese), 14 January 2016.
23. Assam Legislative Assembly Proceedings of March 1945.
24. The struggle for the restoration of the status of the Assamese language has a long history. In the immediate pre-Partition years, a certain section of the Bengali intelligentsia put forth the idea of a separate Purbachal Pradesh comprising Cachar and the hill districts of Assam. This move, along with

other moves, aimed at stalling the process of Assamese becoming the language spoken by the majority of the people of the Assam Valley, added to the Assamese–Bengali divide.

25. Refer to editorials on the topic in Assamese newspapers such as *Amar Asom* edited by Homen Borgohain.

26. The census of 2001 revealed that Assamese speakers had gone down by some 2 per cent from that of 1991 and constituted 48 per cent as against the 28 per cent of Bengali speakers. Assamese-speaking people made up 57.81 per cent of the state's population in 1991 but this percentage fell to 48.80 per cent in the 2001 Census. By contrast, the number of Bengali speakers grew from 21.67 per cent in 1991 to 24.54 per cent in 2001. During the 2001 Census, of the total population of 2,66,55,528, 1,30,10,478 persons were Assamese speakers and 73,43,338 were Bengali speakers. In the 1991 Census the total number of Assamese speakers was 1,29,58,088 (57.81 per cent) and the Bengali speakers was 48,56,532 (21.67 per cent). As per the 2011 Census, Assamese speakers (1,30,10,478) made up 41.74 per cent of the total population (3,11,69,272) whereas Bengali speakers (73,43,338) made up 23.5 per cent.

27. Clause 6 of the Assam Accord, referring to Assamese identity, reads: 'Constitutional, legislative and administrative safeguards, as may be appropriate shall be provided to protect, preserve and promote the cultural, social, linguistic identity and heritage of the Assamese people.'

28. Incidentally, the Bodos had actively participated during the initial stages of the Assam Movement (1979–85) with the hope that the interests of the indigenous people would eventually be safeguarded.

29. Initially, the Sabha, after quite some deliberation in the Sanmilita Sahitya Manch, decided that all those who had got Indian citizenship up to 25 March 1971 and all those whose mother tongue happened to be Assamese or any of the indigenous language of Assam were actually Assamese. Later, it clarified its position by stating that 'all Indian citizens who live in Assam and who speak Assamese language as the mother tongue or either [as] their second or third language, irrespective of their origin, ethnicity, caste or religion, are inseparable part of the greater Assamese society and hence, are Assamese'. Refer to 'It Is Govt. Duty to Define Assamese People: Sabha', by staff reporter, *The Assam Tribune*, Guwahati, 14 March 2015.

30. Refer to Chandan Kumar Sarmah, *Asomiya Kun?* (Assamese) (Guwahati: Span Publications Pvt. Ltd, 2006), pp. 74–6.

31. In March 2015, the speaker of the Assam Assembly put forward a definition of 'Assamese' as provided in the 1951 Census that stated that anyone speaking Assamese or tribal dialects plus Bengali in Cachar could be called

Assamese. This definition was strongly refuted by both the Congress and All India United Democratic Front members and the speaker's report could not go into the Assembly's proceedings. Refer to 'Ruckus in House over Speaker's Report', by staff reporter, *The Assam Tribune*, Guwahati, 1 April 2015.

32. Although there had been a demand from some quarters that the definition of 'Assamese people' be changed to 'people of Assam', the All Assam Students' Union has been consistently maintaining that the different ethnic communities of the state come under the inclusive term 'Assamese'. In this, it seems to have achieved some success, especially when several such ethnic bodies accepted the Speaker's definition. Refer to 'Replace "Assamese" with "Indigenous People": BSS', by staff reporter, in *The Assam Tribune*, 8 March 2015 and 'AASU, 26 Ethnic Bodies Meet Speaker', by staff reporter, *The Assam Tribune*, 22 March 2015.

33. The 1930 Line System Committee had described immigrants as 'persons coming from the districts of Bengal and the Surma Valley but not including tea garden coolies and ex-coolies'. Nirode Barooah, *Gopinath Bardoloi, 'The Assam Problem' and Nehru's Centre* (Guwahati: Bhabani Print and Publications, 2010), p. 44.

34. Ismail Hussain, *Aami Kidore Asomiya Halo?* (How Did We Become Assamese?) (Guwahati: Akhar Prakash, 2013), pp. 15–21.

35. Homen Borgohain, 'Asomar Na-Asamiya Musalman', in Hussain, *Aami Kidore Asomiya Halo?*, pp. 20–1.

36. 'Replace "Assamese" with "Indigenous People": BSS', by staff reporter, *The Assam Tribune*, 8 March 2015. By 'indigenous', the Bodo literary organization was referring to the indigenous tribes of Assam such as the Bodo, Mishing, Karbi, Rabha, Tiwa, and so on.

37. Though the question of a cut-off date to identify immigrant Muslims as foreigners has a long contentious history in the state, the Assam Accord fixed the cut-off date at March 1971. But given the time that has elapsed between the Accord (1975) and today, it would be totally utopian to try to identify foreigners on this basis. The dividing line seems to be increasingly drawn today between immigrants who have accepted Assamese as their mother tongue for all practical purposes and those who continue to speak Bengali. Successive presidents of the Asom Sahitya Sabha, the premier Assamese literary organization of the state, have maintained that the Assamese-speaking immigrant Muslims who have come from East Bengal/East Pakistan/Bangladesh and settled in the state and accepted its language are to be seen as Assamese.

38. Refer to 'Immigration and Identity Transformation in Assam', in Misra, *India's North East*, pp. 162–208.

39. This is borne out by the fact that as many as twenty-five ethnic organizations representing different communities joined hands with the All Assam Students' Union in March 2015 to demand reservations in local bodies, state assembly, and the parliament for 'indigenous and Indigenous Assamese' people. The ethnic bodies declared that the state 'has become vulnerable to the fundamentalist forces along with illegal infiltration'. Regarding the definition of the term 'Assamese', these organizations declared that all persons whose names figured in the NRC, prepared on the basis of the 1951 electoral rolls, belonging to any caste, community, religion or language, or tribes and their descendants would qualify to be called 'indigenous and indigenous Assamese'. Refer to 'Constitutional Safeguards: AASU, 26 Ethnic Bodies Meet Speaker', by staff reporter, *The Assam Tribune*, Guwahati, 22 March 2015, p. 10.

40. The All Assam Goria Moria Desi Jatiya Parishad is today the most representative body of the indigenous Assamese Muslim community. The Gorias, Morias, and the Desis are three indigenous Muslim groups who form the basis of the indigenous Assamese Muslim community. The Federation of Indigenous Muslims (FIMOA) is another body of the indigenous Assamese Muslims who are demanding reservations for their community as also control over *wakf* property (a religious endowment or property dedicated to society). Refer to Syed Miraz Ahmed, 'Indigenous Muslim Sit-in to Press Demands', *Assam Times*, 20 December 2013. Refer also to 'Strands of Belonging', an interview published in *The Hindu* of 11 March 2015 with Nazrul Haque and Malini Bhattacharya by Sangeeta Baruah Pisharoty.

41. The indigenous Assamese Muslim finds himself under increasing pressure from the immigrant neo-Assamese Muslim as well as from those who uphold the idea of a broader pan-Muslim brotherhood.

42. For a detailed discussion on this issue, refer to Udayon Misra, *The Periphery Strikes Back: Challenges to the Nation State in Assam and Nagaland* (Shimla: IIAS, 2000), pp. 182–7.

APPENDIX I

The Assam Gazette Extraordinary,
No. 33,
4 November 1939

Resolution on the Line System Committee's Report

Extracts from the proceedings of the Government of Assam in the Revenue Department, No. 5216-R, dated the 4th November 1939.

1. The report of the Line System Committee and criticisms on its recommendations have been under the careful consideration of the Government for some time past. Meanwhile the demand for early orders both from official and non-official quarters has grown in insistence. In view of the importance attached to the problem of regulating settlement of land by all communities inhabiting the Assam Valley, the present ministry have considered it fit to announce their general policy in the matter. That policy, it will be clear, is one of planned settlement in the interests of cultivators themselves and to protection of interests of the indigenous people, particularly the tribal and backward classes. Government trust that these objects will command general approval and that in carrying them out they will secure the co-operation of all classes and communities.

2. The question of land which has been reserved from settlement for definite purposes, such as village grazing grounds, professional graziers' reserves and the like, can be disposed of in a few words. These reserves are areas in which settlement is forbidden to all persons-immigrants or non-immigrants. All persons, therefore, in occupation of land within these reserves, shall be evicted.

3. Next comes the question of land available for settlement. The need of regulating settlement in the case of this kind of land arises from various causes. One of these is the fact that cultivable land is limited,

while the demand for land from the steady flow of immigrants and the natural increase of the provincial population is unlimited. The problem of landless people is already rearing its head up in certain parts of the province, and the Government believe that it will ease matters if settlement were limited strictly to actual cultivators and in proportion to their individual resources subject to the total area held by a cultivator's family not exceeding 30 bighas. Another, and, in a sense, a more important consideration which necessitates regulation of settlement is the need of giving protection to the less advanced people from the more advanced ones. This question in an extreme form is presented by the areas peopled predominantly by tribal classes or classes equally backward. Elsewhere it is mixed up inextricably with general considerations which go to make up for community of interests in human life such as language, culture and mode of life. With the assimilation of immigrants into the country of adoption and the advance of the indigenous communities living next to them, the problem will become gradually less acute. But the process of assimilation or advance is necessarily a slow one and it is during this period that precautions are necessary for preventing hardship or conflict and that restriction need at all be rigorous.

4. The restrictions constituting the so-called Line System which have been in existence in the province for over ten years were primarily intended against the unending flow of Bengal immigrant cultivators and took the form of constituting certain areas in which settlement of land with such immigrants was prohibited. Government agree with the Committee that in future the unit for such restriction or prohibition should, where possible, be larger. They consider that in the submontane areas it should be possible to constitute whole *mauzas* or compact parts of *mauzas* inhabited predominantly by backward and tribal classes into 'prohibited areas'. Elsewhere where the whole village or a larger compact area is predominantly peopled by backward or tribal classes such village or area may be constituted a 'prohibited area'. Within the prohibited areas so constituted immigrant cultivators shall not be allowed land either by settlement or by transfer of annual *pattas*, and any immigrant so taking up land or by squatting shall be evicted.

5. This policy will be given effect to also in the case of the immigrants who have encroached into or acquired land in areas which were hitherto prohibited areas constituted in the interests of the aforesaid tribal or backward classes. In other areas which were hitherto

constituted prohibited areas in the interests of indigenous people other than the tribal or backward classes, Government propose a relaxation, namely where the number of immigrant families in a village is substantial, i. e. 15 or more in number and the occupation dates from before 1st April 1937, or where any immigrant has been in bonafide occupation of the land for over 12 years before 1st April 1937 and has been paying or pays the revenue due in respect of the land for the period of occupation, such persons will not be disturbed in their present possession in the village provided they pay the premium fixed for the land; they shall however not be entitled to extend their possession in the prohibited area. Where, on the other hand, in a village the number of such families is less than 15 and the occupation or land is not of the type mentioned above or the other condition regarding payment of premium or revenue are not satisfied the immigrant shall be liable to eviction except in regard to periodically settled land, but will be given preference in the settlement of land available for immigrants elsewhere in the district or in the neighbouring district. In cases where valuable consideration has been proved to have passed from the immigrant to the previous settlement holders prior to 1st April 1937 in respect of land from which the immigrants are liable to be evicted under this orders, it will be open to the Deputy Commissioner concerned, after going into the merits of each case, to recommend to Government that premium should not be charged to the immigrants in respect of lands allotted to them elsewhere and that the transferors should be penalised by non-renewal of all their annual *pattas*.

6. Within the prohibited areas constituted or reconstituted after the issue of these orders settlement with indigenous persons other than those belonging to the tribal or backward classes in whose interests a particular prohibited area is constituted or reconstituted shall be allowed only to bonafide agriculturists for cultivation and of a quantity of land not exceeding 30 *bighas* in all per family. No *pattas* issued to such persons shall however be converted into periodic *pattas*. The transfer of an annual *patta* in such an area to an immigrant will entail the cancellation or the non-renewal of all the annual *pattas* held by the transferor in the village or its neighbourhood.

7. Outside the prohibited areas squatting shall be prohibited except where fluctuating cultivation prevails and the Deputy Commissioner considers that such cultivation should be allowed to

continue. Settlement will be on application, but the authority competent to grant settlement will be entitled to refuse settlement to an applicant who is not a bonafide cultivator or settlement with whom is likely to be contrary to local welfare.

8. For the purpose of the above orders the term 'immigrant' shall include any one who comes from outside the province for the purpose of taking up land for cultivation and does not include inhabitants of Sylhet and Cachar migrating into the Assam Valley. Government consider that bonafide cultivators from the Surma Valley are entitled to be treated on the same plane as indigenous cultivators. The term 'backward classes' includes scheduled classes.

9. It has been alleged that women who have married immigrants and have allowed their husbands to cultivate their lands have in some places been held to be liable to eviction. Government consider that such women must be left undisturbed in the enjoyment of the property that belonged to them and cannot be disturbed merely on the ground that their husbands are immigrant cultivators and are cultivating their lands.

S.P. DESAI
Secretary to the Government of Assam
Revenue Department

APPENDIX II

SAADULLA–BARDOLOI AGREEMENT*

After mutual discussion on the points raised in the letter dated 18th March 1945 from Messrs. G.N. Bardoloi and R.K. Chaudhuri To Honourable Sir Mohammad Saadulla, Premier of Assam, and his reply therein (contained in his letter dated 19-3-1945) it is agreed as follows:

I Restoration of Civil Liberties

(a) Two-thirds of the security prisoners now in jail should be released within April, 1945. All M.L.A.s and prominent Congressmen shall be released forthwith. The remaining security prisoners shall be released as early as possible but not later than June 1945.

(b) Convicted political shall also be released forthwith except those convicted for offences of grave and heinous nature such as sabotage, but their cases shall be reviewed and released after examination of their cases on merit.

(c) Ban on public meetings, assemblies and processions etc. shall be forthwith withdrawn from all places except areas and Sadar subdivision of Lakhimpur District. But there will l be no such ban in Dibrugarh town and Khowang area on the south bank and Sisi Dhemaji mauzas on the North Bank of the subdivision. There shall however be no ban anywhere against such meetings, assemblies and processions held in connection with elections to local bodies and legislatures.

(d) Ban, if any, against Congress Committees in the province shall be withdrawn.

(e) All restriction orders on M.L.A.s shall be forthwith withdrawn (so also in cases of all other political except in a few cases requiring scrutiny).

II Procurement and Supply

The policy of the Government in this matter shall be reviewed and revised with a view to provide adequate supplies to the people, remove corruption and to secure more popular support and co-operation.

III Land Settlement

(a) The policy of land settlement embodied in the Government Resolution of 15th January, 1945 will be modified as follows:
      Paragraph 8 of the Resolution shall be substituted by the following:

In order to raise the standard of living of our cultivating classes, the government shall provide on application for land in the planned settlement an economic holding which shall be at least 20 (twenty) bighas for an applicant of a family of five persons or less. In no case shall a family or an applicant get more than 30 (thirty) bighas.

Para 4 shall be deleted.

(b) In explanation of Paras 3 and 15 of the aforesaid Resolution provisions shall be inserted for the purpose of creation of tribal blocks side by side with blocks meant for other communities in planned settlement areas where the tribal people have their villages and homes.

(c) The last sentence in para 15 of the resolution shall be deleted.

(d) Paragraph 18 (c) shall be re-written as follows:

Subject no (a) and (b) above, the Professional Grazing Reserves shall be kept intact, and the Deputy Commissioners will be directed to see that they are kept free of encroachment by eviction of trespassers, past, present and future. But individual cases of hardship arising out of the policy of such eviction shall be reported to Government for decision.

(e) In order to carry out the Government policy thus revised and the spirit of the memorandum submitted by leaders of parties, the consent of the leader of the Congress and the Nationalist Coalition

Party will be taken in the selection of the Member in charge of the Revenue portfolio.

IV Local Board Constituencies Seats

The reconstituted Cabinet shall have the option of re-opening the question of distribution of seats with a view to allay widespread criticism against it.

V Reconstitution of the Cabinet

(a) The present Cabinet will resign on the 23rd of March 1945 and will be reconstituted by Sir Muhammad Saadulla so that the members of the Cabinet may take their seats in the House on the 24th March 1945 before prorogation.

(b) The Cabinet shall be reconstituted in the following manner:

   (i) Five Muslims including the Premier to be selected by the Muslim members of Sir Muhammad Saadulla's Party.

   (ii) Five non-Muslims by the opposition in the following manner:

   (1) 3 Caste Hindus

   (2) 1 Plains Tribal

   (3) 1 Scheduled Caste

   In selecting (2) opinion of the group shall prevail.

   The Scheduled Caste representative will be taken from the members of the community either by selection or by election under the supervision of the opposition.

   (iii) We wish that the Hills tribal and Indian Christians are represented by a seat in the Cabinet to be selected by them, if an 11th seat is available.

Shillong   Sd—Syed Muhammad Saadulla
22/3/45   Gopinath Bardoloi
                   Rohini Kumar Chaudhuri

Note

* S.M. Saadulla Papers, Sub-File 7, Nehru Memorial Museum and Library, New Delhi.

APPENDIX III

SYED SAADULLA'S LETTER TO
LIAQUAT ALI KHAN*

Shillong
The 25th March, 1945.

My dear Nawabzada Liaquat Ali Khan Saheb,

You may have read in the press or heard on the radio about the political development in Assam recently. I want to apprise you of the full details of the situation and also to secure advice on one point. These political events must be studied in their proper background which I detail as under:

Assam Legislative Assembly consists of 108 members of whom only 34 are Moslems. Unfortunately, 4 Moslems cast their lot with the opposition since 1938. Three of them were members of the Congress Coalition Cabinet which ruled the Province for 13 months in 1938–39. I have been running the Ministry with the support of other non-Moslem smaller groups which formed the Coalition called 'Assam United Party'. In this group were 2 Caste Hindus, 2 Scheduled Hindus, 5 Plains Tribals (hill people settled in the Plains for centuries who have been allotted separate seats under the Constitution), 4 Hill Tribals, 3 representatives of Labour, one Indian Christian and one from the women constituency. The Europeans, a group of nine, generally supported me. All told, I could count on the support of 57 members while 54 gave a bare majority in the House. You must, therefore appreciate that the majority is extremely tenuous and the defection of one or two spells disaster for the Ministry.

During this Budget Session starting from the 1 st March, for some reason or other, there was a large number of absentees in the House from my group. Unfortunately, there is hardly much party discipline among the Moslems. One Moslem of my party actually sat with the Opposition without giving any reason or even resigning from my group. This emboldened one of the hill representatives of my party to vote also with the Opposition on a crucial division on 17th March on the vital land settlement policy. We narrowly escaped from a defeat as the voting was 39 for Government against 38 of the Opposition. On the same day, on another cut motion, one Moslem member remained neutral while we averted a disaster by the good offices of the European Group who brought down to the Assembly Chamber one of their members from sick bed in hospital. This time there was a tie of 39 against 39, the Speaker giving his casting vote for the Government. I was so dissatisfied with the conduct of our Moslem members that I was on the point of resigning from the Ministry. For some reason which I cannot fathom, the Leader of the Congress Opposition, whose strength is 32, and the Leader of the Nationalist Independent Group with a following of 17, who always voted against the Government, started parleying with me to form a stable government. The Congress proposal was to give me full support, although not coming into the Cabinet themselves, if I took three Hindu Ministers from amongst the Nationalist Independents. I consulted my party, the Assam United Party, who by three fourths majority, gave me a mandate to grasp the hand of co-operation extended by the Opposition. After mature deliberation and prolonged discussion and also with the full approval of my party, I have now re-formed the Ministry yesterday. In these negotiations I have been more than able to safeguard the interest of the Moslem community and never have deviated from the creed and policy of the Moslem League. The following tabular form will give you at a glance the position of my previous Cabinet and the present one:

	Previous	Present
Moslems (including myself)	5	5
Caste Hindus	2	3
Scheduled Hindus	1	1
Plains Tribal	1	1
Hills Tribal	1	nil
	10	10

In the present Cabinet all the previous 5 Moslem and the Plains Tribal Ministers have found place. The Scheduled Hindu members have changed their representatives in the Cabinet—but the new one was a member in my 1937–38 Cabinet and later on, of the Congress Coalition Government.

Since 1937 I was giving the hills people a seat in the Cabinet, as they have 6 members—from the hills—including the Woman seat of Shillong. There are two Indian Christians amongst my party. I used to take these 8 members as a unit and took one of their members in the Cabinet. In order to give three seats in my present Cabinet to the Caste Hindus which they more than deserve on the ground of the size of their number, having 41 seats in the legislature, I had to drop the seat for the representative of the hill tribes from the Cabinet. From 1939 this representative was Miss Mavis Dunn, B.A., B.L., B.T., a highly qualified and the only lady member in the Assembly. Both the opposition leaders have felt that the non-inclusion of the hill representative in the Cabinet has been an injustice done to that group, and have recommended to increase the number of seats in the Cabinet from 10 to 11 to enable me to take a Minister from the hills group. The Moslem strength in the Cabinet from 1939 has been 50 per cent, but the percentage will be reduced a little if I include a hill representative in the Cabinet. I have every hope, if this lady is again selected by her group and the two Christians, she will always be siding with me and the Moslems, and the practical effect of her inclusion in the Cabinet will really strengthen the position of the Moslem Ministers. I would, therefore, request you to get permission from the Quaid-e-Azam Mr. Jinnah to increase the number of Ministers to 11. This group, barring one member, has been steadfast in its support to me. If I fail them now, I am afraid, they will lose their faith in me as not safeguarding the group's interests. This will be harmful to the Moslem interests in future. A reply by wire is solicited on this point.

You may have been perturbed at the Press report about the land settlement policy of my Government. Rest assured, the Government Resolution on the subject which was published on 15th January 1945 represents the maximum measure of concession obtained from the Hindus and the Plains Tribal people. In my opinion as well as in the opinion of my supporters, barring 9 members, this is the best that could be got from the Hindus. It is no use devising greater concession for which I could not obtain sanction of the Legislature. I can assure all the Moslem Leaguers that the interests of the Moslem immigrants into Assam are safe in my hands and settlement with them is going apace. In the 4 lower districts of the Assam Valley these Bengali immigrant Moslems have quadrupled the Moslem population during the last 20 years.

Yours sincerely,
S.M. Saadulla
Nawabzada Liaquat Ali Khan,
Guli Rana, 15, Hardinge Avenue, New Delhi.

Note

* S.M. Saadulla Papers, Sub-File 7, Nehru Memorial Museum and Library, New Delhi.

APPENDIX IV

A

NOTE

ON

Assam's Stand

vis a vis
British Government Statement
of
6th. December, 1946.

BEING

AN APPEAL

To

Congress Working Committee, Members of All
India Congress Committee and Members
of the Constituent Assembly

Published by the Publicity Department of the
Assam Provincial Congress Committee
Printed at New Press, Gauhati—Assam
by S.R. Bez.

Contents

APPEAL.

On the very day of announcement by the British Cabinet Mission of their Statement of May 16, 1946, the Assam P. C. C., which was in session at Gauhati, sent a telegraphic message to the Congress Working Committee in session in New Delhi, intimating the universal feeling of apprehension of the people of Assam, and lodging emphatic protest against the Grouping Scheme clauses in the State Paper and Shri G. N. Bardoloi, who was then in New Delhi, was also instructed telegraphically to meet Congress Working Committee and represent Assam's case and acquaint the Committee with Assam's strong opposition and her refusal to accept the Grouping Plan.

Accordingly, Shri G. N. Bardoloi met Congress Working Committee and submitted a Memorandum on 19th May, 1946. On June 10, 1946, the Assam Congress Delegation headed by M. Tayyebulla, President A. P. C. C., met the Congress Working Committee at New Delhi where Mahatma Gandhi was also present, and submitted a Memorandum and urged upon Congress Working Committee to lend full support to Assam in her decision not to accept under any circumstances whatsoever, the provision of decision by simple majority of votes in Section 'C' in the matter of settling her constitution. Maulana Abul Kalam Azad, the then Congress President, gave on behalf of the Congress Working Committee, full assurance of support and also conveyed through the Assam Delegation a message of sympathy and support to the people of

Assam. This allayed, for the time being, to a great extent the anxiety of the people of the province.

In July, the Assam Legislative Assembly elected Assam's ten representatives to the Constituent Assembly including the three Muslim League members and gave a clear Mandate in a Resolution which was passed without division not to go into Section and accept the Group Plan of H. M.G. State Paper.

On September 25, 1946, the Assam P. C. C. President M. Tayyebulla and the A. I. C. C. Members of Assam met Mahatmaji and other Congress leaders at New Delhi during the A. I. C. C session and obtained farther [sic] assurances of strong support to Assam. Mahatmaji advised on the very line of his recently published Srirampur Note on 17th December, 1946, wherein he advised Assam not to go into the Section if full assurance is not given by the Congress (Vide Annexure III).

But H. M. G Statement of December 6, 1946, which now seeks to alter and add to the 16th May State Paper fundamentally, has given a rude shock to the people of India in general and to the people of Assam in particular, by its interpretation of the Grouping Clause and thereby raised a deep universal feeling of alarm and resentment in the province. Assam finds herself in grave peril,— facing a crisis indeed.

On December 9, 1946, Shri G. N. Bardoloi on behalf of the Assam Members of the Constituent Assembly, submitted a Memorandum to the Congress Working Committee in regard to the stand of Assam vis-a-vis H.M.G. Statement of December 6, and represented Assam's case fully. (Vide Annexure I).

On December 10, 1946, President A. P. C. C. sent a telegraphic message to Congress President and the Members of the Working Committee and Mahatma Gandhi (at Srirampur) conveying Assam's decision not to accept under any circumstances whatsoever to submit to simple majority vote in Section C for the settlement of Assam's constitution as contemplated in the recent H.M.G. Statement and asked for assurances of support. (Vide Annexure II).

On December 17, Shri Bejoychandra Bhagavati Secretary Assam P. C. C. and Shri Mahendra Mohan Choudhury, Secretary Assam Congress Parliamentary Party, were deputed to meet Mahatma Gandhi at Srirampur and seek his advice. Mahatmaji handed over to them a Note giving his advice, which was published in the Press on December 23, 1946. (Vide Annexure III).

Shri G. N. Bardoloi and prominent Assam Constituent Assembly Members thereupon met the Congress Working Committee at New Delhi and acquainted them of the new position of Assam and Gandhiji's advice in the matter of Grouping and Section.

On return from New Delhi, Shri G N. Bardoloi made a full statement before the Provincial Congress Working Committee on Dec. 26, 1946, regarding the position of Assam obtaining in the counsels of the Congress Working Committee and Constituent Assembly. The Working Committee thereupon having reviewed the whole matter adopted a Statement which will speak for itself. (Vide Annexure V).

To place the decision and point of view of the Assam P.C. Working Committee contained in Statement, Deputation was appointed to meet the Congress Working Committee at New Delhi during the A. I. C. C. session as well as to meet A. I. C. C. members and others and make all possible efforts to obtaining the fullest support and a final decision of the A.I. C.C. in the full satisfaction of the people of Assam.

The question of Assam, and of N.W.F.P. and the Sikhs, vis-a-vis Grouping and Section is today a vital issue of All India importance before the Indian National Congress and the whole country. The A.P. C.C., therefore, appeal to the Congress Working Committee, members of the A.I.C.C. and the Members of the Constituent Assembly to lend their fullest support to the Just and righteous cause of Assam in their hour of grave crisis in her national life when her very existence is in peril.

Published by Shri Siddhinath Sarma, General Secretary, ASSAM PROVINCIAL CONGRESS COMMITTEE.

To

THE PRESIDENT, INDIAN NATIONAL
CONGRESS, NEW DELHI.
New Delhi, 9th. December, 1946.

Dear Friend,

On account of the recent statement of the British Cabinet with reference to Sections and Groupings, and the method of work therein, we the members of the Constituent Assembly from Assam elected, according to Congress directions deem it our duty, to make the following observations in order to emphasise the attitude which we have been all taking on these very important questions:

1. It may be recalled that soon after the Cabinet Mission's proposals of 16th May, 1946 was published, Srijut Gopinath Bardoloi submitted a memorandum to the Congress Working Committee on the 19th May, criticising the proposals not only on account of their falling far short of the Congress claim that the Constituent Assembly was the sovereign authority, but also how they would perniciously affect the province of Assam. What interpretation HMG give today was visualised in that memorandum and the fact that Assam shall be forced to enter into Group 'C', that her constitution be framed by the majority of members sitting in the Section and that there would be no room, for revision of the Constitution as framed by the Section, was clearly pointed out. On the 10th June a Deputation from the Assam Provincial Congress Committee which was led by the President himself waited upon the members of the Working Committee with another memorandum which stressed on the evils of the Cabinet Mission's proposals, in almost identical terms. On both these occasions President Maulana Azad and the members of the Working Committee were pleased to assure both Sjt. Bardoloi, the leader of the Congress Assembly party as well as the deputationists of the Assam Provincial Congress Committee that the case of Assam would receive proper consideration at the hands of the W.C. and that necessary direction would be given for action to be taken by the Legislative Assembly in this behalf.

2. While Sjt. Bardoloi was here he requested the W.C. to give him a draft of a resolution to be moved in the Assam Legislative Assembly

determining what attitude the elected members of the Constituent Assembly should adopt regarding the whole question. Such a resolution could not be handed over to Sjt. Bardoloi at that time but a resolution drafted by a member of the W.C. was sent to President Maulana Azad for approval with a letter through a special messenger. After going through the draft Maulana Sahib replied to the above letter on the following lines: 'The present problem is only concerned with Groupings and you already know the decision of the W.C. about it. You should therefore bring a motion in the light of the above decision. The wording of which may be formulated by the Board mentioned above (Selection Board of Constituent Assembly members).'

Accordingly the Board adopted the draft resolution with slight modification and that resolution was adopted in the House without any division. It will be seen that the main points stressed therein are:

(i) That the representatives elected by the Assam Assembly alone shall frame and settle the constitution of Assam in a meeting or meetings in which only they i.e, the representatives elected by the Assam Legislative Assembly to the Constituent Assembly shall take part.

(ii) That the said representatives shall not take part in any meeting or meetings of any Section or Group of provinces for the purpose of settling the Constitution for the province of Assam.

(iii) That the said representatives shall resist all or any attempt made to set up a Group Constitution for the settlement of questions relating to any subject or subjects in which the Province of Assam is interested or concerned being dealt with by any such group of Provinces on the basis of majority of votes.

On 22nd July, 1946 Pandit Jawaharlal Nehru who became the President of the Congress in the meanwhile wrote to Sri Bardoloi that you should not boycott the section which he said from a cursory reading of the Resolution passed by the Assam Legislative Assembly regarding Grouping, that there was some confusion in the resolution regarding Section and Grouping. He added 'That a Section may definitely decide not to form any Group and yet may continue as a Section to consider

Provincial Constitution. Thus making the provincial constitution representatives of the province need not be out voted by Others.' In reply to this it was pointed out to him by Sjt. Bardoloi that all that was meant in the resolution was that the provinces should be allowed, to function as a unit in the Sections and that the Section should not be made to consist of so many members from the provinces. He pointed out that the provincial constitution must be framed by the province in question alone. On the Broadcast speech which given by Pandit Jawaharlal Nehru after his assumption of the Office as the Head of the Interim Government defining his Govt's attitude towards Sections and Groupings, it was further pointed to him by Sjt. Bardoloi that his declaration for going into Sections without at the same time making any reference to the method of discussion in the section created great confusion in the minds of the people of Assam. To that letter he was pleased to reply on 27th September 1946 as follows:

> I fully appreciate the feeling in Assam in regard to Sections or Grouping. I think that our position safeguards your sentiments completely. Having accepted the document of May 16th we have inevitably to accept going into Sections, but the question arises as to how we shall function in these Sections. You are right in saying that I did not go into this matter in my broadcast because I did not wish to raise controversial issues there. But our position is clear that Provincial autonomy must be maintained and, a province must decide both about Grouping and about its own constitution. It is true that we have accepted the Federal Court's decision in regard to interpretation and we must abide by that decision of ours. But in no event are we going to agree to a Province like Assam being forced against its will to do anything.

It is possibly not necessary for us to mention here that the Working Committee in their sitting both in July and August had made it unequivocally clear that provinces would frame their own constitution and shall be free to go to Group Constitution or not as they liked.

H. M. G. have now given a completely different interpretation from what the Congress Working Committee gave and on the basis of which they held out assurances to the people of Assam. If H. M. G.'s proposals are to be accepted both our constitution as well as Grouping will be determined by the majority of the Constituent Assembly members sitting in Group' C ', with the inevitable result that we shall be thrown entirely at the mercy of the Muslim League both for our provincial constitution as well as our Grouping. With this perspective of a Section before us we, the members of the Constituent Assembly from Assam, can have but only one decision; and, that is that we refuse to go to that Section. We feel that our position is being rendered still worse by the attitude of the Working Committee in agreeing to accept the decision of the Federal Court in all matters of controversy between the Congress and the Muslim League. H.M.G. have already announced that their latest interpretation of the Statement of 16th May, was based on the best legal advice and that it was the essential part of their Scheme. We cannot in these circumstances think that there is any scope for the decision of the Federal Court.

Moreover, the mandate of the Assam Assembly leaves us no room for acting in any other way than to refuse to go to Section.

It seems quite clear to us:

(1) That under no circumstances could the Working Committee agree to the interpretation which has been put to Section 19(5) & (6).

(2) That their previous decision to abide by the arbitration of the Federal Court cannot hold good under the existing altered circumstances.

(3) That in view of the British Government's attitude of trying to impose condition upon the Constituent Assembly according to their sweet will, the Constituent Assembly should declare itself as a Sovereign Body and should proceed to frame the constitution according to their old view point not only in reference to Sections and Grouping but on all other matters.

We shall be grateful to be informed about the decision of the Working Committee.

Yours sincerely,
Sd/- Gopinath Bordalai and others.

ANNEXURE II.

1. Congress President Kripalani.
2. Vice-President Nehru Interim Govt.
3. Sardar Patel.
4. Dr. Rajendra Prasad.
5. Chairman Constituent Assembly.
6. Gopinath Bardoloi Member Assembly
7. Bejoychandra Bhagavati Secretary, Assam Congress Care Gopinath Bardoloi.
8. Mahatma Gandhi, New-Delhi.

Assam can under no circumstances accept British Government interpretation section deciding matters by simple majority votes or federal court decision as biding on Assam's grouping with Bengal.

Assam shall resist any forcible compulsory imposition of constitution notwithstanding approval by Muslim League as against all canons of democracy self-determination. Assam's case special and peculiar. Assembly July resolution Assam Congress directive mandate must stand Assam must be left free to settle own constitution in Sovereign Constituent Assembly pray help Assam in gravest peril by advising and permitting members never to accept section C majority decision or any federal court decision of compulsory grouping wire assurances allaying universal deep feelings.

President Tayyebulla
Secretary Siddhisarmah
Assam Congress.

ANNEXURE III.

GANDHI'S ADVICE TO ASSAM

Two Assam friends Sri Bijoy Chandra Bhagabati and Shri Mohendra Mohan Chaudhury saw Gandhiji on the morning of 5.12.46 on behalf of Shri Bardoloi. They asked him what Assam was to do with regard to the question of Grouping. It was question of life and death for Assam. They did not wish to be grouped with Bengal. Some people told them that they would be helping the League if they stay out. Assam could not be allowed to stand in the way of the progress of the rest of India and so on. They had asked the Working Committee. There did not seem to be any clear guidance from them. So they had come to him for advice. In reply GANDHIJI SAID: 'I DO NOT NEED A SINGLE MINUTE TO COME TO A DECISION FOR ON THIS I HAVE A MIND. I AM A CONGRESSMAN TO THE VERY MARROW, AS I A MAIINLY THE FRAMER OF THE CONSTITUTION OF THE CONGRESS AS IT STANDS TODAY. I TOLD BARDOLOI THAT IF THERE IS NO CLEAR GUIDANCE FROM THE CONGRESS WORKING COMMITTEE ASSAM SHOULD NOT GO INTO THE SECTIONS. IT SHOULD LODGE ITS PROTEST AND RETIRE FROM THE CONSTITUENT ASSEMBLY. IT WILL BE A KIND OF SATYA-GRAHA AGAINST THE CONGRESS FOR THE GOOD OF THE CONGRESS.

Rightly or wrongly the Congress has come to the decision that it will stand by the judgment of the Federal Court. The dice are heavily loaded. The decision of the Federal Court will go against the Congress interpretation of grouping as far as I can make out for the simple reason that the Cabinet has got legal advice which upholds their decision. The Federal Court is the creation of the British. It is a packed court. To be consistent the Congress must abide by it whatever it may be. If Assam keeps quiet it is finished. No one can force Assam to do what it does not want to do. It must stand independently as an autonomous unit. It is autonomous to a large extent today. It must become fully indepen-dent and autonomous. Whether you have that courage grit and the gumption I do not know. You alone can say that. But if you can make that declaration it will be a fine thing. As soon as the time comes for the Constituent Assembly to go into sections you will say "Gentlemen, Assam retires". For the independence of India it is the only condition. Each Unit must be able to decide and act for itself. I am hoping that in this, Assam will lead the way. I have the same advice for the Sikhs. But your position is much happier than that of the Sikhs. You are a whole province. They are a community inside a province. But I feel every individual has the right to act for himself, just as I have.'

Q. But we are told that the framing of the constitution for the whole of India cannot be held up for the sake of Assam. Assam cannot be allowed to block the way.

A. There is no need to do that. That is why I say I am in utter darkness. Why are not these simple truths evident to all after so many years? If Assam retires it does not block but leads the way if to India's independence.

Q. The League has said that the Constitution framed by the Constituent Assembly cannot be imposed on unwilling Units. So if some parts do not accept it, the British Parliament won't accept it.

Gandhiji flared up at this question. 'Who is the British Government? If we think independence is going to descend on our heads from England or somewhere, we are greatly mistaken. It won't be independence we will be crushed to atoms. We are fluctuating between independence and helpless dependents. The Cabinet Mission's Plan lies in between. If we act rightly there will be the full blown flower of independence. If we react wrongly the blossom withers away. Mind you, the League standpoint is quite correct. If they stand out the Constituent Assembly cannot impose its Constitution on an unwilling party. The British Government has not say in the matter one way or another.

The British cannot interfere with the working of the Constituent Assembly. Supposing the vast majority including the Muslims and others from a constitution, you can defy the British Parliament if it seeks to interfere. Power is in your hands. Some such thing happened in Ireland only recently. And De-Valera is no non-violent fighter. The position of India is far better than that of Ireland. If we have not the penetration we will lose the advantage we have as it is apparently being lost to-day.

If Assam takes care of itself the rest of India will be able to look after itself. What have you got to do with the constitution of the Union Government. You should form your own constitution. That is enough. You have the basis of a constitution all right even now.

I have never despised the 1935 constitution. It is based on provincial autonomy. It has the capacity for fullest growth, provided the people are worth it. The hill people are with you. Many Muslims are also with you. The remainder can be too, if you act on the square.

You will have to forget petty jealousies and rivalries and overcome your weaknesses. Assam has many weaknesses as it has much strength for I know my Assam.'

'With your blessings we can even go outside the Congress and fight', the friends put it.

Gandhi replied that in 1939 when there was the question of giving up the Ministry, 'Subhash Babu opposed it as he thought Assam's was special case. I told Bardoloi that there was much in what Subhash Babu had said and although I was the author of that scheme of boycott I said Assam should not come out if it did not feel like it. But Assam did come out. It was wrong.'

The friends said 'Maulana Sahib had then said that exception could not be made in the case of Assam'.

Gandhiji said, 'Here there is no question of exception, Assam rebelled, and that civilly. But we have that slavish mentality. We look to the Congress and then feel that if we do not follow it slavishly something will go wrong with it. I have said that not only a province but even an individual can rebel against the Congress and by doing so save it assuming that he is on the right. I have done so myself. Congress has not attained the present stature without much travail. I remember in 1918 there was the provincial conference of the Congress workers of Gujarat at Ahmedabad. The late Abbas Tyabji Sahab was in the chair. Ali brothers had not joined hands with me fully as they did later on. The late Shri Patel was there, and I moved the non-cooperation resolution. I was non-entity then. A constitutional question arose. Could a provincial conference anticipate the decision of the Congress? I said "Yes". A provincial conference and even a single individual could anticipate the Congress for its own benefit. In spite of opposition of old hands, the resolution was carried. That paved the way for the Congress to pass a similar resolution at Calcutta. India was dumbfounded at the audacity of a provincial conference passing the resolution.

We had formed a Satyagraha Sabha outside the Congress. It was joined by Horiman, Sarojini Devi, Sankarlal, Umar Sobhani, Vallabhbhai the mischief making Sarder. I was ill. The Rowlatt Act was passed. I shook with rage. I said to the Sardar I could do nothing unless he helped me. Sardar was willing. And the rest you know. I was rebellion but a healthy one. We celebrate the 6th of April, to the 13th. You have all these historical instances before.

I have given you all this time to steel your hearts, to give you courage. If you do not act correctly and now, Assam will be finished. Tell Bardoloi I do not want Assam to lose its soul. It must uphold it against the whole world. Else I will say that Assam had only manikins and no men. It is an impertinent suggestion that Bengal should dominate Assam in any way.'

The friend asked if they could tell the people that they have rebelled against the Congress with Gandhiji's blessings.

'Talk of God's blessings', said Gandhi, 'They are much richer. Tell the people even if Gandhi tries to dissuade us, we won't listen.'

ANNEXURE IV.

Resolution of the Assam Legislative Assembly. July 16, 1946

THE RESOLUTION.

Premier Bardoloi then moved the following motion:

Whereas this Assembly after a very careful consideration of the statement made by the British Cabinet delegation and the Viceroy on May 16 last is of opinion that the province of Assam has an undoubted claim to have the constitution of the province framed and settled by its own representatives, elected to the Constituent Assembly, and that it will be detrimental to the interests of the province of Assam to form any section or sections or group or groups with any other province of British India for the purpose of settling the constitution for the province of Assam, and

'Whereas this Assembly is of opinion that no group constitution should be set up for any group of provinces including therein the province of Assam and that no provincial subjects in which the province of Assam is interested or concerned should be dealt with by any such section or group of provinces, this Assembly directs its ten representatives elected by it as laid down in the said statement of May 16 last to act in the manner as set forth:-

'That the said representatives shall frame and settle a constitution for the province of Assam at a meeting or meetings at which only they, that is, the representatives elected for the Constituent Assembly, by the Assam Legislative Assembly shall take part.

'That the said representatives shall not take part in any meeting or meetings of any section or group of provinces for the purpose of settling the constitution for the province of Assam:

'That the said representatives shall resist all or any attempt made to set up a group constitution for the settlement of questions relating to any subject or subjects in which the province of Assam is interested or concerned or for any such questions being dealt with by any such group of provinces on the basis of majority of votes and;

'That the said representatives shall take part in the meeting of the Constituent Assembly for the purpose of framing and settling the Union Constitution and in all matters relating to the Union Constitution.'

ANNEXURE V.

Statement of Assam Provincial Working Committee 26 Dec 1946.

Read Memorandum submitted to the Congress Working Committee at New Delhi by Shri G. N. Bardoloi on 9th December '46 and Assam P. C. C. President's telegrams to Congress President and certain members of the Congress Working Committee and Mahatma Gandhi, dated 10 December '46, also Shri G.N Bardoloi's letter, dated New Delhi, December 10, 1946 to Mahatmaji; and Mahatmaji's directions given in his letter sent through Shri Bijoy Chandra Bhagabati, M.L.A., Secretary Assam P.C.C. and Shri Mohendra Mohan Chaudhuri, M.L.A., Secretary of Assam Congress Parliamentary Party, who met Gandhiji at Srirampur (Bengal) on, 17 December 1946.

Heard Shri. G. N. Bardoloi, who upon his return from New Delhi today made a statement before the Assam P.C. Working Committee about Constituent Assembly and Congress Working Committee, with special reference to the matter of Section and Grouping.

The Working Committee of Assam P. C. C. hereby endorses the aforesaid telegrams of President Assam P. C. C. and Bardoloi's Memorandum to the Congress Working Committee.

The Working Committee, Assam P. C. C. appreciate the stand taken by the Congress Working Committee in maintaining 'the interpretation of British Government in regard to the method of voting in the section is not in conformity with provincial autonomy, which is one of the fundamental base of the Scheme proposed in the Statement of May 16'. The Committee, however, feel that the Statement of Congress Working Committee of 23 December, 1946, is not enough to assure the province of Assam of sufficient safeguards against the repugnant declaration of H. M. G. statement of 6 December, 1946, seeking to determine, provincial Constitution, as well as group Constitution, by simple majority of votes of the provinces sitting together in a Section: The Committee are of opinion that the recent interpretation of the British Government on this subject, has not only gone beyond the Statement of May 16, to the detriment of the provinces like N.W. F. P. and Assam, but it is also against the assurances and safeguard given to the Sikhs for their protection. Assam can, under no circumstances, accept the interpretation of

H. M. G. Statement of December 6. Assam must be left free to settle her own constitution in sovereign Constituent Assembly.

The W. C. of the Assam P. C. C. is of the considered opinion that, so far as the province of Assam is concerned, Assam's entry into the Section in the existing circumstances will be suicidal. In terms of the statement of H. M. G., Assam decides to go into the Section, she cannot by the dissociation of her Constituent Assembly members except the Muslim League group, from section C, claim to be unrepresented and thereby avoid a constitution imposed on her.

The Committee is further of opinion that if the Working Committee cannot give assurance of protection to these provinces and to the Sikh Minority, they should carry on the work of the Constituent Assembly regarded, as a sovereign body, in accordance with its own interpretations and in complete disregard of the HMG statement of 6 December.

The Assam P. C. Working Committee's decision to stay out of the Section is determined by the general principle of self-determination, autonomy for the provinces and fundamental, principles of democracy, for which the Congress stands; while conceding to the Muslim League demand for framing a provincial constitution, or a group Constitution, by the strength of simple majority of votes of other provinces in the Section, is nothing but concession to coercion and force.

The Committee, therefore, strongly urge the Congress Working Committee and the A. I. C. C. to give clear and unequivocal direction to the provinces aforesaid and give full assurances of protection to the minorities. The Committee accordingly requests the Congress President and the A. I. C. C. to issue special directions to Assam in this behalf.

This W. C. hereby deputes the President, Assam P. C. C., the Assam A. I. C. C members and Sjts. D. Sarmah, B. Bhagawati, Secy, A.P. C. C. and O. K. Das to meet the Working Committee in this behalf; and Sjts. G. N. Bardoloi and S. N. Sarma, General Secy, A. P. C. C to acquaint Mahatma Gandhi at Srirampur with the present position of this province in reference to the recent British Govt's Statement.

APPENDIX V

SYED SAADULLA'S LETTER TO MOHAMMAD ALI JINNAH*

Shillong

The 10th April, 1947

My dear Quaid-e-Azam,

Mr Abdul Matin Chaudhury who is going to attend the meeting of the Central Committee of Action at Delhi on the 20th of April, has requested me to send you a short note on the present political situation in Assam.

The position is hopeless from any point of view. On the 19th February, a meeting of the Council of the Provincial Muslim League was convened in a sub-divisional headquarter of the Sylhet district where a Committee of Action was created who were authorized to devise ways and means to counteract the eviction policy of the Congress Government. I was nominated a member in my absence without my consent. It is alleged that the President of the Provincial Muslim League verbally told the members on the 19th February, that the meeting of the Committee of Action will be held at Dhubri on 2nd March. That is probably the reason no notice was sent to me of this meeting on the 2nd of March though I was not present at Maulivibazar where the Council meeting was held. Only three out of nine members of the Committee of Action were present at Dhubri where the Committee of Action is supposed to have clothed the President of the Provincial Muslim League with dictatorial powers. One member of the Committee of Action who was present at Dhubri on the day—an M.L.A.—asserts that there was no meeting of the Committee of Action at Dhubri. The President convened a meeting of the Working Committee of the Provincial Muslim League to be held at Nowgong on the 9th March, 1947. Three M.L.A.s out of twelve members of the Parliamentary Party who are members of the Working Committee, attended this meeting at Nowgong on the 9th where a civil disobedience movement for Assam to be launched by the Muslim League was decided upon. On the 10th March, The President, Maulana Abdul Hamid Khan, started civil disobedience at Tezpur and courted arrest. A list of 52 members were drawn up by the President at Nowgong which would offer civil disobedience at Tezpur on successive dates.

Thus it will be apparent that the Working Committee declared civil disobedience on the 9th March, without taking any steps to prepare the country for such a move. They took no approval for their scheme from the Central Committee of Action as is necessary under the Muslim League Constitution. The civil disobedience movement thus launched was against the eviction policy of the Congress Government which they have adopted since February, 1946.

The Parliamentary Party, consisting of 31 Muslim League M.L.A.s was ordered by the Working Committee to abstain from the session of the Assembly, although they had no powers to dictate to the Parliamentary Group. To preserve the unity of the Muslim League, the Parliamentary Committee acted as directed by the Working Committee and withdrew from the Assembly Session. We sent representatives at Delhi to place the situation in Assam before the Central Committee of Action who deputed Chaudhury Khalique-uz-Zaman to Assam. The resolution adopted by the Working Committee of the Provincial Muslim League at the instance of Chaudhury Khalique-uz-Zaman may have been shown to you by your secretary as it appeared in the Press. For the prestige of the Muslim League Organization, and as we are presented with a fait accompli by the President of the Provincial Muslim League, we are forced to adopt the resolution of the civil disobedience movement. Ever since 30th March, my co-workers have been doing their level best to organize the people for launching of the movement vigorously when the approval of the Central Committee of Action will be obtained. But, up till now, except in two areas, the response has been poor. There is absolutely no funds even for the travelling expenses of the co-workers, not to speak of any relief to sufferers from the movement. I have borrowed Rs. 2,000/- from a certain fund to carry on. It was out in the Press that Bengal is raising a lac of rupees to help us and we have also appealed to the All India Muslim league to help us with a lac of rupees. Uptill now, in spite of the promise of help by the acting Secretary of the Bengal Provincial Muslim League who accompanied Chaudhury Khalique-uz-Zaman to Shillong, not a single farthing has been received by me so far from this source. I know that a draft of Rs.1,000/- was sent by the Bengal Treasurer in the name of our General Secretary at Guwahati. But I do not know what will be the fate of that draft as the General Secretary has already been detained by the Government for violating Section 144 at Dhubri. The Muslims are not at all prepared to launch (a) big civil disobedience movement; they are disorganized and, as I stated, for want of fund, workers in sufficient numbers could not be sent to the different areas to arouse the people.

The Congress Premier and myself met on the 3rd April to negotiate a peaceful settlement; but uptill now nothing concrete has emerged which I can place before you. The entire Assam Valley Hindus, Tribal people and also the Tea Garden labourers are dead set against the Muslim immigrants from Bengal. We can expect no help, no sympathy from them in the Assam Valley in our civil disobedience movement, and we are in a minority in the Assam Valley. Please therefore, give your best thoughts on the situation in Assam and guide the Committee of Action who are meeting at your place on the 20th April, and give directions what to do. If a vigorous civil disobedience movement is to be carried on, it will surely mean much loss of innocent lives and destruction of property. It is a moot point whether by launching such a movement we can dislodge the present Ministry with our 31 Muslim League Members in a House of 108—and yet, 'Down with this Ministry' is the slogan of this movement.

The Congress Government has raised the false cry that the movement is specially designed to for bringing Assam into the Pakistan Zone. The varied geographical position of Assam will compel her ultimately to align herself with Bengal, for, Assam has got no outlet to the outside world except through Bengal and an alienated Bengal can use the strangle hold on the economic life of Assam. Our chief export is 4,000 million pounds of tea which must be exported through Calcutta or Chittagong ports and Assam is dependent, except rice, for every article of daily dietary like salt, sugar, dal, wheat products etc. to other parts of India and these articles must be moved through Bengal to reach Assam.

In the future constitution of India if Assam becomes an independent State or a part of Hindustan while Bengal enjoys Pakistan, Bengal will have the whip-hand over Assam to make Assam ask for Grouping with Bengal. Therefore, in my opinion, it is immaterial if Assam, under her present Masters, proves intransigent and refuses to join in the grouping. Muslim League need not, on the score of Assam alone, object to sit in the Constituent Assembly. As the letter has become inordinately long, I will close here; but I have instructed Mr. Abdul Matin to give you all further materials about Assam's present and future position verbally to you.

With best regards and sincerest wishes,
Yours fraternally,
S.M. Saadulla

To
Quaid-e-Azam Mohammad Ali Jinnah, Delhi.

Note

* S.M. Saadulla Papers, Sub-File No.7, Nehru Memorial Museum and Library, New Delhi.

APPENDIX VI

THE IMMIGRANTS (EXPULSION FROM ASSAM) ACT, 1950

(10 of 1950)

(1st March 1950)

An Act to provide for the expulsion of certain immigrants from Assam

Be it enacted by Parliament as follows:

1. Short title and extent: (i) This Act may be called the Immigrants (Expulsion from Assam) Act, 1950.
   (ii) It extends to the whole of India.
2. Power to order expulsion of certain immigrants: If the Central Government is of opinion that any person or class of persons, having been ordinarily resident in any place outside India, has or have, whether before or after commencement of this Act, come into Assam and that the stay of such person or class of persons is detrimental to the interests of the general public or any section thereof or of any Scheduled Tribe in Assam, the Central Government may by order
   (a) direct such person or class of persons, to remove himself or themselves from India or Assam within such time and by such route as may be specified in the order; and
   (b) give such further directions in regard to his or their removal from India or Assam as it may consider necessary or expedient; Provided that nothing in this section shall apply to any person

who on account of civil disturbances or the fear of such disturbances in any area now forming part of Pakistan has been displaced from or has left his place of residence in such area and who has been subsequently residing in Assam.

3. Delegation of power: The Central Government may, by notification in the Official Gazette, direct that the powers and duties conferred or imposed on it by Section 2 shall, subject to such conditions, if any, as may be specified in the notification, be exercised or discharged also by

   (a) any officer subordinate to the Central Government;

   (b) the Government of Assam or any officer subordinate to that Government;

4. Any authority empowered by or in pursuance of the provisions of this Act to exercise any power may, in addition to any other action expressly provided for in this Act, take or cause to be taken such steps, and use or cause to be used, such force, as may in its opinion, be reasonably necessary for the effective exercise of such power.

5. Penalties: Any person who

   (a) Contravenes or attempts to contravene or abets the contravention of any order made under Section 2, or

   (b) Fails to comply with any direction given by any such order, or

   (c) Harbours any person who has contravened any order made under section 2 or has failed to comply with any direction given by any such order shall be punishable with imprisonment which may extend to three years and shall also be liable to fine.

6. Protection to persons acting under this Act: No suit, prosecution or other legal proceedings shall lie against any person for anything which in good faith is done or intended to be done under this Act.

7. The Act was subsequently amended to include the States of Nagaland, Meghalaya and the then Union Territories of Arunachal Pradesh and Mizoram. Sate Amendments After of the States of Nagaland, Meghalaya and Mizoram.

APPENDIX VII

THE ASSAM OFFICIAL LANGUAGE ACT, 1960*

An Act to declare Official Language of the State of Assam†

Preamble

Whereas Article 345 of the Constitution provides that the Legislature of a State may by law adopt any one or more of the languages in use in the State as the language to be used for official purposes of the State and for matters hereinafter appearing:

It is hereby enacted in the Eleventh Year of the Republic of India, as follows:—

Short title extent and commencement

(1) This Act may be called the Assam Official Language Act, 1960.

(2) It extends to the whole of the State of Assam.

(3) It shall come into force, on such date as the State Government may, by notification, in the official Gazette, appoint and different dates may be appointed for different official purposes and for different parts of the State of Assam:

Provided that the date of dates appointed by the State Government in respect of any of the parts of the State of Assam shall not be later than five years from the date the assent to this Act is first published in the official Gazette.

Definitions

2. In this Act, unless there is anything repugnant in the subject or context, —

(a) 'Autonomous District' means an area deemed as such under paragraph 1(1) of the Sixth Schedule to the Constitution of India.

(b) 'Autonomous Region' means an area deemed as such under paragraph 1(2) of the Sixth Schedule to the Constitution of India.

(c) 'District Council' means a District Council constituted under paragraph 2 of the Sixth Schedule to the Constitution of India.

(d) 'Mohkuma Parishad' means a Mohkuma Parishad established under the Assam Panchayat Act, 1959. (Assam Act XXIV of 1959)

(e) 'Municipal Board' means a Municipal Board established under the Assam Municipal Act 1956 and shall include Town Committees established under the said Act. (Assam Act XV of 1957)

(f) 'Prescribed' means prescribed by rules made under this Act.

(g) 'Regional Council' means a Regional Council constituted under paragraph 2 of the Sixth Schedule to the Construction of India.

Official language for official purposes of the State of Assam

3. Without prejudice to the provisions of Article 346 and 347 of the Constitution of India and subject as hereinafter provided, Assamese shall be used for all or any of the official purpose, of the State of Assam:

Provided that the English language, so long as the use thereof is permissible under Article 343 of the Constitution of India, and thereafter Hindi in place of English, shall also be used for such official purposes of the Secretariat and the offices of the Heads of the Departments of the State Government and in such manner as may be prescribed:

Provided further that, —

(a) All Ordinance promulgated under Article 213 of the Constitution of India;

(b) All Acts passed by the State Legislature;

(c) All Bills to be introduced or amendments thereto to be moved in the State Legislature; and

(d) All Orders, Regulations, Rules and Bye-laws issued by the State Government under the Constitution of India or any law made by Parliament or the Legislature of the State shall be published in the official Gazette in the Assamese language.

Safeguard of the use of language in the Autonomous Region and in the Autonomous District

4. Notwithstanding anything in Section 3, only languages which are in use immediately before the commencement of this Act shall continue to be used for administrative and other official purposes up to and including the level of the Autonomous Region or the Autonomous District, as the case may be, until the Regional Council or the District Council in respect of the Autonomous Region or the Autonomous District, as the case may be, by a majority of not less than two-thirds of the members present and voting decide in favour of adoption of any other language for any of the administrative or official purposes within that region or district.

Safeguard of the use of Bengali language in the district of Cachar

5. Notwithstanding anything in Section 3, the Bengali language shall be used for administrative and other official purposes up to and including the district level in the district of Cachar until the Mohkuma Parishads and Municipal Boards of the district in a joint meeting by a majority of not less than two-thirds of the members present and voting decide in favour of adoption of the official language for use in the district for the aforesaid purposes.

The use of English as official language in respect of examination conducted by the Assam Public Service Commission

6. Notwithstanding anything in Section 3, any examination held by the Assam Public Service Commission, which immediately before the commencement of this Act used to be conducted in the English

language shall continue to be so conducted till such time as the use thereof is permissible under clause (2) of Article 343 of the Constitution of India:

Provided that a candidate shall have the right to choose the language in use in the State of Assam, which was the medium of his University examination.

Rights of the various linguistic groups

7. Subject to the provision of this Act, the State Government may be notification issued from time to time, direct the use of the language as may be specified in the notification and in such parts of the State of Assam as may be specified therein:

Provided that —

(a) The rights of the various linguistic groups in respect of medium of instruction in educational institutions as laid down in the Constitution of India shall not be affected;

(b) The State shall not, in granting aid to educational and cultural institutions, discriminate against any such institutions on grounds of language;

(c) The rights to appointments in the Assam Public Services and to contracts and other avocations shall be maintained without discrimination on the ground of language; and

(d) In regard to noting in the offices in the region or district if any member of the staff is unable to note in any of the district language, the use of English shall be permitted by the Heads of Departments so long as the use thereof is permissible under Article 343 of the Constitution of India.

Power to make rules

8. The State Government shall have the power to make rules for carrying out the purposes of this Act.

Notes

*   Published in the *Assam Gazette*, Extraordinary, 19 December 1960.

† The Act was amended in 1961 to include the following: 'Without prejudice to the provisions contained in Section 5, the Bengali language shall be used for administrative and other official purposes up to and including the district level in the district of Cachar.'

APPENDIX VIII

IMMIGRATION TIMELINE
1900–50

1901: Census report takes note of increase in immigrant population in Assam. In 1891–1901 there was a marked increase of immigration from neighbouring East Bengal. Of the 5,10,672 immigrants during this period, as many as 4,18,360 were from Bengal, primarily from the Mymensingh district.

1911: Census report refers to the 'peaceful invasion of Assam by advancing hordes of Mymensinghia army'. Colonial administration contemplates measures to check immigration and occupation of land held by indigenes.

1916: Director of Land Records proposes regulation of immigration and settlement rules for the immigrants. Prelude to the Line System. According to some scholars, the measure, though apparently meant to streamline immigration, was actually intended to prevent occupation of land belonging to the indigenous population.

1920: Line System adopted as an administrative measure in certain districts such as Kamrup and Nowgong. Its aim was to protect the lands of autochthons from Bengali Muslim immigrants.

1921: Census report refers to the continued large-scale immigration into Assam of Muslim peasants from East Bengal, especially from Mymensingh. Demographic change in the districts of Goalpara, Nowgong, and Kamrup.

1925: Resolution moved in the Legislative Council for the protection of indigenous land from immigrant occupation. Conference of colonial officials held at Shillong to work out amendments to the Assam Land and Revenue Regulations of 1886 with the aim of prohibiting the transfer of land belonging to the indigenous Assamese people to immigrants. Move fails to materialize.

1928: Colonisation Scheme put into effect. Large areas of Nowgong district and Barpeta and Mangaldai subdivisions opened up for settlement by immigrants. Deputy commissioners of districts asked to evolve their own strategy to deal with immigration and occupation of land in Assam. As many as 59 grazing, forest, and village reserves opened up for settlement in Nowgong district alone during the next six years.

1931: Census Commissioner S.C. Mullan, ICS, predicts that unchecked immigration would radically alter socio-cultural profile of the region and affect the future of the Assamese people as a whole. The census superintendent of Assam observes that

> probably the most important event in the province during the last twenty five years—an event, moreover, which seems lively to alter permanently the whole future of Assam and to destroy more surely than did the Burmese invaders of 1829, the whole structure of Assamese culture and civilisation—has been the invasion of a vast horde of land hungry Bengali immigrants; mostly Muslims, from the districts of Eastern Bengal.

He further states that

> by 1921, the first army corps of the invaders had conquered Goalpara. The second army corps which followed them in the years 1921–31 has consolidated their position in that district and has also completed their conquest of Nowgong. The Barpeta subdivision of Kamrup has also fallen to their attack and Darrang is being invaded. Sibsagar has so far escaped completely but the few thousand Mymensinghias in North Lakhimpur are an outpost which may, during the next decade, prove to be a valuable basis of major operations.

1937: Syed Muhammad Saadulla becomes prime minister of Assam. Steps initiated to speed up immigration of Muslim peasants into Assam.

1937: Assamese middle-class concerns regarding immigration grow as immigrant lobby demands scrapping of the Line System. Government appoints Line System Enquiry Committee under the chairmanship of Mr F.W. Hockenhull.

1938: Line Committee Report published. Assamese strongly support the Line System while immigrants oppose it. Line Committee favours continuance of the Line System and suggests strong measures to prevent alienation of tribal land; disfavours settlement of land with post-January 1938 immigrants.

1939: Gopinath Bardoloi-led Congress Coalition Government publishes report on the Line Committee's findings. Government Resolution endorses Line Committee recommendation of putting a stop on settlement of land by immigrants who came after January 1938. But, government resigns before steps are taken for implementation.

1939: Saadulla forms government with support from the Muslim League. Assam Provincial Muslim League in its first provincial conference demands the scrapping of the Line System.

1940: Lahore Resolution of the AIML leads to quick politicization of the land issue in Assam. In the following years Muslim immigration into Assam would come to be linked with the demand for Pakistan.

1940: Land Development Scheme introduced by the Saadulla government with the aim of boosting immigration. Although cut-off date for new settlements was fixed at 1 January 1938, under government patronage unauthorized encroachment and occupation by immigrants upon government land in Brahmaputra Valley districts continued. Tribal reserves further opened up.

1940–1: Large-scale settlement of immigrants by Saadulla government. Over 1 lakh bighas of land in Brahmaputra Valley districts allotted to immigrants between 1939 and 1941.

March 1942: Saadulla ministry falls and Governor's Rule proclaimed. Governor scraps the Land Development Scheme.

August 1942: Saadulla comes back to power and initiates steps to revive his Land Development Scheme.

1943: Bengal Legislative Assembly passes resolution demanding the scrapping of the Line System in Assam and calls for the unrestricted flow of migrants into the state.

August 1943: Saadulla ministry adopts a new resolution on land settlement, which entails further opening up of grazing reserve areas and wastelands, in the districts of Nowgong, Darrang, and Kamrupas as part of the Grow More Food programme ostensibly aimed at helping the war economy.

1944: Muslim League Conference demands the total scrapping of the Line System and demands resignation of the Saadulla ministry.

Saadulla's rift with Maulana Bhasani widens and he warns Bhasani
that unrestricted occupation of Assamese and tribal land could
prove to be counter-productive.

December 1944: Saadulla bypasses the Muslim League and convenes
the All-Party Conference to discuss the land issue.

January 1945: Government Resolution on land passed. Government
decides to keep PGRs intact. Resolves to speed up efforts to settle
immigrants who came to Assam before 1938 as also Assamese
landless. Proposal laid to give special protection to tribal people.
Government Resolution opposed by both Muslim League and
Congress on different grounds. Muslim League wants all curbs on
immigration to go and the Congress feels that local officials had
been vested with too much power which could be misused in favour
of immigrants.

March 1945: Assam Assembly debates the immigration issue at length.
Obvious divide between the Muslim League and Congress members. The issue of alienation of tribal/Assamese land gains major
focus. Gopinath Bardoloi strongly opposes government's land policy,
which he terms as 'anti-tribal' and 'anti-Assamese'.

1945: Saadulla works out understanding with the Assam Congress
and independent legislators, resigns, and reconstitutes his ministry;
forms coalition government with Congress support from outside.
Tripartite Agreement stresses on need to prevent further alienation
of land belonging to the indigenous people and prevention of further encroachment on government reserves. Stiff opposition from
Muslim League.

October 1945: Congress withdraws support from the Saadulla ministry on the plea that the terms of the Tripartite Agreement relating
to immigration and land occupation have not been implemented.
Saadulla government falls.

January 1946: Gopinath Bardoloi forms government in Assam following Congress victory at the polls. Muslim League secures thirty-one
of the thirty-four seats reserved for Muslims, while Congress sweeps
the general constituencies.

February–April 1946: Bardoloi government initiates measures to
evict encroachers from PGRs. Muslim League draws up plans
for 'direct action' against the Congress government on the land
question. At a Guwahati meeting, Mohammad Ali Jinnah warns

Bardoloi government to stop eviction. Agitation grows in immigrant Muslim areas.

June 1946: Announcement of Cabinet Mission Proposals and polarization of Assam politics. Saadulla and Muslim League support Grouping. Congress and hill leaders oppose it. Assam Assembly adopts resolution opposing Grouping. Gandhi supports the Assam Congress move. The land and immigration issue becomes a part of the Muslim League strategy to make Assam a part of the Eastern Zone of the proposed Pakistan.

1946–7: Assam Provincial Muslim League launches civil disobedience movement against Bardoloi government's move to evict encroachers from government reserves. League leader, Maulana Bhasani, appeals to immigrants to forcefully occupy government land.

1947: Assam district of Sylhet goes to Pakistan through a referendum. Percentage of Muslim population in Assam goes down. Muslim League's civil disobedience movement fails to take off.

1947: Huge influx of Bengali Hindu refugees into Assam. The official figures released in 1951 put the number of refugees at over 3 lakhs. By 1961 the figure crossed 6.5 lakhs. Another 4.5 lakhs immigrants entered Assam in 1968.

1948: Assam Land Revenue Regulations of 1888 amended to provide reserve belts and blocks in different regions with the purpose of protecting the tribal land from being taken over by immigrants.

May 1949: Assam chief minister, Gopinath Bardoloi, writes to Nehru asking for introduction of Permit System in Assam in view of large-scale immigration of Muslims (estimated at 5 lakhs) into Assam from East Pakistan.

January 1950: Undesirable Immigrants (Expulsion from Assam) Ordinance passed by Government of India.

1950: Communal riots in parts of lower Assam. 1,00,000 Muslim immigrants are reported to have left lower Assam for Pakistan following the riots.

1950: Nehru–Liaquat Pact provides for return of majority of the displaced immigrants.

15 October 1950: Passport/visa regime put in place. Prior to this date East Pakistanis did not need passports to enter Assam.

February 1950: Debate in parliament on illegal migration into Assam. All the members from Assam make forceful pleas to save Assam

from being swamped by immigrants from East Pakistan. Total unanimity among members on the need to prevent immigration and
expulsion of illegal Muslim immigrants.

1950: Indian parliament passes legislation to discourage immigration from East Pakistan. Immigrants (Expulsion from Assam) Act
adopted in February 1950.

BIBLIOGRAPHY

Ahmed, A.N.S. 'Problem of Identity, Assimilation and Nation-building: A Case of the Muslims of Assam'. In *Politics of Identity and Nation-Building in Northeast India*, edited by Girin Phukan and N.L. Dutta. New Delhi: South Asian Press, 1995.

———. *Nationality Question in Assam: The EPW 1980–81 Debate*. New Delhi: Akansha, 2006.

Ahmed, Imtiaz, Abhijit Dasgupta, and Kathinka Sinha, eds. *State, Society and Displaced People in South Asia*. Dhaka: The University Press, 2004.

AICC Papers, P–4. New Delhi: Nehru Memorial Museum and Library.

Alam, Javed. 'Conceptualising State-Society Relations in India'. *Studies in Humanities and Social Sciences*, vol. II, no. 1 (Shimla: IIAS, 1995).

Anderson, Benedict. *Imagined Communities: Reflections on the Origin and Spread of Nationalism*. London: Verso, 1983.

Antrobus, H.A. *A History of the Assam Company: 1839–1953*. Edinburgh: 1957.

Assam Legislative Assembly Proceedings, 1940–1947, compiled under the provisions of the Government of India Act of 1935. Shillong: Government Press.

Azad, Maulana Abul Kalam. *India Wins Freedom*. New Delhi: Orient Longman, 1988.

Bagchi, P.C. *India and China, a Thousand Years of Cultural Relations*. Bombay: Hind Kitab Ltd, 1950.

Bandopadhyaya, Sailesh Kumar. *Quaid-i-Azam Mohammad Ali Jinnah and the Creation of Pakistan*. New Delhi: Sterling, 1991.

Banerjee, A.C. *The Eastern Frontier of British India*. Calcutta: A. Mukherjee and Bros, 1934.

Banerjee, Ashis. *Federalism and Nationalism: A Historical Survey*, Occasional Paper 3. New Delhi: Nehru Memorial Museum and Library.

Barooah, Nirode Kumar. *David Scott in North-East India 1802–1831: A Study in British Paternalism.* New Delhi: Munshiram Manoharlal, 1970.
———. *Gopinath Bardoloi, Indian Constitution and Centre-State Relations: 1940–1950.* Guwahati: Publication Board, 1990.
———. *Gopinath Bardoloi, 'The Assam Problem' and Nehru's Centre.* Guwahati: Bhabani Print and Publications, 2010.
Barpujari, H.K. *Assam in the Days of the Company 1826–1858.* Shillong: North Eastern Hill University Publications, 1996.
———, ed. *Political History of Assam: 1826–1919,* vol. 1. Guwahati: Government of Assam, 1977.
Barua, Birinchi Kumar. *History of Assamese Literature.* New Delhi: Sahitya Akademi, 1964.
Barua, Harendra Nath. *Reflections on Assam Cum Pakistan.* Calcutta: H. Goswami, 1945.
Barua, K.L. *Early History of Kamrupa.* Shillong: self-published, 1933.
Baruah, Amarjyoti. 'Assam's Nowhere People'. *Down to Earth* (1 October 2015).
Baruah, Lily Mazinder. *Lokapriya Gopinath Bardoloi: An Architect of Modern India.* New Delhi: Gyan Publishing, 1992.
Baruah, Sanjib. *Durable Disorder: Understanding the Politics of Northeast India.* New Delhi: Oxford University Press, 2005.
———. 'Assam: Confronting A Failed Partition'. *Seminar,* vol. 591 (November 2008).
Basu, Durga Das, ed. *Shorter Constitution of India,* 12th edition. New Delhi: Wadhwa and Company, Law Publishers, 1996.
Bhagabati, Dhiren. 'An Economy That Was Shattered—Problems of Meghalaya's Border Areas'. *Journal of North East India Council of Social Science Research* (Shillong: October 1991).
Bhuyan, Arun Chandra, ed. *Political History of Assam 1920–1939,* vol. II. Guwahati: Government of Assam, 1978.
Bhuyan, Arun Chandra and S. De, eds. *Political History of Assam 1920–1939,* vol. II. Guwahati: Publication Board of Assam, 1991.
Bhuyan, S.K. *Anglo-Assamese Relations: 1711–1826.* Guwahati: Lawyer's Book Stall, 1974 (1949).
———. *Lachit Barphukan and His Times.* Guwahati: Department of Historical and Antiquarian Studies, 1947.
———. *Studies in the Literature of Assam.* Guwahati and New Delhi: Omsons Publications, 1985 (1955).
Bishnuram Medhi Papers. New Delhi: Nehru Memorial Museum and Library.
Bordoloi, B.N., ed. *Alienation of Tribal Land and Indebtedness.* Guwahati: Tribal Research Institute, 1986.

————. *Transfer and Alienation of Tribal Land in Assam*. Guwahati: B.N. Bordoloi, 1991.

Brass, Paul R. *Language, Religion and Politics in North India*. London: Cambridge University Press, 1974.

————. *Ethnicity and Nationalism: Theory and Comparison*. New Delhi: SAGE Publications, 1991.

————. *The Politics of India since Independence*. New Delhi: Foundation Books, 1992.

Chakrabarty, Bidyut. 'The "Hut" and the "Axe": The 1947 Sylhet Referendum'. *The Indian Economic and Social History Review*, vol. XXXIX, no. 4 (October 2002).

————. *The Partition of Bengal and Assam 1932–1947: Contour of Freedom*. London: Routledge, 2004.

Chalam K.S. 'Dalit Muslim Relations in Pre-Partition Bengal: Paradigm Shift in Dalit Discourse'. *Mainstream*, vol. LI, no. 22 (18 May 2013).

Chand, Tara. *History of the Freedom Movement in India*. New Delhi: Publication Division, Government of India, 1972.

Chatterjee, Suniti Kumar. *Kirata-Jana-Kriti: The Indo-Mongoloids, Their Contribution to the History and Civilization of India*, reprint. Calcutta: The Asiatic Society, 1974 (1951).

Chatterji, Joya. *Bengal Divided: Hindu Communalism and Partition, 1932–1947*. Cambridge: Cambridge University Press, 1994.

————. *The Spoils of Partition: Bengal and India 1947–1967*. New Delhi: Cambridge University Press, 2008.

Chaudhuri, Sujit. 'A God-Sent Opportunity'. *Seminar*, no. 515 (February 2002):

Chaudhury, P.C. *The History and Civilisation of the People of Assam to the Twelfth Century*. Guwahati: Department of Historical and Antiquarian Studies, 1959.

Chaudhury, Valmiki, ed. *Dr. Rajendra Prasad: Correspondence and Select Documents*, vol. III. New Delhi: Allied Publishers, 1984.

Constituent Assembly Debates, vols I–X. New Delhi: *Lok Sabha Secretariat, 1999*.

Dainik Asam (Assamese). Guwahati: 18 September 2015.

Dainik Janambhumi (Assamese). Guwahati: 13 January 2015; 8 September 2015.

Das, Durga, ed. *Sardar Patel's Correspondence 1945–50*, vols III and V. Ahmedabad: Navajivan Publishing House, 1972.

Das, J.N. 'Genesis of Tribal Belts and Blocks in Assam'. In *Alienation of Tribal Land and Indebtedness*, edited by B.N. Bardoloi. Guwahati: Tribal Research Institute, 1986.

Dasgupta, Anindita. 'Partition Migration in Assam: The Case of the Bengali Bhadralok'. In *State, Society and Displaced People in South Asia*, edited by Imtiaz Ahmed et al. Dhaka: The University Press, 2004.

————. 'Remembering Sylhet: A Forgotten Story of India's 1947 Partition'. *Economic and Political Weekly*, vol. XLIII, no. 31 (2 August 2008).

Datta, P.S., ed. *Autonomy Movements in Assam*, documents, 1st edition. New Delhi: Omsons Publications, 1993.

————, ed. *Ethnic Movements in Poly-Cultural Assam*. New Delhi: Vikas Publishing House, 1990.

Deb, Saptarshi. 'The Construction of the Sylheti Identity in Assam'. M. Phil thesis submitted to the Department of History, School of Social Sciences, University of Hyderabad, 2015.

Dev, Bimal J. and Dilip Kumar Lahiri. *Assam Muslims: Politics and Cohesion*. Delhi: Mittal Publications, 1985.

Dhulipala, Venkat. *Creating a New Medina: State Power, Islam and the Quest for Pakistan in Late Colonial India*. New Delhi: Cambridge University Press, 2015.

Diamond, Jared. *Guns, Germs and Steel: A Short History of Everybody for the Last 13,000 Years*. London: Vintage Books, 1998.

Dutta, Binayak. *Religion and Politics in Eastern India 1905–1947*. Varanasi: Pilgrims Book House, 2009.

————. 'Violent Parting: Recovering the History of Violence in Sylhet on Partition and After (1947–1950)'. *The Heritage*, vol. IV, no. 1 (Guwahati: 2013).

————. 'The "Stout Fanatical Mahomedan" and Mullan's Burden: The History of Bengali Immigration in Colonial Assam (1871–1931)'. *Man and Society: A Journal of North-East Studies*, vol. XI (Shillong: ICSSR North Eastern Regional Centre, Winter 2014).

Government of Assam, Directorate of Economics and Statistics, Planning and Development Department. *Economic Survey of Assam 2011–12*.

Government of Assam, Home and Political department. *White Paper on Foreigners' Issue*. Dispur, Guwahati, October 2012.

Government of India. *Papers Relating to the Reconstitution of the Provinces of Bengal and Assam (Shimla)*. New Delhi: D.K. Publishers, 1983 (1906).

Gopal, S., ed. *Selected Works of Jawaharlal Nehru*, vol. I. New Delhi: Orient Longman, 1984.

Gopinath Bardoloi Papers. New Delhi: Nehru Memorial Museum and Library.

Guha, Amalendu. *Planter Raj to Swaraj: Freedom Struggle and Electoral Politics in Assam: 1826–1947*. New Delhi: Indian Council of Historical Research (ICHR), 1977.

————. 'Little Nationalism Turned Chauvinist: Assam's Anti-Foreigner Upsurge, 1979–80'. *Economic and Political Weekly*, vol. XV, nos 41–3, special number (October 1980).

————. *Medieval and Early Assam: Society, Polity and Economy*. Calcutta: K.P. Bagchi and Company, 1991.

Hasan, Mushirul. *India Partitioned: The Other Face of Freedom*, vols I and II. Delhi: Roli Books, 1995.

———. *The Partition Omnibus*. New Delhi: Oxford University Press, 2001.

Hussain, Ashfaque. 'The Making and Unmaking of Assam–Bengal Borders and the Sylhet Referendum'. *Modern Asian Studies*, vol. XLVII, no. 1 (2012).

Hussain, Ismail. *Aami Kidore Asomiya Halo?* (How Did We Become Assamese?) Guwahati: Akhar Prakash, 2013.

Hussain, Monirul. *The Assam Movement, Class, Ideology and Identity*. New Delhi: Manak Publications, 1993.

Jalal, Ayesha. *The Sole Spokesman: Jinnah, the Muslim League and the Demand for Pakistan*. Cambridge: Cambridge University Press, 1985.

Kakati, Bani Kanta. *Assamese, Its Formation and Development*. Gauhati: Lawyer's Book Stall, 1972 (1941).

Kar, M. *Muslims in Assam Politics*. Delhi: Omsons Publications, 1990.

Khan, Khurshid Ahmed, ed. *Speeches, Statements and Messages of the Quaid-i-Azam*, vol. II (1938–41). Lahore: Bazm-e-Iqbal, 1996.

Kumar, Chanchal. 'Federalism in India: A Critical Appraisal'. *Journal of Business Management and Social Sciences Research*, vol. III, no. 9 (September 2014): 31–43.

Lahiri, Nayanjot. *Pre-Ahom Assam: Studies in the Inscriptions of Assam between the Fifth and Thirteenth Centuries A.D.* New Delhi: Munshiram Manoharlal, 1991.

Mahajan, Sucheta, ed. *Towards Freedom: Documents on the Movement for Independence in India*, 1947, part 1. New Delhi: ICHR and Oxford University Press, 2013.

Mansergh, Nicholas and Panderlal Moon, eds. *Constitutional Relations between Britain and India: The Transfer of Power: 1942–47*, vol. VII (*The Cabinet Mission 23 March–29 June 1946*). London: Her Majesty's Stationery Office, 1983.

———, eds. *Constitutional Relations between Britain and India: The Transfer of Power: 1942–47*, vol. IX (*The Fixing of a Time Limit, 4 November 1946–22 March 1947*). London: Her Majesty's Stationery Office, 1983.

———, eds. *Constitutional Relations between Britain and India: The Transfer of Power: 1942–47*, vol. XII (*The Mountbatten Plan, Viceroyalty, Princes, Partition and Independence, July–August 15 1947*). London: Her Majesty's Stationery Office, 1983.

Medhi, S.B. *River Transport and Economic Development in Assam*. Guwahati: Publication Board, 1978.

Misra, Sanghamitra. *Becoming a Borderland: The Politics of Space and Identity in Colonial Northeastern India*. New Delhi: Routledge, 2011.

Misra, Tilottoma. 'Assam: A Colonial Hinterland'. *Economic and Political Weekly*, vol. XV, no. 32 (9 August 1980).

———. *Literature and Society in Assam: A Study of the Assamese Renaissance 1826–1926*. Guwahati and New Delhi: Omsons Publications, 1987.

Misra, Udayon. *The Periphery Strikes Back: Challenges to the Nation State in Assam and Nagaland*. Shimla: IIAS, 2000.

———. *India's North-East: Identity Struggles, State, and Civil Society*. New Delhi: Oxford University Press, 2014.

Moon, Panderlal. *Divide and Quit*. New Delhi: Oxford University Press, 1998 (1941).

Nag, Sajal. *India and Northeast India: Mind, Politics and Process of Integration (1946–1950)*. New Delhi: Regency Publications, 1998.

Nag, Sajal, Tejimala Gurung, and Abhijit Chaudhury, eds. *Making of the Indian Union: Merger of the Princely States and Scheduled Areas*. New Delhi: Akansha Publications, 2007.

Nilachal (Assamese weekly). Guwahati: 10 June 1970.

North Eastern Council. *A Saga of Commitment and Achievement: Glorious 35 Years of Existence*. Shillong: n.p., 2007.

Pannikar, K.N., ed. *Towards Freedom: Documents on the Movement for Independence in India*, 1940, part 1. New Delhi: ICHR and Oxford University Press, 2007.

Percival, Archibald. *Wavell: The Viceroy's Journal*, edited by Penderal Moon. London: Oxford University Press, 1978.

Phukan, Girin. *Assam's Attitude to Federalism*. New Delhi: Sterling Publications, 1984.

Pirzada, Syed Sharifuddin, ed. *Foundations of Pakistan: All India Muslim League Documents*, vol. II, 1924–27. Karachi: National Publishing House Ltd, 1969.

Prasad, Rajendra. *India Divided*. Bombay: Hind Kitabs, 1946.

Rammohan, E.N. *Insurgent Frontiers*. New Delhi: India Research Press, 2005.

Rao, M. Govinda and Nirvikar Singh. *Political Economy of Federalism in India*. New Delhi: Oxford University Press, 2005.

Ray Chaudhury, Ambikagiri. *Ambikagiri Raychoudhury Racanavali*, introduction by Sayendranath Sarma. Guwahati: Publication Board, 1986.

Saikia, Joydeep. *Documents on North East India*. New Delhi: Institute for Defence Studies and Analyses (IDSA) and Shipra Publications, 2010.

Samaddar, Ranabir, ed. *Reflections on Partition in East*. Delhi: Vikas Publications, 1997.

Sarkar, Sumit, ed. *Towards Freedom: Documents on the Movement for Independence in India*, 1946, part 1. New Delhi: ICHR and Oxford University Press, 2008.

Sarma, Atul. 'Why the Northeastern States Continue to Decelerate'. *Man and Society: A Journal of North East States*, vol. I, no. 1 (Shillong: ICSSR, Spring 2005).

Sarma, Kumar Chandan. *Asomiya Kun?* (Assamese). Guwahati: Span Publications Pvt. Ltd, 2006.

Schendel, Willem Van. *The Bengal Borderland: Beyond State and Nation in India, 1945.* New Delhi: ICHR and Oxford University Press, 2008.

Sherwani, Latif Ahmed. *The Partition of India and Mountbatten.* Karachi: Council for Pakistan Studies, 1986.

Singh, Jaswant. *Jinnah: India, Partition, Independence.* New Delhi: Rupa and Co., 2009.

Singh, K.S., ed. *People of India,* vol. IX. Calcutta: Anthropological Survey of India and Seagull Books, 1993.

Syama Prasad Mookerjee Papers. New Delhi: Nehru Memorial Museum and Library.

Syed Saadulla Papers. New Delhi: Nehru Memorial Museum and Library.

Thapar, Romila. *The Past as Present: Forging Contemporary Identities through History.* New Delhi: Aleph Book Company, 2014.

The Assam Tribune. Guwahati: 8 March 2015; 14 March 2015; 22 March 2015; 1 April 2015; 7 June 2015; 18 September 2015; 28 November 2015.

The Telegraph. Kolkata: 6 February 2014.

Verghese B.G. *India's Northeast Resurgent.* New Delhi: Konarak Publishers, 1996.

Wills, Ian Bryant. *Jinnah's Early Politics: Ambassador of Hindu Muslim Unity.* New Delhi: Permanent Black, 2005.

World Bank. *India: Investment Climate and Manufacturing Industry.* Washington DC: World Bank, 2004. Available at http://siteresources.worldbank.org/INTKNOWLEDGEFORCHANGE/Resources/491519-1199818447826/IC-IndiaUpdateDraft.pdf.

Zaidi, Z.H., editor-in-chief. *Quaid-i-Azam Mohammad Ali Jinnah Papers, Prelude to Pakistan,* vol. I, part 2. Lahore: National Archives of Pakistan, 1998.

Zaman, S.M., ed. *Quaid-i-Azam and Education.* Islamabad: National Institute of Historical and Cultural Research, 1995.

INDEX

ABOUT THE AUTHOR

Udayon Misra is former Professor of English Literature at Dibrugarh University, Assam, India. He was National Fellow at Indian Institute of Advanced Study, Shimla, and at the Indian Council of Social Science Research, New Delhi, India. His most recent work, *India's North-East: Identity Movements, State, and Civil Society*, was published by Oxford University Press in 2014. Other publications include *The Periphery Strikes Back: Challenges to the Nation-State in Assam and Nagaland* (2000), *North-East India: Quest for Identity* (1988), and *The Raj in Fiction* (1987). Misra writes for several leading newspapers in Assamese and English, and contributes regularly to the *Economic and Political Weekly*.